M000306423

Author, Vic Mills
September 1967

 *situation*

 *normal*

 all

 *fouled*

 up

Vic Mills

with illustrations by
Pamela Hohner,
Michael Mills,
and S.E. Price

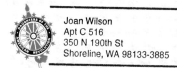

Dedicated to all who have served.

ACKNOWLEDGEMENTS

When I first began this grand excursion into writing, I cloistered myself away in a back bedroom/office each evening. A scheduled two-hour session with the computer would, in a flash, become six. My love and thanks to my family for putting up with me and with my extremes.

My late brother, Richard G. Mills, encouraged me to write this story. He was a hawk in lamb's clothing and taught me much about honor.

Thanks are due to a late friend of many, many years, Robert Bruce Axmann MacKay, who read a portion of a poorly written, misspelled and incomplete first draft, and persistently encouraged me to move forward with the telling of this story — "This is very important. Finish it!"

Nothing happens in the world of writing without editors and proofreaders. Although I was born in America, at times I think of English as a second language because I do so poorly with it. Because of that, I wish to humbly thank a dear family friend, Marci Williams, an educator, who was the first person to read the beginning pages of what I had so crudely written. Graciously accepting the challenge, she was soon laughing at some parts and showing concern at others. For her three years of teaching and encouragement, and for help on the final rewrite, I offer my deep appreciation and thanks.

Once the draft was completed, the next task was to find an editor. Instead of one I got two, in Larry and Gloria Campbell. Both are writers, and Gloria teaches college courses. They took a rough (and the key word here is "*rough*") manuscript and put it into a form suitable for a publisher to see. And like magic, I received my first rejection. I was elated. Thanks, too, to Kay Gordon for her assistance in formatting.

I also wish to express my gratitude to the artists. Pamela Hohner has incorporated firm but gentle beauty into her artwork. Her design of the cover is perfect, along with her sketches (pages 97, 142, 247 and 265) attest to her insight and ability to see beyond the written word. Pam also did the cover design. My son Michael created several fine sketches for the book (pages 17, 64, 74, and 196) along with S.E. Price (pages 272 and 287). Walt Burville Studio, Gig Harbor, WA, computer-enhanced the cover graphics .

Vic Mills

Contents

Life is full of surprises. When my friend Vic Mills asked me to read his manuscript about experiences in Vietnam, I thought to myself, "Can I take one more story of blood and tears about Nam?" But for once I kept my mouth shut, and I'm glad that I did. At 2:30 a.m. the next morning I finally finished reading the manuscript. I couldn't lay it down!

Vic's story of his tour of duty as an M.P. in Vietnam reveals a whole new slant on that conflagration. I chuckled when Vic and his buddies put their native Yankee smarts into play to outsmart the Viet Cong. I raged when inept, unscrupulous officers and non-coms put liquor, women and self-preservation ahead of the welfare of their men. I sweat some blood when Vic was nearly court-martialed for trying to protect vulnerable Vietnamese women. I marveled at Vic and his friends setting up an orphanage for the Vietnamese children. In short, I ran the full gamut of emotions.

This is not just a war story. This is a heartwarming account of a handful of M.P.s who refused to let fear, outrageous decisions from some of their commanders, the constant threat of enemy infiltration, heat, insects and snakes destroy their morale. Their innate desire to learn their jobs thoroughly, stick together, perform under pressure and return home intact brought them through the toughest of experiences.

To my thinking, Vic Mills has written one heck of a fine story--one that really needs to be told.

Lawrence T. Campbell
U.S. Army Veteran, W.W.II
Co-editor, Sundial Press
and
Author of *Coming Home Journal of a Sagewalker*

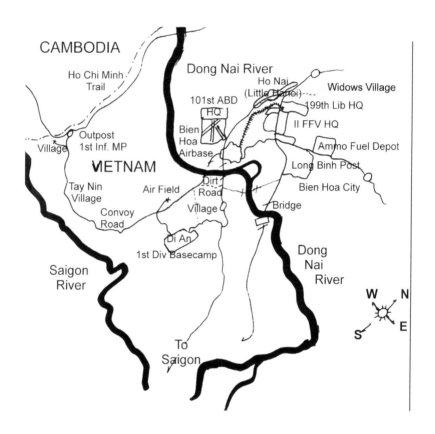

SNAFU

PROLOGUE

By the end of 1967, the war in Vietnam had already been going hot and heavy for three years. Our military presence there had ballooned from 50,000 men in 1964 to half a million soldiers. By all assessments, it would continue for an unforeseeable length of time.

In 1962, under President Kennedy, the Family Deferment Act was passed. It stated that any young man between the ages of eighteen and twenty-five who was married with a dependent child would automatically be deferred from the draft and reclassified as 4-A instead of 1-A. I had dutifully registered with the Selective Service in July 1960. Without a thought about the military buildup in Southeast Asia, I was married in September 1963. Fourteen months later on Veterans Day, 1964, my son Micheal was born.

From the spring of 1963 to early 1966, I worked in the construction trades as a carpenter's apprentice and got to know several Vietnam vets who were in the same program. Most said little about their experiences. Those who did talk about Nam told some unbelievable horror stories. Those of us who only saw the fighting on TV news had little understanding of the living hell those men had endured.

In all honesty, my own life was far from tranquil. Right from the start my marriage was shaky, at best. When it finally broke up, I decided to move to Washington State with a friend. I had known little about Vietnam and the war, but because of the imminent change in my draft status, I began to follow every news broadcast. The draft rules were confusing. After I received the Selective Service notice advising me of the change in my status (from 4-A to 1-A), I tried to enlist, just to get it over with.

I approached all branches of the military with the exception of the Marines, but they all gave me the same answer: because I was still legally married (for three more months) and I had a dependent, I could not voluntarily join the military. But the Army could still draft me! In April of 1967 they did.

As my induction date drew nearer, I started to think of ways to improve my physical conditioning. I had gotten an interim job driving for Seattle Transit. None of the buses was equipped with power steering. As a result, my arms and upper body were in fairly good shape; I just needed to work on my legs and improve my wind. I started running, usually in dress shoes. I ran to catch buses and to get to the grocery store. It was an easy way to exercise. Within a few weeks, I could comfortably run a mile or so. This surprised me, since I had never been very good at athletics.

I stayed with Seattle Transit until the end of March, when I took my military leave of absence and a two-week vacation prior to my induction. I stored some things in the basement of a friend from Transit and left for sunny California to visit my 2-year-old son and the rest of my family. I had a wonderful time, said my good-byes, and headed for the San Francisco International Airport. My return flight on United Airlines to Seattle would begin my stint with the Army. That was quite a flight, and a story in itself.

Chapter One
MY ODYSSEY BEGINS

The roar of the trijets filled our ears, and as the plane accelerated down the runway, we were pressed hard against our seat backs. It was a two-hour flight from San Francisco to Seattle. As I settled into my window seat for a short nap, the harsh glare from the huge woman overflowing from the seat next to me set the tone for the flight.

Takeoff was flawless, and we lifted off into the clear blue sky. We were airborne for less than five minutes when suddenly the engines lost power, and the roar was replaced with a low-pitched, whispering whine. My seatmate screamed in terror, "We're going to crash! We're going to crash!"

"Lady, we're okay!" I yelled back. "The engines are still burning. The pilot is in control." I was certainly hoping this was the case.

The plane had ascended to about four thousand feet. Food carts full of little trays had been brought out as the flight attendants prepared to serve lunch. There had not been the slightest warning of trouble. The engines, indeed, were still running, although they were barely audible. A sudden floating sensation confirmed two unwelcome facts: one, we were no longer going up; and two, gravity still worked, and the plane was coming down.

Due to the unexpected weightlessness, trays of food, and everything else not fastened down, were going every which way. I saw our stewardess bounce off the cart, and as she was thrown against a nearby seat, I reached across my neighbor and made a grab for her. "Hold on miss, I've got ya," I said, reeling her in onto my lap.

Over the years, even as a child, I had found flying very enjoyable. I had even logged several hours of lessons, so I knew what was normal, and recognized what was not. We were in trouble.

A few screams and cries pierced the tension. In the midst of it all a 10-year-old boy seated nearby was having a ball, enjoying the ride, much to the consternation of his panic-stricken mother.

The plane had circled toward the northwestern part of the Santa Cruz Mountain Range. The mountains there were only about two thousand feet in elevation. Skyline Boulevard, an old state highway, ran southeast to Highway 9, one of the scenic routes to the town of Santa Cruz. I knew the area quite well, having been raised there. Crossing over the mountains, I could see we were coming down and Skyline Boulevard was coming up. Still buckled in, I maintained my hold on the stewardess. At only a few hundred feet above the mountains and the highway, I could tell the make and model of vehicles below. Then the plane slowed its descent and began to level off.

"Tell me, does your pilot give this kind of tour often?" I asked in a hoarse whisper.

There was no response. It's difficult to talk when your heart and stomach are in your throat. The stewardess, I'm sure, was not really comfortable; she was partially draped across the feet and legs of my *friend* in the next seat. "Please," the woman complained, "can't you get her off me? Get her off my feet."

"Hold tight for a few minutes, ma'am," I answered.

Still coming down, we crossed over Highway 1 near Half Moon Bay and continued west out over the ocean at perhaps no higher than five hundred feet. We could see that the mountains were behind and slightly above us. Then the engines once again roared their power. A collective sigh from passengers and crew alike blended with the sound of the jets as the plane began to climb once more.

"Thank you for catching me, sir. That was fast thinking," the attendant told me as she struggled to her feet. Turning to the lady next to me, she added, "I do apologize, ma'am, for stepping on your feet." The woman simply glared at her indignantly.

"Smile, it won't hurt!" I suggested to my seatmate.

Except for a few cuts and bruises, no one was seriously injured. The cabin crew was marvelous in picking up the mess as well as in keeping our spirits high. During those few minutes when the plane was dropping, the prospect of combat hadn't seemed quite so frightening.

Why we didn't return to San Francisco International, as I had thought we might, has always been a mystery. Instead there was an unscheduled stop in Portland an hour and a half later. The thirty-minute layover turned out to be over an hour.

Entering the terminal, I wanted to find someone in charge. I stopped by the ticket counter, along with a dozen of my fellow passengers, and we found a ticket agent. "Excuse me, sir," I began. "I'd like to speak to someone in charge."

"Are you all on flight 301 from the Bay Area?" he asked, looking us over.

"Yes, we are."

With a stoic expression on his face he said, "Just a moment, I'll see if someone is available."

He turned around and picked up the receiver of a wall phone. We couldn't hear what he said, but in a moment he hung up the phone. "There will be someone right out," he said. Then, gesturing to a waiting area, he added, "If you would, please take a seat."

Fifteen minutes later, a man carrying a clipboard and paper approached our little group and announced, "If you are on flight 301 to Seattle, I need to have you print your names, phone numbers, and mailing addresses."

As he began to pass the clipboard around, several people tried to ask the man questions. "Answers will be given in due time, but we need this information first, please."

"Excuse me, sir," I said. "I'm in transit for Army induction. I have no idea where I'll be."

"Okay, just fill out your full name, and on the address line write 'U. S. Army.'"

The airline personnel said that they knew nothing about our harrowing experience. Either they really didn't know what had happened or they were ordered to be quiet. I chose to believe the latter. A short time later, a flight officer approached us and explained that the plane had been checked over by the ground crew and that we should board for the final leg of our flight.

In Seattle I spent two nights at the Savoy Hotel across from the King Street Train Station. The Army Induction Center was on Seattle's waterfront a half-mile away. Returning from dinner my second evening, I found some unexpected visitors waiting by the door to my room. They were well dressed, not unlike the Mormon missionaries.

"Hi," one began. "Are you Vic Mills?"

"Yes, I am," I reluctantly acknowledged.

"My name is Clifford," the leader began. "These are my friends, Sean and Valerie. We're part of a Vietnam antiwar group in the Northwest based out of British Columbia. If you're not busy, may we come in for a few moments? It may be vital to you."

The three sat down and explained their mission. "You don't have to go to the Army and kill or be killed fighting in Vietnam," Sean announced.

Clifford then added, "You've been working the past four months driving a bus here in Seattle. There's a similar job waiting for you up north."

In short, they offered me a free trip to Canada, complete with employment and an apartment. "I appreciate your concern," I answered. "But this is not an option for me."

I believe they were conscientious and meant well, and I certainly don't condemn those who chose that route if they did so from an honest conviction. Thanking the protesters for their kind offer, I walked the three to the door. The young woman stopped, then turned around and smiled. With a kiss on my cheek she said, "God bless you, Vic Mills, and keep you safe." I will always be curious as to how they knew about me and about my being in the hotel.

Officially, I was inducted out of my home state of California. Had I changed my address, my basic training would probably have been at Fort Ord, near Monterey. Instead I was sent to Fort Lewis, which was quite fortunate for me. Fort Ord came under quarantine just after my induction due to widespread meningitis; hundreds of trainees became ill and a few even died. During my whole time in the military, I was convinced that there was a divine force safeguarding me. There were many such instances that went far beyond mere coincidence or luck.

The ride to Fort Lewis took only an hour and a half. With a sergeant on each of the eight buses, the caravan left the Army's induction station shortly after noon. Mine was the last bus in line, and while en route we became separated from the rest of the group. After clearing the main gate, the sergeant on our bus gave the driver what seemed to be some final instructions, then quietly got off. We didn't know it then, but it would take several days before the Army would realize where we were.

There were two rows of barracks where we were let off, four buildings on each side of the street. An hour later it began to rain. Curious and damp, we decided to look inside some of the unlocked buildings. Figuring that someone in authority would be showing up soon, we went into the first barrack, suitcases and gym bags in hand. Except for rolled up mattresses on a few bunks, there was no bedding. We had arrived on the Army's doorstep, but there was no one home.

By 4:00 p.m. the rain had let up and most of us were getting hungry. We flagged down a young soldier driving by and asked where we could eat. Surprised by the size of our group, he said pointing, "There's a coffee shop on post about a mile away."

Breakfast for me had been at nine that morning, and we hadn't eaten lunch. Those of us who had money took the walk and pooled some cash in order to bring back something to eat for the others.

It was getting late when we returned from the coffee shop, and still the Army hadn't shown up. Since it was turning dark, the talk soon turned to settling in for the night. April in the Northwest is rather chilly, so our next chore was to locate some blankets and more mattresses. Everyone went hunting. We scrounged up twelve blankets stored in two adjacent buildings. We were still short by two-thirds, and the night was cold. There was no furnace. The next day we managed to scrounge up the rest of what we needed.

It soon became obvious that we couldn't keep eating out, and we managed to attach ourselves to some mess halls in the area using a variety of excuses. A couple of times we even tried the truth, hoping someone would take pity and come to our rescue. No one believed us.

Someone found a volleyball in one of the barracks and another guy had brought a football. So, besides running and doing a few calisthenics, we played a lot of volleyball and touch football to fill our waiting time.

One morning I thought we were finally discovered. It was our fourth day there, and we had a good touch football game going. I had gone inside for a few minutes to shave—hard to do without warm water. Anyway, a station wagon stopped abruptly at our barracks, and an officer (a major, I think) got out and walked slowly up to the group. I think he was a little perturbed that no one in the group called "attention" or saluted as he approached.

"Who's in charge here?" he asked.

Hearing a voice of authority, I hurried back outside and, as I walked up to him, said, "We have no one in charge, sir." Another recruit and I then introduced ourselves, and my new friend added, "We're waiting for processing into basic training. We've been here for several days."

"You know these buildings are off-limits," he informed us. "They haven't been used in years." That was totally believable.

The officer continued to ask questions, and we answered the best we could. As he drove away most of us felt relieved and truly thought our vacation would be over within the hour. But it wasn't to be. It took another few days before the shit finally hit the fan. At 4:30 on the morning of our eighth or ninth day, the real Army showed up with a vengeance. It was still dark outside when two sergeants came through the barracks banging on garbage cans and yelling for us to "Hit the floor!" It was a rude awakening in every way, but it was something we were going to have to get used to. Although these DIs (drill instructors) showed little humor, I spotted a smirk or two on their faces when they heard how long we had been in the abandoned barracks and how we had survived.

"Okay, listen up, children," one of the sergeants shouted. "My name is Sergeant Carter. I want you to pick up your bags and go outside. The DI there will instruct you what to do next." Taking a look around at us he added, "*And, I strongly suggest you do exactly what he says, quickly. Fall out—now!*"

There was a light rain falling as we formed up into two soggy lines to receive our first lesson on how to do the "military walk" or march.

"Start on your left foot," the second drill instructor yelled. "It is the foot generally found next to your right foot. Ready, au-tin-hut [attention]! Right face, forward, harch [march]! Left, yer left, yer left, right, left."

We even learned how to count—up to four: "Hup [one], two, three, foe [four]." Military lingo was a language unto itself.

Half an hour later we moved into what would be our home for the next ten weeks. We were immediately issued uniforms, class "A"s and fatigues, along with boots and shoes. Then we were turned loose to shower and shave. With an abundance of hot water, no one had to tell us twice. That was one pungent shower, as thirty-five dirty, rain-wet GIs hit the shower—our first in many days.

Before the Army, my only experience with a coal-fired furnace had been in an old farmhouse where I had stayed with a friend. That's when I first learned about "clinkers," the fused debris of spent coal, and about furnace cleaning. I found my coal-stoking experience invaluable when I was introduced to our barracks' heating system.

"Private Mills and Private Marsh," Sergeant Carter called out in formation the next morning.

"Here, Sergeant," we both yelled in unison.

"You are our two firemen. Our furnace is your furnace. I give it to you. *Do you understand?*"

"*Yes, Sergeant,*" we chorused.

Continuing, our DI added, "You will report for boiler training at zero-eight-hundred this morning."

Training? Ha! Thirty minutes was all it took to tell us what we already knew, "Don't let the barracks catch on fire!" As I understood our responsibilities, we were to make sure the fire in the boiler never went out at night and that the barracks didn't burn down. The furnace had a huge cylinder, eight feet high and six feet wide. Cleaning this monster meant getting covered from head to toe in soot. It permeated just about everything and coated the insides of our noses, mouths, and ears.

Because of our lateness in starting basic training, our group was separated from the rest of the company and brigade for a five-day crash course in playing catch-up. Early morning PT (physical training) and chow were our only contacts with the rest of the trainees.

Up till then we still hadn't been taught simple military courtesy or how to identify the ranks of commissioned and noncommissioned officers. There was an incident that clearly showed just what we didn't know. It was the second or third night in our new barracks, and we were busy polishing our new boots and shoes and getting familiar with our newly issued gear. Our DI, Sergeant Carter, lived in the barracks, and his room was at the top of the stairs. He was out at the time, and I was standing near the top step of the second level, when I heard someone come in the side entrance of the main floor. At first I thought it might be Carter returning, but he was a rather small man, and this guy was huge. When he reached the last step, he hollered at me, since I was the closest, "Aren't you supposed to say something, soldier?"

The dumb look on my face certainly didn't help my cause any. This man was easily twice the size of Sergeant Carter and louder, as he continued to yell, "Recruit, you'd better say something, and fast!"

"Good evening, sir," I finally blurted out.

"*Don't call me sir!*" he shouted. "I'm no *officer*. I am a *sergeant!*" he yelled even louder.

He walked up and down the length of our floor for a few minutes yelling unintelligible directives. Carter soon returned, and although he was a bit drunk, he tongue-lashed the other man for interfering. "Sergeant Smith, what the hell do you think you are doing with my men?"

"Oh, I just came up to see you, and . . ." he meekly tried to explain.

"Shut your face, and take it with you as you leave . . . and don't let the door hit you in the ass on your way out. You have no business interfering."

Half of the next day was dedicated to learning rank insignias for all the services and proper military courtesy. At the end of the session Carter added, "When in doubt, just salute the sonofabitch." I did that a lot.

The background of the recruits was varied. Most were in their late teens. A few came from colleges where they had enlisted for the reserve programs;

some others came from the courts, where a judge had offered two options—prison or the military. Some of these court recruits made it into sensitive security and intelligence areas—a frightening reality of the system.

I was surprised at the large number of young recruits who were unable to fill out the forms and do the written tests. Many could not read and write above the third-grade level. Most were recent high school graduates. Some had played sports and did well with physical agility tests, but they couldn't understand the written tests or many of the oral commands. The Army offered them no support.

A few days after getting our new haircuts, the sergeant told us to fall in.

"Okay, listen up," Sergeant Carter began. "We have a short march for you before we break for lunch. Tin-hut! Right face. Forward, harch. Yer left, yer left, yer-left-right-left."

A couple of blocks later, the kid behind me said softly, "Oh shit, we're heading for the infirmary." That and similar refrains raced through the ranks in seconds. This was one part of basic training we all hated—when we were "shot" for real. I had never had a shot before, not even a vaccination, so this was all new to me. When the medicine odor reached us, the marching pace began to drag.

"Come on, guys, let's keep up the pace," Carter urged. "It will soon be behind you."

When we reached our destination, a sergeant came out and said, "Fall out. Rest in line. Smoke if you've got 'em and listen up for your name."

Standing or sitting in line and seeing how some of the men came through the ordeal had me convinced that I wanted to go home; anybody's home. I knew, of course, that shots were given with needles, but I didn't know that an air gun was also part of their arsenal. Our medical records determined how, where, and with which weapons we were to be shot.

Everyone was affected differently. I lost almost everything I had eaten since birth; others became light-headed, and a few passed out. One of the sergeants and an orderly brought us cups of 7-Up and orange juice to help settle our stomachs.

The next day, still sore from the shots, we merged with the rest of the main training group.

Over the next two weeks it became increasingly difficult for me to move my left arm and shoulder during physical training. It was nearly impossible for me to do push-ups. I often felt nauseated and weak. Early one morning before we were ordered to fall out for company formation, our head drill instructor, a sergeant first class, came into the shower area to talk to me. I was the last one there.

"Private Mills? Mills, are you in here?" he called out in his Tennessee drawl.

"I'll be right there, Sergeant. I'm around the corner," I hollered back. Still dripping wet with a towel around my waist, I hurried to where he was waiting.

"At ease, Mills. You may continue drying off while we talk." As I gingerly worked the towel around he explained, "Up till now you have been doing great in all your training. What's going . . ." his voice dropped off when he noticed my left shoulder. The air-gun inoculation had festered to about the size of a golf ball. He lightly touched an area near the wound to inspect it, but the pain was so intense that I nearly passed out.

The sergeant yelled at someone near the door, "Private, go get the lieutenant on the double."

"On my way, Sergeant!"

I hadn't totally blacked out, but the sergeant helped me to a bench along the wall. Looking at my shoulder, he said, "This answers my question. You sure as hell can't train with that."

As he helped me with my shirt he asked, "Why didn't you report this to me or one of the other DIs?"

"You see, Sergeant, I've had no experience with shots and didn't know what a bad reaction was."

One of my buddies brought my trousers to me and I slid them on. Our lieutenant hurried in and asked, "What's going on here, Sergeant?"

"Good morning, sir. Private Mills has a seriously infected inoculation on his left shoulder. I'm going to take him to the infirmary. I'm placing him on the sick list."

I had lost some weight and was dehydrated. After two nights in the infirmary the doctor placed me on light duty for a couple of days. In less than a week I was back to my regular strength.

We usually had Sundays off, which to me meant church, though many of the guys caught up on their sleep and letter writing. We couldn't leave the post or the company area without permission. Transportation to chapel was supplied by our DIs. My first such ride was pretty tense; I was told not to speak. The sergeant had a bad hangover and wasn't very coherent. When he dropped me at the chapel, I tried thanking him, but he just growled, "Don't thank me for doing my job."

After that I usually walked, since it only took about fifteen minutes. Interestingly, this same sergeant asked me each week if I needed a lift. Thanking him, I explained that I would walk. One rainy Sunday morning, though, he stopped alongside me, insisting I ride. Half-joking and half-serious, I asked if he would like to come in for the service. He smiled slightly and said, "Thanks, no."

I knew that my chances of going to Vietnam were high. Because of this, I asked a lot of questions whenever something wasn't clear to me. The fighting going on in Nam was no joke, and the training was serious business. Many of the younger guys were reluctant to ask questions. At times they'd ask me to explain what was going on. We'd talk about it, but I told them that if they were serious they should ask the instructors. There is no such thing as a stupid question; stupidity lies in not asking.

My questions, however, encouraged heckling from one guy. Bill was one arrogant SOB, and he took none of the training very seriously. As a Canadian citizen, Bill couldn't be sent to Nam unless he volunteered, and I didn't think he would ever do that. After a while his badgering became more than a nuisance--it became vicious. When I was assigned as squad leader, he seemed determined to make my life difficult.

James, our acting platoon guide, Sergeant Carter, and the other DIs were very aware of Bill's haranguing. They were especially concerned about how it might affect the other men. Their talking with him did nothing to help the situation.

When Bill was left alone, he would go through our things and make a mess, usually just prior to an inspection. My foot and wall lockers seemed to be one of his preferred targets. He even took some of my T-shirts and wrote "The Question Man" on them. As far as any of us knew, Bill had never stolen anything, but his actions lost us all privileges and irritated the hell out of us.

One Sunday afternoon James and one of our DIs found me in the dayroom. James said, "Hey, Mills, you gotta come and see this. Bill has really flipped."

As we approached the barracks we could see my footlocker dangling by a heavy cord from the second-floor window. My newly purchased olive drab T-shirts hung tacked to the locker lid with Bill's inscription: "The Question Man."

Looking up at the window, I muttered, "This is definitely annoying."

The sergeant growled, "This has gone too far."

"Sergeant," I began, "he's a member of my squad. Could you give me a few minutes alone with him? You know, turn your back?" As the noncom (NCO) thought about my request, I added, "No one will get hurt; bruised maybe, but not hurt." He finally agreed and headed back to the orderly room to wait.

Knowing that Bill craved an audience, James waited downstairs to keep any of the guys from going up. As I started up the steps, I didn't have a clue what I would say or do. But enough was enough. Up till then, no one had ever challenged him. We'd grumble a little, fix whatever had been messed up, and get on with life.

Stretched out on my bunk, Bill pretended to be asleep. I sat down on the next bunk. Slowly he turned his head toward me, opened one eye, and gave me a Cheshire Cat grin.

"No more, Bill," I said. "This stops here. Now!"

Before he could say anything, and in less than a heartbeat, I grabbed my mattress with both hands. Pulling up and over with all my might, I rolled him off the bunk and onto the floor. With a swooping motion, I followed him across the bare springs. Landing on top of him, I pinned him to the floor with his arms and legs tightly wrapped up in the bedding and the mattress. He couldn't move. Only his head and part of his shoulders protruded.

With my left arm around his throat, I locked that hand onto my right forearm. He could still breathe, but only with my permission.

"You dumb shit, listen closely," I began. "I know you can't be sent to Nam. We all know that. But most of us are going whether we want to or not. Your cutting up and heckling might be detrimental to someone's survival. Do you understand?"

He nodded quickly.

"I'm going to release you now," I continued, "and you will immediately pull my locker back in the window, remake my bunk, secure all my gear and anyone else's you've messed with. If this does not happen, I will continue this conversation at a later time. Do you understand?"

Bill nodded again.

He must have taken me seriously because as I left the building with James to meet with the sergeant again, the locker was already out of the window. A few days later, a fresh package of T-shirts was left on my bunk. Sarge couldn't understand the change in Bill.

"What did you do to him, Mills?" the DI asked.

I shrugged. "Oh, Bill and I just had a very enlightening talk—slightly one-sided."

My own upbringing had been pretty strict. I was used to discipline, and according to some of my instructors, my conduct was not typical for a new recruit. Because I was older than the other recruits and was in fairly good physical condition, the cadre suspected that I might be a plant by the Army brass, or even Congress. Some unfortunate and unexplained accidents had happened to recruits going through basic training in all branches of the military. These had resulted in serious injuries and, in a few cases, death. The Vietnam man-buildup gave a sense of urgency, and training often took a few shortcuts. Families' complaints to elected officials had resulted in the placement of young military officers or noncoms posing as raw recruits as part of the investigation, so the idea that I might be a pigeon wasn't that far-fetched.

As a result of high scores on written exams, I was regularly singled out as a possible candidate for Officer Candidate School (OCS), or helicopter pilot training. Twice a week I was told to report to the captain's office. He made a strong case, but I still refused.

Perhaps I was wrong to decline the Army's offer, but I really didn't want to fly choppers. Besides, it would have required a three-to-five-year commitment. Another problem I had with OCS was that there seemed to be a lot of bickering and friction between the officers and noncoms. It didn't instill much respect for their leadership abilities.

Late one Saturday afternoon in the barracks, one of the guys hollered, "At ease." We had a noncom visitor.

"Carry on," the first sergeant yelled. Then just as loudly he asked, "Where's Mills? Front and center, Mills!" he bellowed.

We had returned from a ten-mile hike only minutes before. I was upstairs putting my gear away. "Here, First Sergeant," I said. "I'll be right down."

Coming to attention at the bottom of the stairs, I said, "Private Mills reporting to the First Sergeant as ordered."

"As you were, Private. I've got a letter here for you." Handing me an envelope he added, "This damn thing has been around the country a few times; even visited the Marines once."

The return address read "United Airlines." For a quick two seconds I was baffled. As I opened the letter a check fell to the floor. Sarge picked it up and handed it back to me. The letter contained three short sentences. I knew the sergeant was curious to know, so I handed him the letter.

"What kind of inconvenience were you caused?" he asked, handing the letter back to me.

I gave him a quick rundown on the exciting flight from San Francisco to Seattle just weeks earlier. He could hardly believe it.

"Damn," one of my buddies groaned, "I think I'd rather be shot at. At least then you can shoot back."

"They didn't explain what happened in this letter, that's for sure," the First Sergeant mused.

The Army's training was rigorous. There were times when I would be so tired in the morning that I wondered if it was possible to fall asleep while doing physical training. I think I came close.

Although I had never been known for my athletic abilities, I found after a short time that I was actually doing pretty well. Running was tough for me, but after a couple of weeks I was up at the front of my squad, and many times we were at the head of the company.

The low crawl was my least favorite exercise. There were two kinds of low crawl. One, more for drill than practical use, required us to move alligator-like, palms flat and chest just a couple of inches off the ground, as fast as we could for about twenty yards. The other was more like what you might see in the movies. We moved forward on our elbows and knees with packs, heavy steel helmets that refused to stay on, and rifles cradled across our arms. It was like swimming on dry ground and paddling with our elbows. It didn't take long for our shirts and pants to be torn at the elbows and knees.

The real fun came during several nights of low crawling under barbed wire while machine guns fired live ammo just above our heads. Flares were shot off with an occasional ground blast to simulate grenades, land mines, or mortars. It seemed pretty real, and people reacted to this exercise in different ways.

On the second or third night of the drill, a guy from another company who had missed this exercise was scheduled to go through with my squad. About halfway through, he became panicked, crying and yelling, "I can't stand this! I can't stand this! I've gotta get out of here." He was so scared that he tried to stand up. My buddy Tom and I were in the lanes on either side of him. About three feet above us was wire, and live rounds were being fired above that. The lanes were divided by wire as well. Tom yelled out to me, "Vic, grab his right arm—I have his left!"

A man behind us grabbed a boot and a leg, and the three of us wrestled the kid to the ground. The exercise was halted and we *carefully* untangled ourselves from the wire. As the medics in the first-aid tent were treating us, Sergeant Carter said, "If you guys hadn't pulled the kid down, he could have been killed. Good job."

The tear gas exercise was another nightmarish ordeal. We put on our gas masks as we moved into a small steel-sided building. Once inside we formed a circle. Then a canister or two of C-4 gas was set off in the building. After a short lecture, the trainer said, "Okay, everyone take off your masks and jog around the circle."

This procedure was designed to get us used to low levels of gas before we donned the masks again. We emerged from the building with burning skin, puffy eyes, and tears streaming down our faces, desperately trying to catch our breath. It hurt just to breathe—a little like when I lived and worked in Los Angeles.

Next to marching, the Army really enjoyed long hikes into the country. Sometimes the hikes even had a purpose. I don't recall the exact distances, but we would hike for hours at a time. Usually we would set up a camp or bivouac for a few days.

On one of these maneuvers we were warned of a simulated gas attack scheduled to occur during the night. There had been other similar tests. During evening chow, James and I sat a short distance away from the other guys and talked about being gassed. I proposed a change of plans. He didn't much care for my idea, but I argued, "Look, James. If this was the real thing, real combat, we'd try anything to counter such an attack, right?" I knew he would have to agree. "We're supposed to pretend this is combat. . ."

James finally agreed and we worked out the details. Later we met with the other squad leaders to fill them in. The other three guys went for it. We told our guys that at midnight they were to grab their rolled up sleeping bags, low-crawl out of the tents, and move a few yards away into the woods.

At about 2:00 a.m., gas canisters were thrown into our tents, but we weren't there. One of the responsibilities of a soldier during a gas attack is to put on his gas mask and holler "gas attack" several times as loudly as possible, which we did—from the trees.

Earlier that evening, we had *accidentally* found one new gas canister. The sergeants and lieutenant shared one larger, six-man tent. None of these men carried a gas mask. They had no reason to. About an hour after we were gassed, we returned the new canister we found by rolling it into the cadre's tent, minus the pin. What a verbal explosion! They ran outside, hacking, coughing, and making an effort at a few crude expletives, and we quickly found they had no sense of humor. Hell, I figured the five of us were headed for the guardhouse.

The two sergeants and the lieutenant were beyond angry, and rightfully so. It had been a damn fool thing to do. Our company commander really chewed out James and me. "What the hell were you thinking of?" he asked. "Where did you get such a plan?" he demanded. He listened as we explained our reasons. After a few moments he looked at us, and trying hard not to crack a smile, he said before dismissing us, "Good thinking, men—but *don't* do it again." They still wouldn't fire us. I guess the Army still needed live targets in Nam.

Basic training also meant training with firearms. When I was about eleven years old I found out what recoil was all about. My older brother had bought a Winchester, lever-action, 30.30, similar to those seen in western movies. Not only did it knock me on my butt, it also left my shoulder black-and-blue for weeks after. Even so, I liked shooting.

All through basic, we trained with the M-14, a gas-operated, semi-or fully automatic rifle, which fired the NATO's 7.62 mm (.308) caliber ammo. The M-16 was actually the military's weapon of choice in Nam. It fired the smaller, but hotter, .223 caliber. The story was that there weren't enough of the newer rifles to use in training, but we did fire a few rounds through them.

My skill on the rifle range again raised suspicions that I might be a plant. My scores were high, and I became quick at disassembling, cleaning, and reassembling my weapon. I wasn't the quickest, but I never put it together incorrectly and my time was always among the best. As a result, Sarge sometimes had me help out with the training.

The military was starting to pick up on the freestyle shooting technique that civilian police and other government agencies were pioneering. It was more like shooting from the hip at close range, rather than taking time to shoulder a weapon and use the sights. I had played around with freestyle for years and found it worked really well during the rapid-target-fire qualifying exercise.

This exercise was a simulated-combat walking range. Twelve or fifteen targets, shaped like men, would suddenly pop up, one or two at a time. Some would be in front of us, others off to the left or right. The range must have been around three hundred meters long and fifty to seventy-five meters wide. We didn't walk the whole length; some targets were over two hundred meters away. The usual M-14 magazine held twenty rounds, but to qualify we could only use ten rounds on this course. This training probably benefited the guys who would later infiltrate jungles and rice paddies. In that kind of combat, the lighter M-16 would have worked better, but there were complaints from GIs about the M-16's range, striking power, and reliability in combat.

Like many units, the recruits in my basic training outfit represented a wide variety of backgrounds, personalities, and skills. One very different type of individual was Tom. Quiet and friendly, he kept to himself most of the time. He aced all of the written tests. He was just twenty-one and had already earned a master's degree in mathematics. For all his intelligence, however, he possessed very little physical ability, nearly failing all of the agility tests and the rifle range. He could run, rope climb, and do push-ups and overhead bars, but he was painfully slow. Yet he was one of the kindest, most gentle people I had ever met; he always had a kind word for everyone.

Having Tom in our training group was a blessing in disguise. He helped to unite all of the guys to stand by one of their own. Quite often, after we finished one test, some of us would go back to help Tom. Watching him do the routines would have been sad if it hadn't been so comical. One of the funniest was bayonet practice. We were to charge up a short hill with fixed bayonets, screaming at the top of our lungs, and attack poor defenseless bags of straw. Tom was pathetic. He had probably never killed so much as a bug in his life. He tried so hard, but he couldn't run well, and he couldn't sound mean.

We worried about him. In combat, his lack of physical aptitude could endanger him and those around him. It didn't seem right that such an intelligent, kind person be used for the military's folly. Toward the end of basic training a few of us asked to speak with the CO. Tom's making it through basic training had been a committee effort. We felt there must be some role for him other than that of combat soldier.

We met with our captain and our head drill instructor, and much to everyone's surprise, they listened to us and agreed. After graduation, we got our orders for advanced individual training (AIT). Tom was sent to Washington, D.C., as a noncombatant. We were told that because of his education, he would start out either as a warrant officer or a second lieutenant. He was spared any further physical training. During the graduation ceremony, the battalion commander, without mentioning any names, gave our company a verbal commendation for helping one of our own.

With everything done and the ink still drying on our orders, the company held a talent show for the whole brigade during the last day of basic. I had brought my Gibson guitar, and kept it secured in the orderly room when I wasn't playing it. Our Tennessee sergeant liked country music and could play a little guitar too. We sang a lot of familiar tunes, including Roy Orbison's "Sweet Dreams." I still remember this performance and its contrast with what was to come.

Chapter 2
AIT and MP School

After finishing basic training, I was ordered directly to AIT at the Military Police School at Fort Gordon, Georgia, outside of Augusta. I waited at SeaTac Airport, hoping for a better flight than the one I'd had to Seattle some ten weeks earlier. Our departure was delayed by two hours due to mechanical problems, but once we were underway most of the flight went fine. Just outside of Chicago we did run into a pretty serious lightning storm that kept us circling the airport for an hour. Flying above the storm, I watched the dancing light show in the sky below.

"I don't see my Atlanta flight listed on the board," I said to the lady behind the ticket counter when we had finally landed.

Looking at my ticket she said, "Sorry, soldier, your connecting flight left over an hour ago."

"How long of a wait do I have?"

"I'm terribly sorry, but the thunderstorms have delayed many flights," she smiled apologetically. "The next plane to Atlanta won't be until 9:00 this evening." Writing on the envelope she added, "Please report to this gate number thirty minutes ahead of departure time."

With several hours to wait, I headed for the USO's corner of the terminal. Two young high school girls greeted me.

"Hi, where ya from?"

"Originally, or twenty-four hours ago?"

With giggles the older of the two said, "All the above."

"Well, I had just moved to Seattle from the Bay Area. Then the President sent me this personal little note about straightening out the U. S. Army. And here I am."

"Well," the girl said with a grin, "what can we get for you? We have writing materials, sandwiches, doughnuts, cold drinks, and coffee." Pausing for a moment as if searching for something more, she finally added with the enthusiasm of a drum roll, "Oh! And the always popular . . . Army bunk beds."

Since I had been on the go for over twenty-four hours, I opted for the bunk and four hours of sleep.

My connecting flight arrived in Atlanta a little past midnight. I was a whole day and a half behind schedule. One more short flight would take me to Augusta. The final leg of the trip was on an old thirty-passenger, twin-engine DC-3. It had been a long time since I had flown on anything old enough to have been at Kitty Hawk! Two hours and three rough stops later, we were on the ground at the Augusta airport. To my surprise, someone was actually there to meet me.

Dawn was just breaking when I was dropped off at the company's orderly room. I think it was Sunday, but days and dates were getting fuzzy. This was my first time in the South, and two things immediately impressed me. One, it seemed very warm for 4:30 in the morning, even though this was just the end of June; and two, our first sergeant was on hand that early on a Sunday morning.

"I've been waiting for you and two others," he told me. "You're the last one, Mills. Rough flight?" he asked.

"Which of the three would you like to hear about, First Sergeant?" I answered.

"Well, boy, I've certainly been on a few like that myself." As first sergeants go, he made a great first impression. While he was checking me in, he asked, "When did you eat last?"

"While circling O'Hare about twenty hours back, First Sergeant," I responded.

"Come on, let's take a walk over to the mess hall for a cup of coffee and a doughnut, and a little conversation," he told me. As we sipped the dark, steaming beverage he said, "You missed orientation late Friday. Most of the guys have been here for two or three days already." Taking a sip he added, "Nothing to be concerned about. You didn't miss much."

Then he led me to the barracks. With the exception of one soldier still on fireguard duty, everyone else was asleep. Top (the nickname for first sergeants) showed me to a bunk and said to come see him when I felt like getting up. The narrow, iron, Army bunk always seemed better suited for torture than for sleep. However, I hadn't been to bed, other than that nap in Chicago, since late Thursday night, so I settled in.

It was just past noon when I finally regained consciousness. I was extremely hungry and uncomfortably hot. After the cool, late spring of the Northwest, Georgia's steamy heat had me sweating profusely. What made me even more uncomfortable was that I hadn't been able to shower for three days. I headed for the showers, and once I got in, it felt so good to get clean that I didn't want to turn the water off.

After leaving Fort Lewis Friday morning, I hadn't eaten anything other than snack food and a bad airline sandwich. At my new mess hall a young cook filled me up with some ham, pancakes, and eggs. I added some juice, milk, and coffee. It wasn't quite home cooking, but it was good. With almost eight hours of sleep, a hot shower and hot food, I felt nearly human. Afterwards I wandered back to the orderly room to chat with the first sergeant.

After this visit I began adjusting to the new group, gradually familiarizing myself with command and rules. Most of rules that had been covered in the orientation I had missed were ones common to other posts. However one was different, and I had to learn about it the hard way.

It was on my way out of the mess hall.

"Hey you," the guy manning the hot, sudsy rinse water yelled after me. "You're s'posed to rinse this stuff."

With a glance back I said, "Who are you kidding?"

I had cleared my dishes and set them in the container of soapy water as I had been taught back at Fort Lewis, and I thought this was standard operating procedure (S.O.P.) on all bases. It wasn't! If I had been more observant I could have saved myself a bit of embarrassment. As it was, I continued putting my dirty dishes in the container after all meals.

Everything seemed okay until breakfast on Tuesday morning, my third day there. Our head instructor, a sergeant first class whom I had had the pleasure of meeting before, sent word for me to report to him at the front door of our barracks ASAP. In Army language that meant "five minutes ago." I had no idea why he wanted to see me; but the guy who came for me said, "He's pissed at you about something!" Hell, I hadn't been there long enough to get into any trouble.

The sergeant was a big man, about 6 feet 4, and 230 pounds of angry granite. When I reported to him he quickly seemed to be 9 feet, 13 inches tall and about 800 pounds; and he was right in my face. He yelled something about following procedures. I had absolutely no clue why he was so upset. He was speaking so loudly that I couldn't understand much of what he said. Sarge used snuff, and as he continued yelling, I became liberally baptized with little brown droplets of spit. He awarded me three days of KP (kitchen police) duty.

As I found out, the guy at the mess hall who I had thought was joking about rinsing my dishes, hadn't been. He and another kid had reported me several times to their mess sergeant, but hadn't been able to read my nametag. Well, I finally got caught.

Ironically, the group training for that morning was going to be something called "running the gauntlet." This outing had all the earmarks of a visit to hell. That little adventure was canceled for me. I put my gear away and reported to the mess sergeant instead. The same kid who had turned me in came over saying, as we shook hands, "Hey, my name's Pryce. We finally caught your ass."

"Yeah, I guess. I had thought the rules would be the same on any post."

"Well, come 4:00 or 5:00 this afternoon, you'll be glad you screwed up. You'll be even gladder I pigeoned on ya." Then with a big grin he added, "You just wait and see what them boys look like when they come back. Come on, I'll show ya around."

Back then the military still used KP as punishment, although it was a rotating assignment as well. From what I was hearing, though, this was going to be more like a weekend pass than a penalty. Most of the guys really hated to pull KP, but it was easy duty.

A couple of hours after the company left for their fun and games in the humid, 90-degree plus weather, one of our DIs, Staff Sergeant Reddig, came by the mess hall to get a cup of coffee.

"Hi, Mills. How ya makin'out?"

"I'm fine, Sergeant. Pryce here explained what the problem was."

Glancing first at Pryce, then over at the mess sergeant, then back at me, Reddig said as I poured his coffee, "Grab a cup for yourself and join me."

"Thanks, Sergeant," I responded as the head cook gave me the nod.

"You know, we didn't realize you had missed orientation until Top told me a little while ago." Sipping his coffee and looking stern at me, Reddig added, "You aren't a screw-up, are ya, Mills?"

"No, Sergeant," I responded emphatically. "I am not. This is all very serious to me."

Softening his gaze he said, "Top and I have been looking over your file, and it didn't appear to us you're a screw-up either." Sitting back in his chair and pausing, he added, "But you really lucked out missing today's exercise." Then he explained a little about the "gauntlet" and continued, "The first sergeant and I will straighten things out later with Sergeant Clausen. There won't be any record of this in your file. Now you'd best get back to work."

From what I saw of the guys when they came back, Reddig and Pryce had been right. I did luck out. Providence was truly watching over me. I do believe that the "gauntlet" would have made one hell of a worse punishment than washing a few pots and pans.

A few nights later, my kitchen tour now in the past, Sergeant Clausen called me out of formation. The rest of the company was dismissed. "Smoke if you like, Mills," he said.

"Thanks, Sergeant, but I don't smoke."

"I wanted to have a few words with you," he said slowly. "Sergeant Reddig and the first sergeant seem to think I was wrong about you. So tell me, why the hell didn't you tell me you missed orientation when I was chewing you out?"

"Actually, at the time I didn't think it appropriate or healthy to do so, Sergeant," I replied.

He smiled slightly and nodded in agreement.

"Private Zimmerman, your acting squad leader, is in the hospital and will not finish this training. You're taking his place as head of 3rd Squad."

It sure wasn't what I was expecting, nor was it a responsibility I wanted, but I accepted anyway and came to attention saying, "Thank you, Sergeant!"

Georgia is a beautiful state, even with the heat and humidity. The insects, however, were something that none of us enjoyed very much. There were so many biting bugs they had to fight for a space on our bodies. One pest, the gnat, was even more aggressive than the mosquito. Mosquitoes were a bother at night as we slept, but those tiny gnats buzzed around our heads, flying in our eyes and ears, and even up our noses. They liked to bite too.

The Army had us form up in lines for almost everything, and the gnats always lined up in perfect formation with us. Each GI had his own personal little swarm. Form up a line of hot sweaty bodies and the gnats would surely be there.

Once while waiting in the chow line, one of our DIs announced, "You will all stand at attention. And, you will not hurt any of my gnats. You will not swat at or wave at them."

This was impossible. When our lieutenant came over to us by way of the open field and saw us being tortured, he asked a soldier, "Why are all your men at attention with all these damn bugs buzzin' around you?"

"Sir," the GI answered, "the sergeant placed us at attention, and we're ordered not to harm any of the sergeant's gnats, sir."

Waving a few off from in front of his own face, the lieutenant yelled, "Detail, rest in place. Smoke if you wish. Hunting season for gnats is now open."

Everyone let out a loud sigh of relief. When the sergeant came out of the mess hall, the lieutenant quietly, but soundly, rebuked the noncom, "In the future, Sergeant, if you wish to protect your gnats and skeeters, you do so outside with your men, and you follow the same orders you give them."

The sergeant glumly replied, "Yes, sir." Then, turning to the rest of the group, he said, "Everyone, move into the mess hall."

While waiting in line, I mentioned to one of the guys, "I think I know how we can at least get rid of these gnats." The others close by seemed interested. After many days of putting up with these bugs, I remembered something I had used while growing up around the citrus orchards of California: bay leaves. Back home, I would slide a bay leaf or two inside the sweatband of my cap. Western gnats do not care for the bay tree at all. I misappropriated a few bay leaves from the mess hall and soon found out that the southern gnats don't care for the leaf either. From then on, I kept bay leaves with me all the time, especially during marches and bivouacs, or whenever we had to form a line. One day the lieutenant saw what I was doing and asked, so I shared the secret with him. The results were great!

Since I was quite familiar with the workings of a kitchen, KP duty was not a punishment. While growing up in a household with two brothers and two sisters, we had learned how to cook many different foods, including some pastries. My downfall was in the cleanup department; I didn't do very well there at all. I still don't.

Early one Sunday morning around 0800, I came into the mess hall to grab a bite. There was a bus due through the fort within the hour that I could catch to get to church. I was a lot earlier than the other guys; almost everyone else was still sleeping.

The mess sergeant, who probably had a hangover, was in a sour mood when I asked for some scrambled eggs. He said coarsely, "Cold cereal or hot oatmeal, but if eggs are what you want, then you best get your ass back here and fix 'em yourself, 'cause I ain't."

"Okay, Sarge. My cooking won't get you into trouble, will it?" I asked.

"No trouble. Just don't make too much noise—my head's about to split."

I surprised him, because I did just what he had suggested. Now, scrambled eggs are one thing, but I hadn't had a good omelet in months, so I thought I might just as well cook up something I would really like. I found some sliced ham and mild cheddar in the cooler, and also some bacon, which had been cooked for somebody else. The omelet was perfect. The young sergeant ate that one—a real work of art. I had to make another one for myself—this time a Denver omelet with ham, cheese, a little green onion, a slice or two of tomato, and a bit of green pepper. It was mighty good.

My cooking expertise qualified me to become this sergeant's favorite private. I was on mess hall detail several times after that. We got along just fine, even though I had to double up on study time for my MP training.

Whenever I had a two-day pass, I'd try to go into town. The bus route took us right through what was then called the colored district. One Saturday while on my way into Augusta, I met a young black couple. They got on the bus right at the gate. The husband was in the Army Reserves. From what they told me, the area was city-owned housing, and it was nearly impossible to get even the simplest of repairs done. His brother and sister-in-law rented a duplex. They had two small kids, and the family had been without a working bathroom for several months. The reservist and his brother once made some basic repairs, paying for the parts themselves. The city nearly evicted them for their efforts.

Because of where I had been raised, I had known only a few people of color. I'd worked with two in construction whom I considered friends, and thought nothing of it. However, the blacks in my company warned us that Caucasians had to be cautious about associating with them or with other blacks outside of duty. The local whites could bring reprisals against both for breaking the racial code. In 1967 I certainly couldn't tell that Mr. Lincoln had won much of anything for these people.

I had to deal with some other strange treatment as well. Apparently my file from basic still had a notation in it that I might be a plant, because at times I was asked some very odd questions. One day my squad was weeding and policing the grounds around the company area. I had been working several yards away from the rest of the detail when Sergeant Reddig came over to me and, out of the blue, he asked, "Hey, Mills, how's it going?" Then in a quieter voice he said, "I want to ask you something."

"Sure, Sergeant, what is it?" I queried.

"Tell me, do you think I handle the men all right?"

The sergeant was a good man, and I wouldn't have minded going into combat with him, but his question caught me off guard. I stood there for a moment studying his face and finally responded, "Fine, Sergeant, but I can't say anymore now."

Apparently my choice of words gave him the wrong impression. He smiled and said "Thanks! I understand," then walked away.

Our MP training consisted of a lot of spit-and-polish and some of the most rigorous physical training anywhere. I had never run so much in my life; we ran up to five miles every other day on the quarter-mile track, in addition to our usual full-pack runs.

When we weren't running, marching for miles and miles, setting up bivouacs, or doing some other physical training, our barracks were inspected once or twice a week. Sometimes we were surprised with an inspection in the middle of the night. This gradually eased off, but the general's inspections usually came without warning. Of course, we had gone through inspections during basic, but these in AIT were taken to a much higher level.

Before I was made acting squad leader, my company had never passed an inspection. As a result, the guys received extra duty with little or no time off. My acting platoon guide, a kid from Oklahoma named Billy Joe, had just turned nineteen. We called him BJ. He worked hard and had a lot of self-confidence, but he wasn't cocky. I asked him to call a meeting of squad leaders to discuss the inspection problem. We met with the whole company. We suspected there had been a little sleight of hand, either by our drill instructors or by some people from another company. Often, after we had thoroughly cleaned, our cadre would find candy or gum wrappers on the floor or on a windowsill, and a cigarette butt or two in the latrine. Often our gear had been rearranged.

We figured we could get away with a clandestine guard for a week or two before the inspectors caught on. Whenever members of our group were assigned to KP or garbage detail, we kept watch by feigning nature calls in order to get back into the barracks to check things out.

Once a sergeant from a rival company was spotted going into our barracks about half an hour before a scheduled inspection. Our watcher and another guy, who was on light duty for a day, removed the planted cigarette butts and wiped up the water that had been spilled on the latrine floor. They also checked for any out-of-place gear. We passed that inspection and aced every one from then on.

Training included many hours of judo, and we all had the bruises to show for it. We had touched on hand-to-hand combat in basic, but this training was far more intense. We needed to learn how to break up bar fights or stop any other disorderly conduct. As MPs, we would need to disarm, temporarily immobilize, and handcuff any out-of-control GI. In reality, I think we learned just enough judo to get into trouble. Even so, we were required to learn it.

We also learned that there were two facets to military police work—security and investigations. We were to provide security and traffic control as well as investigate accidents and crimes committed against the military on or off post. Much of our training and classroom instruction focused on security and on the "Uniform Code of Military Justice," though in practice, as I found out later, it was short on "uniform" and contained very little "justice."

Our security training included camping trips or bivouacs. These usually meant more marches and long hikes with all our gear. Often temperatures hit the high nineties to low hundreds with like humidity. We would be out two or three days and then march, hike, or crawl back. Many of these outings also included compass reading and map making.

While returning from one of these bivouacs, we were informed that our class "A" pictures would be taken as soon as we got back to the company area. We put on our Class "A" dress-green jackets with our ascots, ribbons, and white caps, and lined up for the photo session, even though we had been out in the field for two or three days and were still filthy. Later my family asked why I looked so angry and mean in that picture. I explained about having been in the field and told them, "Some of Georgia's best-kept secrets were still crawling on me. I was not in a good mood!"

After we finished with the pictures, our company was given a long weekend off, but we had to stay on post. That was a nice way of letting us clean our gear and ourselves and go to the mess hall for a meal. After dinner, some of the guys went to the post theater to see a movie. BJ and I grabbed some shorts and hitched a ride some distance from the company area to the post swimming pool, where I discovered protocol, Beverly, and a different kind of Georgia warmth.

We arrived at the pool around 8:00 p.m. The weather had cooled some from the near 110 degrees to the mid-90s. I am not much of a swimmer, but the pool was certainly refreshing. There had been two other swimmers in the water when we got there, but one left almost immediately after our arrival. After his dip, BJ became interested in playing eight ball in the game room with another soldier. I stayed in the water for a long time with the other swimmer, a young woman. We introduced ourselves as we passed each other.

"Hi, I'm Beverly, but call me Bev," she called out.

"I'm Vic. You can call me Vic," I answered, and she gave a quick giggle.

My thought was that she was also in the Army or a dependent because the rec center was only open to military personnel and their families. The rules stated that there was no rank on the premises. Everyone arrived and played in civvies—so you really couldn't tell the other person's status.

After awhile we got out of the pool and dried off. We drank some pop and talked. We each volunteered a little. I told her I was about midway through MP school, and she said she was assigned to the post supply or something like that. The thought that she might be a PFC or Specialist 4th Class danced briefly through my mind, but other than that first short exchange we didn't talk Army. We joined BJ to shoot a little pool, then I found an old guitar and strummed some tunes, and we talked about our hometowns. Bev was from a little town in the Midwest. She shared pictures of her family, and I showed her snapshots of my son. Suddenly I didn't feel that home was so far away.

BJ hitched a ride back to the barracks around ten, and I barbecued a couple of hamburgers on the patio grill for Bev and myself. It was a clear night, and the stars came out as the sunlight faded across the horizon. It was quiet and peaceful, one of the few times I enjoyed a Georgia evening, and the second time I had ever seen fireflies.

Bev drove me back to my company area and gave me her phone number as she dropped me off. I had to pull duty over that weekend, but over the next few weeks we did spend a lot of off-duty time together. She had a friend who enjoyed being with BJ, so we double-dated, going to movies or dances in town, and hanging out at the pool. BJ was engaged and he made it clear that he was spoken for, but we always had a good time.

I made some other new friends as well. During my first week at Fort Gordon, the chaplain's office told me there was a church of my persuasion in Augusta, and that I could get there easily by bus. That's where I met Wally Wilson and his family. Because of my short GI hair, I still had the look of a raw recruit and I stuck out in a crowd.

At the conclusion of that first service, Wally's wife asked, "Tell me, Vic, what time do you have to be back to the Fort?"

"By 5:00 this evening, ma'am," I replied.

Mrs. Wilson smiled and said, "Well, that's more than enough time."

She gathered her two teenage daughters, who took me by both arms, led me to their car, and took me home to one fantastic southern-style Sunday dinner. After that, the Wilsons took me home with them nearly every Sunday I could get in for church. Occasionally, other people from the church would come for dinner or barbecues as well.

On that first Sunday, the Wilsons dropped me off at the Fort's gate at 4:30 p.m.

"Can you walk to your quarters by 5:00?" they asked.

"Sure. It's less than a mile," I responded. Then, turning to Mr. and Mrs. Wilson, I added, "Thank you for a wonderful Sunday, for dinner, and for all your hospitality."

Waving goodbye as they drove off, I heard the girls giggling wildly in the back seat. Something was very funny, and I wondered what it could be.

The following Wednesday afternoon, as I was working with BJ and the other squad leaders making up a duty roster for the weekend, Sergeant Reddig came looking for me. When I saw him, I immediately announced his presence saying, "At ease." (I was learning.) We stopped what we were doing.

As he approached, Reddig said, "Carry on."

I stood up and said, "Hi, Sarge. What's up?"

"Mills, there's a lieutenant colonel from JAG (Judge Advocate General) at the orderly room asking for you."

"Are you sure he wants me?"

Reddig nodded in the affirmative, and I followed him back to report to this officer.

Why any officer, in or out of my training group, would be looking for me I didn't have a clue. When I walked into the orderly room I came to attention in front of Captain Jake (my CO), snapped a salute, and said, "Private Mills reporting to the captain as ordered, sir."

The colonel's back was to me so I couldn't see his face.

"At ease, Mills. This officer would like to speak with you privately."

I still could not see his face when the colonel suggested in a rough voice, "Let's go outside, Private." Boy, was I ever surprised when he turned around and I recognized *Mr. Wilson*, with a silver oak leaf on his collar. He told me not to say anything until we got some distance away from the building, so I kept quiet.

We walked a few yards before he told me why he had come. "Your final divorce papers were sent to my office by mistake," he began. "When I saw your name on them, I thought I'd just bring them to you myself rather than send them back through channels." Then added, "They had already been sent to Fort Lewis and two or three other posts."

Evidently the Army still had no idea where I was.

"By the way," the Colonel asked, "would you like a ride to the Wednesday evening church service tonight?"

"Yes, sir," I answered, "but I'm not sure I can get a pass. And it's difficult to get a ride back to base at night."

Colonel Wally already had it all figured out. He handed me a pass he had wrangled from the first sergeant. "I'll be back at 5:00 to pick you up, unless you truly prefer Army chow to my wife's cooking."

I was enthusiastic about his wife's cooking. "That would be great, sir."

"I'll get you back in plenty of time, as I have to report back this evening myself," he explained.

Coming to attention and saluting, I said, "Sir, thank you again for these papers and for the invitation. I'll be ready at 5:00."

As he walked to his car, I stuffed the pass into my pocket and headed back to the barracks.

As soon as I walked in, BJ asked jokingly, "Well, are you on your way to the guardhouse?"

"No, the officer just dropped off some legal papers for me. Oh, I'll be going into town for a few hours this evening."

This episode didn't lessen the suspicions that had swirled around me over the past weeks. A colonel asking for a mere private—talk about using gasoline to put out a fire. Boy, it was getting warm! I was beginning to see that the colonel had a sense of humor. Now I knew why his daughters had been giggling when the family drove off the previous Sunday.

On our way into town, Wally explained, "Look, as long as we're alone or with the family, I am just Wally. But on the post or in the company of other military personnel, you'll have to play Army, just as I will. You know, I think my girls have a crush on you." Then with a wink he added, "Come to think of it, my wife seemed to be very happy I was bringing you out for dinner."

"You have a wonderful family, sir."

Colonel Wilson could have gotten into big trouble for socializing with a mere private. I certainly didn't wish that to happen; besides, I figured I had few opportunities left for Sunday dinners.

My CO seemed very curious about a ranking officer's interest in me. My explanation to him and the first sergeant about the misdirected letter from my divorce attorney was all right on the surface, but I never thought he was happy about the situation.

Captain Jake had been in the Army since graduating from high school and was actually a year younger than I. This was his first training command. Some of us from the company had run into him and his wife and baby a few times at the PX and at the rec center. He invited BJ and me to his residence on post twice, almost socially. I think he was concerned about the rumors about a "plant" in his training company. BJ and I thought a lot of Jake. He seemed like a good officer who took care of his men.

Another friend I made during that period was a civilian church volunteer for my denomination. He was a young college student named Gary. Working through the chaplain's office, he regularly visited a couple of other guys and me on post, although I seldom saw any of them at the church service. Gary also attended the church in Augusta and was good friends with the Wilsons. One weekend, I had a two-day pass and nowhere to go, so Gary invited me to go home with him to Columbia, South Carolina. With the pass in my wallet and some overnight stuff in my bag, I took off with Gary. It was great being able to wear civvies, even for just two days.

Even though this was one of the few times I could have legally slept in past dawn, I was up at 5:30 a.m. and driving through the gate by 6:10. The trip took us just over two hours. En route, we stopped at a Denny's for breakfast where I had my first and last experience eating grits. Thanks, but no thanks! Grits could be the reason why the South lost the Civil War.

We finally arrived at Gary's home, where he lived with his parents, his teenage brother, and two sisters. His brother was in junior high. One sister was in high school and the other in college. Both were true Southern belles. I was captivated by their speech. Listening to them talk, I became instant putty. I never knew anyone could take a simple, single-syllable word like my name and create a totally different sound—"Vee-ick"—and make it sound so soft and warm. Their voices instantly changed the atmosphere around me. My toes barely touched the grass as Gary introduced us. It was a marvelous experience. Unfortunately, I didn't have occasion to see the family again, but I'll never forget their warmth and the hospitality they showed to a total stranger.

The following weekend, I was hoping to ride into town with Bev to see a movie. The duty roster usually rotated everyone pretty well, but something happened to change my plans. First, I restricted my squad to the company area for the weekend with extra duty. Later, BJ restricted the whole barracks, which meant that he and I had to stay on post as well.

Here's why. Three days a week we had lectures and films on Vietnam. At 3:00 one Thursday afternoon, we walked outside the lecture hall to wait for the buses that were to take us back to the company area. I hadn't been feeling well for a couple of days due to a cold or the flu. I kept up with the training all right, but I hadn't realized just how tired I was. Since we had a twenty to thirty-minute wait, I sat down on the steps to enjoy the cool shade. Putting my head down on my knees, I promptly went to sleep. Since the buses were so loud and smelly, I figured I would hear them when they arrived, or that if I didn't, some-one in my squad would surely nudge me.

I woke up a few minutes past four. I stood up and stretched, feeling a lot better. As I cleared the cobwebs, I realized the buses had come and gone. There was absolutely no one around. I had slept for an hour, all through the noise and odor of the buses loading and leaving. No one had awakened me. Apparently some people had thought it was funny to leave their squad leader asleep on the steps.

I was only about three miles from the company area, so I started back, walking, then running, and taking shortcuts. In about half an hour, I arrived at the barracks. BJ had been on duty in the orderly room and hadn't gone with us. Back in the barracks, he was sitting on his bunk when I came in.

"You look awful!" he said. "Why didn't you come back on the bus with the other guys?"

"I fell asleep while we were waiting for the bus," I explained. "I'm thirsty as hell," I added as I headed for the water fountain.

BJ had to admit that he would have been annoyed with the men as well, as he chuckled a little. One thing the Army had taught me was the importance of teamwork—sticking together and watching out for a buddy. You don't have to be friends with everyone in the service, but you have to be able to work together regardless of personal feelings. Many times, especially in Nam, I worked with people I did not care for and who did not care for me, but we got the job done just the same.

BJ and I decided we needed to work over the duty roster. We talked it over with Sergeant Reddig, and he agreed. We gave our weekend passes to another company and restricted our own barracks. Needless to say, our guys were not happy. Only one man received a pass and that was only because he was getting married on Saturday morning. He hadn't been at the lecture anyway. (This young man was later killed in action in Saigon during the Tet offensive while carrying six infant children at one time to safety before being cut down. Not exactly the actions of the "baby killers" some people made our soldiers out to be.)

I phoned Bev and explained to her about the changes for the weekend. She stopped by the next night, and we drove up to the rec center, which was nearly deserted. We watched some TV, grilled some hamburgers, and danced to the jukebox.

The following Monday we were awakened by shouting a little earlier than usual. It was 4:00 a.m. "All right, everyone up, get dressed and fall out for inspection," one of our DIs yelled. Amazingly, we were the first barracks. This was a surprise inspection by the Post Commander. It was the very first time a general ever spoke to me. He asked a few questions and, trying not to show my nervousness, I did my best to answer. While the general and his aides did their inspection, Reddig showed up and ran us through a thorough series of physical training drills.

Later on, we were told our barracks received a perfect score on the inspection. Because the men had been restricted to the company area, they had spent a lot of time cleaning. It's funny how things work out sometimes. All of the guys in our platoon were convinced that somehow BJ and the four squad leaders had known about the inspection in advance and that was why we had canceled the weekend passes. According to Sergeant Reddig, even he hadn't been notified of the inspection.

In spite of the events of that weekend, Bev and I had been seeing a lot of each other during my stay at Fort Gordon. The USO club held dances nearly every weekend, so BJ and I and some of the others in the company went a few times. But on those occasions, Bev never came with us. Only later did I finally understand why. Uniforms were required there.

Up to this time, I still didn't know where on base Bev worked or what her rank was. Any effort I made to bring up the subject was quickly and firmly thwarted. Whenever I saw her, on or off post, she was always in street clothes. She had a nice car and lived off post, where I visited her a few times. Since I really enjoyed her company, I decided not to press the subject of rank any further. As long as she wasn't an officer or a noncom, it was really none of my business!

Two weeks before MP graduation, I was in the orderly room working on a duty roster. It was Friday, and my shift went from 3:00 p.m. to midnight. The assignment was fairly easy. There was a radio to listen to and plenty to do.

I had been on duty for about thirty minutes when I heard our company clerk call out, "Tin-hut," signifying that an officer had just walked in and that our CO was out of the building. I was in a large room in the rear, which doubled as an additional office and storage room. The company staff rarely came into that section. When the door suddenly swung open and Top walked in calling me to attention, I was twice surprised, but knew an officer accompanied him.

The old desk and chair we used there must have been left over from Civil War days. They were both badly worn. The chair had five octopus-style legs on rollers, and it swiveled and tilted back uncontrollably; it was not safe in any position.

I tried my best to stand up, but I got stuck halfway between sitting and standing. I was ridiculously off balance because of *that damn chair*. I didn't dare try to see who was there. Besides, I was too busy with my juggling act; I had a potted plant in one hand and a stack of files in the other. Somehow my feet got tangled up with that five-legged octopus.

When I thought I was stable, I glanced up to see who had come in with Top. Beverly! Surprised, I suddenly lost the rest of my balance, falling over backwards, and crashing onto the floor, my back against the wall and my butt on the seat back of the chair. The flowerpot went one direction and the file folders flew the other.

Trying hard not to laugh, Top and Beverly stood there looking down at me.

Barely concealing a smile, Top said, "The lieutenant would like to speak with you, Private."

"Excuse me for a moment, Lieutenant," I answered as I tried to regain my feet as well as my composure.

Bev responded, "No hurry. Take your time."

Top stepped around the desk to help, but I declined saying, "Thanks, First Sergeant, but this is a one-man operation." My feet were still pretty well tangled up.

After a few moments of working out the logistics, I was finally able to get to my feet amidst the debris. Coming to attention, I said, "Sorry, Lieutenant. Good afternoon."

Top had already left the room and was splitting a gut laughing. I must have been quite a sight.

"Okay," she began. "So I surprised you. Now stop playing Army for a few minutes so that I can."

"What do I call you now?" I asked, still stunned.

She just shook her head. "I just received new orders, and I'm being transferred immediately to Japan." Walking over to me, she put a hand on my arm. "I wanted to see you before I left. I could really get into trouble for telling you this, but I found out that you are definitely going to Vietnam."

I had been pretty sure about my going too, but her words sent a shiver up my spine just the same.

Quietly I asked, "What kind of trouble would you—we—have been in over our dating these past few weeks? We could have been sending picture postcards from adjoining cells in Fort Leavenworth, Kansas!"

A little misty-eyed, she said, "I didn't think about getting into trouble. I really care a lot about you, Vic."

After a few minutes, she left. We met Saturday evening at the rec center, and that was the last contact I had with her except for a short note she left with BJ, saying goodbye, wishing me good luck, and telling me to keep my ass down in Nam. She still holds a warm place in my memory for helping me cope with the rigors of military life, and I will always treasure those days.

I was surprised a couple of days later when Top said to me, "The CO and I knew about you and Bev, but I was sure you didn't know her rank, so the captain and I decided to leave things alone. You were just two kids going swimming."

Meanwhile, the rumors of a plant somewhere in the brigade were running rampant, and the *clandestine* meetings with Colonel Wilson seemed to point to me. A situation that drove a few more nails into the box came one day. It was a very nice Saturday afternoon, hot and humid as usual, and I was walking to the PX. When Sergeant Reddig drove up and asked if I would like a ride, I accepted.

As he drove, we talked about possible assignments, as well as some of his experiences in Vietnam. I told him I felt sure I'd be going there. He concurred that there was a good chance. We talked about his wife and kids, and I told him about my son.

When we got to the door of the PX, a funny thing happened. Both the sarge and I were in our civvies and a young E-5 sergeant and his wife were just walking out the door, heading our way. He had several medals on his shirt along with the Vietnam campaign ribbon. I had never met this soldier before. As they approached us and started to pass, he looked me right in the eyes and, with a surprised expression on his face, saluted me saying, "Good afternoon, Captain."

Without thinking, I saluted back and responded to both him and his wife, "Sergeant. Ma'am."

That was just too much for Reddig. With an immediate "'Bout face" he went back and stopped the younger sergeant. I could see them talking as I disappeared into the building.

I really felt stupid. This business of saluting had gotten out of hand; it had become a reflex action. Hell, I saluted nearly anyone regardless of rank—they just had to look important. I quickly made my few purchases and headed back to the company area, hoping to avoid the good sergeant. After hitching a ride back to the barracks, I met BJ coming from the dayroom. He had been somewhat aware from past conversations that I was suspected of being a plant, so I filled him in on this latest incident. He laughed for nearly five minutes. Sergeant Reddig never mentioned the saluting incident, but that evening at chow he stopped by my table and told me, "Mills, now I understand."

Even though Reddig and the others may have wondered about my background, one area where I really could shine was firearms. I did well with the M-14 on the rifle range, making some of the best scores in basic and in AIT. The MPs' sidearm, the Colt .45 caliber semiautomatic pistol, however, was a challenge. Over the years, there had been talk about how difficult the pistol was to shoot and how poor its accuracy, but I just pooh-poohed this talk as grumbling.

I was wrong for several reasons. It was hard to hit much of anything with the .45s we had in training, and I wasn't the only GI who had a problem. Most of the pistols we used were old and worn. The barrel was sloppy in the frame, so when we fired we hit the target in inconsistent patterns. The Army's tried-and-true stance—sideways to the target with arm raised and extended to take careful aim and then squeeze off one round at a time—did not seem very realistic to me.

"I'm sure they do that when in combat," I muttered sarcastically to a buddy. It would have made just as much sense to throw the damn pistol at the target or enemy as to shoot it.

Three of us in the company couldn't hit a bull in the butt at five paces with these guns. I could barely cut the edge of the paper target, firing from only twenty-five yards away. But there weren't enough pistols to go around, so we had to take turns learning to break them down to clean. With permission from our sergeant I inspected a few of the pistols, and realized just how worn they were, how much play each had in the barrel with the breech closed. This explained why most of the guys barely passed that part of the range course, and why a few others of us couldn't.

There wasn't much time left for the two others and me to qualify, and passing this test was a requirement for graduation. The shooting instructor took the three of us down to the range several times for extra practice. Finally I showed him how sloppy the pistol we were using had become. He even fired a few rounds himself. He made our point for us—his rounds hit all over the target and not where he intended.

"Sergeant," I asked, "could I see your weapon?"

He dropped the magazine out, cleared the chamber, and handed his .45 to me. It appeared to be nearly new. The action was tight and flawless, the operation smooth. I asked if I could fire his pistol, using the newer two-handhold method.

"You guys can use your toes if that will get you qualified," he stated. "You're making me look bad."

I don't recall how many rounds we had to fire to qualify. Firing at two targets, some yards apart, I made it! I don't remember my score, but it was good. My two buddies did as well. With a little more practice using as competent a weapon as the sergeant's, I think the whole company would have scored considerably higher. What a difference his pistol made. When we returned to the company area he personally collected all the pistols.

During our eight weeks in MP training, we studied a great deal about military law—the Code of Military Justice, and what the military establishment expected from us, including how we were to handle ourselves if the enemy should capture us. We learned how to control ourselves under stress and how to help subdue an angry crowd or an individual soldier without harming anyone.

Early on we also had to learn how to drive the M-151 jeep with its manual transmission. Some of the guys only knew how to drive an automatic and had difficulty coordinating the clutch with the gas pedal.

We were also required to take some survival training, to learn even more map reading and writing, and to study how to use a compass. We had covered some of this in basic, but the new stuff was much more intense. We had to find our way over open and forested terrain without help, and without getting lost or caught in the swamp. This was a severe challenge. Each group made a map and then switched with another group. Even though I didn't really understand much of the process at the time, I managed to pass this part of the training with a fair score. I think this field training helped me most once I got to Vietnam.

Graduation from AIT made me a part of the Military Police Corps. There was no ceremony. During the last two weeks of AIT, we drilled and marched and drilled. Then someone thought we should march and drill some more!

The end of August in Georgia was the hottest, muggiest weather I had ever experienced. It was a record breaker. Along with the heat and humidity came thunderstorms that seemed to pop up out of the blue. Several violent lightning storms struck the post. One of these happened on a Sunday when I had just returned from church. I had gone to the dayroom to eat a sandwich, drink a cold pop, and watch part of a baseball game with some of the guys. Ten minutes earlier there hadn't been a cloud in the sky, but soon we could hear the distant rumblings that had become so familiar. In a few minutes, the sky darkened, and we saw flashes of light followed by claps of thunder. Outside, rain poured down in sudden torrents. We were nice and dry in the dayroom, and it was still 90 degrees. A big electric fan kept a breeze moving in the room.

Suddenly there was an explosion. The TV went off as all of the power shut down. Then the fireplace chimney caved in, most of it falling onto the hearth. Everyone ran outside. We were in the midst of a magnificent storm. Bricks were scattered over a fifty-yard radius. I had never seen anything like this. Someone said a lightning bolt had hit the chimney and the TV antenna. It had sounded like a howitzer going off. Five minutes later, the storm passed, and the sun came out. Everything returned to calm.

Finally the day of graduation came. To celebrate, we were given a two-week leave, orders to our next duty station, and transportation vouchers. I was headed for the West Coast, family, and then . . . Vietnam.

Chapter 3
A Respite Before the Storm

The flight from Atlanta to Los Angeles was smooth and peaceful. In fact, I slept much of the way. The stewardesses seated another guy and me near the galley in the rear of the plane. It was quieter there and the seats were larger, with more legroom. I suspect they put us there in deference to our uniforms. Anyway, they treated us like royalty. All we did was eat, sleep, and look out the window.

Once in Los Angeles, I had plans to visit my family in the surrounding area, which meant I had to rent a car.

"Are you home for long?" the girl at the rental car agency asked.

"No, just two weeks, then I head on to Vietnam," I answered as she proceeded to fill out the rental forms. "I have family scattered from here to San Francisco."

When I finished up, she took the paperwork, along with my driver's license, military ID, and cash. Excusing herself she said, "I'll be just a minute. I need the manager to approve this," and she disappeared into the manager's office.

A few moments later a fiftyish-looking gentleman returned with her. The young lady handed me my license, a copy of the rental agreement, and the keys to a brand-new 1967 Ford Galaxy hardtop.

"Here's your refund. The car's on us," the man told me as my money was placed back into my hand, along with a voucher for an additional tank of gas.

As my eyes widened with surprise, the man explained, "I have a nephew already in Vietnam. Have a good leave and a safe tour of duty."

After shaking hands and thanking him, I followed the girl out to find my car. She said that the agency had given many GIs bound for Nam a similar deal. Considering the general social unrest about Vietnam, I thought the rental agency's gesture was pretty nice.

"My older brother is over there now," she added somberly. "Be safe!"

Once I hit the road, I picked up my young son Micheal and went to Palm Springs where my mom and sister lived. My mom's apartment was pretty small, so James and I stayed at an inexpensive Best Western motel. Our visit lasted two days, and then we headed for Artesia (a suburb of L.A.) to see one of my brothers and his family.

After taking James home, I pointed the shiny-new, blue Ford northward toward Santa Cruz and the redwoods for visits with another sister and brother and their families. Since my group was scheduled to leave from the Alameda Naval Air Station, I decided to stay around the Bay Area. The Ford had fourteen miles on it when I started out and nearly two thousand by the time I turned it in at Oakland. I wrote a note to the rental agency in L.A., thanking the man and the young lady for their kindness.

My leave was over. My sister dropped me at the naval air station's embarkation area in Alameda. Neither the Army nor the Navy could find copies of my orders anywhere. For a while, they couldn't even verify that I was in the Army. I volunteered to change into civvies and go home right then, but they assured me that the oversight would be cleared up soon, and that I should not do anything too hastily.

Just after morning chow the next day, someone came into the barracks and read off a bunch of names—including mine. The officer told us that we would board buses at noon for the short ride to the Oakland airport. In 1967 the naval air station wasn't set up for DC-8s or Boeing 707s. We were to have all of our gear packed and ready to go in four hours. I still didn't have confirmed orders, only my originals from AIT.

The military is famous for having people stand in lines waiting for someone to show up, and the Navy was no exception. The first line was for the buses that never showed up. We cooked in the hot sun for nearly three hours. Apparently someone had forgotten to inform ground transportation that we needed a ride. The next line was at the military's part of the airport where we waited to board the plane. The Army couldn't find the aircraft, so we waited again. This time the wait was longer, and since it was a hot day I retreated to the shade of a nearby hanger. Within minutes the entire line joined me.

True to form, the Army bused us back to the holding area to wait for further orders, which finally came the next morning at 11:00. We scrambled for our gear and headed for the parking area. There, waiting in all their splendor and glory, were ten buses, some from the Army, others from the Air Force and Navy. It's marvelous how the branches of our military can cooperate— when they can actually figure out what they're doing. Twenty minutes later we pulled alongside a Continental Airlines' DC-8. We exited the buses and formed up again. Fortunately, someone had found my orders, so at least I didn't have to buy my own ticket.

Before leaving Oakland, and up to the time we boarded the plane, rumors were rampant. Someone said that some guy told him that someone else had heard that we weren't going to Nam at all, but first to Hawaii and then on to either Japan or the Philippines. For sure we would have a week's leave in Honolulu. It's amazing how scuttlebutt can overrule common sense.

As we stood in line, again, several officers from all branches of the service took turns explaining exactly what our route was going to be. Much to everyone's surprise, we were indeed going to land in Honolulu for refueling, with a one-day pass to the immediate area. Most of us were happy about this and would have done nearly anything to defer our trip to Vietnam even for one day.

The flight was to be five-and-a-half hours, putting us in Honolulu by 6:30 p.m. We boarded the plane and got as comfortable as possible. Man, was it crowded! As we taxied down the runway, I thought about how nice it would be to have an authentic Hawaiian dinner in a true Hawaiian restaurant. The flight personnel greeted us warmly before takeoff, joking about our captive flight.

"Who's your tailor?" they kidded.

Everyone on the crew was a volunteer, and they worked hard to make this flight as pleasant as possible. The attendants were women in their mid-forties. One said she was going to meet her son for a few hours' visit in Nam.
About half an hour into the flight, I was surprised to see my friend Colonel Wilson stroll up the aisle from first-class into the enlisted men's economy section.

As he looked around, Wally finally spotted me and said, "Oh, there you are, Mills." He stopped at our row, and the two kids sitting next to me nearly killed themselves trying to jump to attention—a tough maneuver while still buckled in.

Wally quickly put his hands on their shoulders, saying gently, "Easy, boys. On an aircraft or ship, only the verbal greeting to an officer or a sergeant is required."

That's a very confusing part of training. Their eyes were as big as coffee cups as he spoke to them, but they began to relax, saying, "Yes, sir. Thank you, sir."

Wally had a reassuring, genuinely kind way about him.

It was finally my turn and I said, "Good afternoon, sir."

"Would you like to come up front for awhile? I have three seats all to myself."

I agreed, and he said to one of the stewardesses, "Private Mills here is moving up front for a little while. Could you serve his lunch there?"

The two guys seated next to me were still looking shell-shocked. "How come you know a colonel?" one of them asked.

I smiled and whispered, "Shhh! I'm a government spy."

Following Colonel Wilson forward, I noticed that he had been promoted to full-bird, and as we walked through the curtained doorway, I said, "Congratulations, sir. I see the Army has given you the bird."

I must have caught him a little off guard because he roared with laughter. Colonel Wilson was a rare man and hard not to like. He not only looked out for the soldiers, but he treated us all with respect. He had a great sense of humor too.

We talked as we ate lunch. He said his wife and daughters wished me a safe tour of duty and hoped that someday we might have another visit. Then he handed me a funny card they had all signed. I felt a real kinship with him and his family.

"Thank you for the card, sir," I said, sliding it into my pocket. "Tell me, how did you know I would be on this flight or even that I would be going to Nam?"

"Officers who are given the bird by the Army," he quipped, "are also given access to certain recruit information as well as passenger manifests."

After an hour or so, I returned to my seat and stretched out for what I thought was going to be a two- or three-hour snooze. My friends were engrossed in watching the shades of blue now contrasting with a few puffy, little white clouds floating by the window.

It seemed I had no more than closed my eyes when I heard the stewardesses talking in loud voices and scrambling between the first-class and general admission sections. I looked at my watch and found that I had actually slept several hours.

My first thought was, "We're getting ready to land at Honolulu," but all this activity was mighty strange for a routine landing. On her way to the rear of the plane, one of the stewardesses stopped near my seat and asked, "Which one of you is Private Mills?" When I responded she told me, "The officer up front wants to see you."

As I stepped through the curtain divider and saw all the commotion, a chill shot through me like never before. An Air Force officer and three or four stewardesses were pounding on the cockpit door. Glancing at my watch, I realized we were actually a couple of hours past our expected landing time.

As I eased into the seat next to the colonel, I asked, "What's going on, sir? This doesn't mean what I think it means, does it?"

He simply placed his two hands together as if to pray. I knew exactly what he meant; I began to pray—did I ever!

"They have been trying to get into the cockpit now for over an hour," Wally finally told me. "One of the stewardesses became curious when we missed landing in Hawaii. And there's no response from the intercom."

While he was talking, an attendant hurried forward past us, telling the group pounding on the door, "Ground control says they have not been able to raise anyone in the cockpit on the radio for three hours now. They want to know what's going on."

Wally leaned a little toward me and explained, "That old saying, 'running on fumes' has real meaning right now. We are about out of fuel!"

We would have to land. The question was *how soon* and *where* we would come down. Technicolor reruns of my flight from San Francisco to Seattle only six months before played in my head.

The Air Force officer took a fire extinguisher off the wall and proceeded to bang on the cockpit door with it. In a short time, three or four minutes (it seemed like three or four hours), the door slowly opened and one of the cockpit crew stuck his head out. He looked as if he had just fallen out of bed. After a brief, animated discussion with the head stewardess and the officer, he quickly disappeared back into the cockpit.

One can only imagine the conversation they must have had in the cockpit within those few seconds. Immediately, the seat belt and no smoking signs came on and the captain quickly announced over the PA system, "We will be making a hard turn to port and a more rapid descent than normal. We have been given emergency clearance for a straight-in approach for Wake Island."

Wake Island was nearly five miles down and eighteen miles southwest of us. Because the situation was so tense, the stewardesses hastily went through the instructions on what to do if we should end up getting wet. In spite of protests from the flight attendants, I went back to help calm down my two seat buddies and any other nervous passengers.

Someone spotted the island below and shouted, "Hey, I've spotted Wake—the small dots down below."

At 25,000 feet, the dots resembled a tiny fishhook. They had been all but invisible at 30,000 feet. We hoped the military landing strip would be long enough for our DC-8, because the plane hadn't been designed for this short of a runway, or the runway for this size of aircraft.

Losing all that sky seemed to take a long time. At first the pilot circled slowly four or five times to drop some altitude. Then he straightened the plane and nosed over into a steep dive, aiming right for Wake Island. The four jet engines were nearly inaudible. All was quiet on board, but no one was asleep. A few had closed their eyes; some lips were moving.

In spite of our circumstances, I couldn't help but appreciate how beautiful the sky was at that time of evening. With all the glory of an approaching sunset, the bright orange horizon was emblazoned on the water as well as in the sky. It seemed a moment to remember—perhaps my last. As we readied for a possible water landing, we hoped and prayed for a dry touchdown. Still, I felt grateful to see this glorious sight.

In a few minutes, we pulled out of our steep descent into the final approach. As the plane leveled off to five hundred feet above the Pacific Ocean, we could all feel the terrific G-force at work. The whining engines returned to half their normal pitch. From my seat just to the rear of the left wing, I could see the faint lights of the field as the plane gently banked. This place didn't look much bigger from five hundred feet! The plane's nose was angled slightly upward. The engines slowed again slightly. We were two miles out from the runway.

As we crossed the outer markers of the runway, the sun was shining on the starboard side of the plane; the left wing and engines were shaded. A large bluish flame belched out, followed by a short stream of light gray smoke. Then there was nothing. The starboard outboard engine had quit. Then a kid hollered out, "Hey, the port outboard engine is out!" Everyone held their breath as the pilot brought up the power on the two remaining engines and lowered the landing gear.

We passed over the boulders along the western shore of the island. Then we saw concrete—the runway coming toward us! Everyone yelled with joy and relief as the wheels touched down. The two remaining engines idled for a moment, then quickly roared back to life as the reverse thrusters and brakes were engaged, making every effort to stop the big plane. This was a shorter-than-we-wanted runway, and being minus two reverse thrusters the two working engines and the brakes were pulling double duty. At the instant we touched down, our speed was much too fast for this strip. We went coast to coast using every foot of runway. As we turned to taxi back to the terminal, our wing extended past the end of the runway, creating long shadows across the rocks.

The two remaining engines quit short of the passenger loading area. When I stepped out onto the ramp, the last remnants of sunlight shone on my face. I thought of the glory and color of the sky just a few minutes earlier, and I felt grateful to God to be alive—that all of us were alive.

Some of us sat in the waiting room and others lounged on the grass outside. That was one flat island. A description said it was a little over a mile across because of the airstrip and about a mile and a half long. Only a few military and civilian families live on Wake.

We saw a plaque honoring a handful of U.S. Marine ground troops, fighter pilots, and a civilian construction crew who held Wake Island following the attack on Pearl Harbor. For nearly fifteen days, about fifteen hundred men kept the much larger Japanese task force from taking the island. They sank several Japanese warships and shot down a score of aircraft. It was an amazing feat.

It was late in the evening, and with the aircraft refueled, we were ordered to reboard the plane. I reclaimed my window seat. Somehow the airlines had quietly flown in a replacement cockpit crew, but none of the stewardesses had left the flight. This part of the trip too was pretty exciting. We taxied to the end of the runway and made our U-turn getting ready for takeoff. We sat there for a long time, and then some of us noticed that a small air-service tractor, barely visible from the plane's landing lights, had moved toward the front of the plane. They must have attached the vehicle to our plane's nose gear because the aircraft slowly began to back up a good distance. In the lights shining from the plane, we could make out the surf splashing over the rocks directly below us. Our wheels must have been backed up right to the crack where the dirt and tarmac met.

Our new pilot introduced himself over the intercom, saying, "Hi everyone. I'm Captain McEvers. It is a beautiful night for flying. Oh, and I had my last solo flight yesterday and wish to assure you, all will be fine."

Actually the captain's brand of humor settled nearly all of us down. He explained how it would be a tricky "giddy-up," pointing out we were very fuel heavy, and that usually a longer bit of concrete would have been preferred. His confidence helped . . . a little. I was about to volunteer to do my twelve-month stint right there on Wake, but the roar of the jet engines reinforced the fact that I was still going to Vietnam, come hell or deep ocean.

As the engine pitch rose and got louder, the plane began to shudder from the tremendous power and thrust. Solid white flames from the jets reached back twenty to thirty feet, the brakes holding us fast. Then there was a lurch forward, and we started our roll. This baby was going to get airborne even if the captain had to climb out and pick her up.

The tremendous roar intensified as we rocketed down the runway. Finally the nose of the plane lifted slightly; but we weren't airborne. The nose rose a bit higher—and still no liftoff. Then a strange thing happened. From underneath the plane there was a loud bang, and I saw rocks and surf whizzing by beneath the window; then a blur of lights that must have been the island's outer markers. Still we didn't climb. With another series of lesser bangs I realized that we had actually rolled or flown off the end of the runway. The first noise had come from the landing gear as it moved to full extension. The sounds that followed had been the landing gear coming up. Looking out the window again, I noticed the angle of the flaps had decreased. As we finally began to climb, everyone let out a cheer.

Through the intercom, the captain asked a few minutes later, "You guys didn't have any doubts, did you?" Once we gained our flight altitude he came through the plane and talked briefly with all of us. As far as the military and the airline were concerned, this whole incident had never happened.

Handcuffed

Chapter 4
SETTLING IN AT NAM

It was mid-afternoon on September 10 when our flight ended at Bien Hoa Air Base, South Vietnam. The last leg of the flight, which included a short stop in the Philippines, was as smooth as Southeast Asian silk. It was hot, and sitting on the plane for an additional twenty to thirty minutes wasn't making things any cooler. An Army captain came on board for a brief two minutes with instructions for all of us: "Officers to the left of the ramp; noncoms straight out; the rest of you to the right."

As hot as it had become waiting on the plane, it was nothing compared to when we were finally allowed to disembark. That first moment when I stepped through the plane's door was like walking into a blast furnace, only stickier. The weather was similar to that of Fort Gordon, only more intense. The sky was clear blue, but the heat and humidity were downright suffocating.

The cockpit crew and stewardesses were lined up near the door wishing us well as we left the plane. I overheard the pilot saying to a major, "Some of the commercial flights are being fired on with small arms as they prepare to land." It was not exactly comforting. Apparently the Viet Cong were not particular about what they shot at, just as long as it had something to do with the U.S.

Following the instructions from the information officer, all of us "green peas" (enlisted men) picked up our duffel bags from the tarmac and waited for a few minutes in our designated area. Then the ever-familiar sound, "Gentlemen, fall in at ease." A very short corporal said, "May I have your attention please. Form two ranks and follow me."

The distance from the DC-8 to the large open-tented area designated as "in-country processing" was about sixty yards. In the time it took us to cover that short distance, we were drenched in perspiration. The sun was intense; the humidity, unbearable. I was glad to be wearing summer khakis.

The in-country processing was probably the most efficient part of my military experience. There must have been a table, a clerk, and a sergeant or lieutenant for nearly every letter of the alphabet. The staff checked our papers and gave us new ones to go with the old ones. Then we were issued two small bottles: salt tablets and malaria pills. (They tasted awful.) We were in, out, and heading for the buses in half an hour.

It was late afternoon, and the temperature and humidity were still high. Sitting on that hot bus, we must have looked as though someone had just hosed us down. Getting underway created a breeze—a hot breeze, but a breeze all the same, and at least we were out of the direct sun. Our destination was the 90th Replacement Battalion where we were to stay for the next three or four days to become acclimated before going to our permanent duty stations. Our body clocks and thermostats needed to adjust to the new time zone and extreme weather.

We left the airbase and entered Bien Hoa. It was a large town by Vietnamese standards, and we got a good tour of it as we drove through. I settled back in my seat and tried to enjoy the ride. Since we had no armed escort, I figured we must be fairly safe. As I looked out the window, I saw street vendors, outdoor markets, and people hurrying along the streets on foot or bicycles. Some rode in strange looking three-wheeled, gas-powered conveyances called Lambrettas. The air smelled foul, like something rotting.

Gradually reality began to kick in. I was in Nam, and there was a war on. My butt was really on the line! In spite of all the heat and humidity, a cold chill shot up my back and was chased by a shiver. I imagined other GIs must have experienced a similar feeling.

We arrived at 90th Replacement without a hitch. I had reached what I thought was to be my home for the next few days. I had already reset my watch to local time. It was 5:30 p.m. So far I hadn't heard a shot fired. In a way, I was a little surprised, even a little disappointed, but I was relieved at the same time. We had been led to believe that the fighting was widespread and without defined battle lines. Except for the choppers overhead and truck traffic on the highway, it was pretty quiet.

After a short formation where our papers were checked for the umpteenth time, we were shown to our bunks and told where to stow our gear and where and how the showers worked. It was really primitive. Water for the showers came from large, black steel tanks. They were perched on a derrick-like platform fifty feet above the showers so the sun could heat the tanks and warm the water, albeit only slightly. Since we were already so hot, the lukewarm shower actually felt cold and quite refreshing. From the shower I went to chow, which really wasn't bad at all.

At night, the sticky heat and mosquitoes were the two biggest problems. It has always been difficult for me to sleep in hot weather. The guys from the South and from the East Coast seemed to fare much better than those of us from the West. My clammy mattress was soaked with perspiration. Showering had been of little help, because as soon as I finished drying off, I was already dripping with sweat. It would take time to get adjusted to these conditions.

By around 2:00 a.m., the air finally cooled off enough that I could sleep soundly, so I wasn't really pleased when the company clerk woke me and another guy at 6:00 my first morning in Nam.

"Transportation will pick you two up at ten hundred hours," he told us.

Thanking him, we rolled over and went back to sleep, but by 7:00 a.m. it was too damn hot to sleep anyway. The other guy and I both sat up at the same time. We shook hands and he said, "Hi, I'm Jerry, from Pennsylvania."

"Hi, Jerry. I'm Vic. How long have you been at the 90th, and where ya headin'?"

"This will be my third day," he answered. "I'm assigned to the 552nd MP

Company."

"Me too!" I told him.

We talked about Fort Gordon. He had been in Echo Company; I had been in Alpha.

As we got ourselves up and headed toward the showers, Jerry asked, "Say, there was a rumor about an undercover man in either Alpha or Delta companies. Think there was any truth to it?"

I played dumb. "I heard that too. Don't know for sure."

Seconds after showering, I was dripping with sweat again. It was unbelievable. We were a little late for breakfast, but the mess cook fed us anyway, and by 9:30 Jerry and I were standing in front of the orderly room waiting for our ride. We didn't have to wait long; the ride was early.

The driver looked at us and said, "If you're going to the 552nd MPs, throw your gear in and let's go."

The 90th Replacement was located at the intersection of two highways. I think Jerry and I both thought the ride would take ten or fifteen minutes, but when we left the compound, the driver turned right and drove to a stop sign an eighth of a mile away. This was the same road that had brought us from Bien Hoa. Turning right again, we drove west for a short third of a mile to the next compound, which was adjacent to 90th Replacement. There we entered the II Field Force Headquarters compound through the first gate. There was an MP on duty. Our driver made an immediate left onto the compound's south perimeter road running parallel to the highway. In between the perimeter road and the highway on our left was a large ditch, perhaps three feet deep. Rolls of barbed wire ran along both sides. As the driver made his turn onto the perimeter road, I reached up to the front seat to tap Jerry on the shoulder and pointed to a sign on a small building.

"The 552nd," I said.

The kid at the wheel said casually, "All of you MPs have to go through headquarters and the provost marshal's office. The guy on the gate is in your unit."

As we stepped inside the HQ building, the sergeant there took a quick look at our orders and said, "Wait outside, boys, your ride will be here in a few minutes."

We searched out what little shade was available and waited. Twenty minutes later an MP jeep showed up with the company clerk in the driver's seat. "Hey, you two guys going to the 552nd?"

"Yeah," we answered.

With our stuff and ourselves loaded into this jeep, we went down the same road we had just come up. In less then thirty minutes after leaving the 90th Replacement, and nineteen hours after arriving in Nam, I was standing at attention, along with Jerry, in the orderly room of the 552nd MP Company.

We got the standard short orientation from Top (the first sergeant) and the CO. The clerk then took us to our quarters. Jerry went to the hootch directly across from the shower and latrine area. My quarters were last in line in the second row. They were the farthest from the latrine, an especially nice location on a windy day. Anyway, I settled in.

The hootches were aluminum structures sixty feet long, twenty feet wide, and twelve to fifteen feet high at the roof peak. Even with the insulation in the ceiling, every window opened, and with the large double doors at each end, there was little or no ventilation. It was hotter than hell, and you couldn't buy a breeze except for heavy winds or storms. It seemed that all the guys had invested in small electric fans, which were fastened to their bunks.

Finally getting settled into the hootch was a relief because my body clock was twelve hours out of whack, and the lack of sleep was starting to catch up with me. I had really looked forward to that three- or four-day stay at the replacement center before being sent to my permanent duty station. Adjusting to a time zone halfway around the world, as well as to the hot, sticky weather, was not easy. In four days, I had been able to sleep in a bed for only six hours. I was virtually living on catnaps.

My first night in Nam had not been exactly restful, and unfortunately my second night was even worse. It was a disaster. There were two guys in the rear of the hootch blissfully asleep. I was exhausted, yet all I could do was lie there trying to find some position that the lumps in the mattress and I could agree on.

A small room at the front door of the building housed the squad leader's quarters. He and a group of guys were playing cards to a background of loud music. My bunk was first in line, diagonally across from him. After a couple of hours of tossing and turning, I went over and knocked on his door.

"Yeah, come in," he roared.

I opened the door and politely asked, "Hi, I was wondering if you could turn the music down a little?"

Two things happened. First, the music got louder, and second, I found myself on the sergeant's shit list, which is not a good list to start out on. As tired as I was, a little voice had tried to warn me. As soon as I opened my big mouth, both of my feet and one of Sarge's boots went in. The next morning I tried to apologize. On the surface he seemed to accept it, but my efforts didn't help much; I was a marked man from then on. That kind of information spreads through camp faster than a napalm barbecue.

Throughout ten of my fifteen months in Vietnam, the food in our mess hall was awful as well as dangerous. I tried eating at the mess for a while, but within a short time I'd have the "latrine boogie shuffle." It finally dawned on me that no one ate there very often.

For the first two weeks, my name was not on the duty roster. This gave me a lot of free time to get acquainted with company operations and II Field Force compound. Eventually I would pull patrol duty, and it would certainly be to my advantage to know the layout. Having made such a "wonderful" first impression, it seemed prudent to stay out of sight and mind and to learn all I could about this place.

The company area was laid out in one long stretch about one hundred yards long and fifty yards wide. Wire fences and rolls of barbed wire seemed to be everywhere. A double roll of this stuff separated us from the 90th Replacement compound.

During my first few days "in-country" I heard many new and strange sounds. A helicopter gunship, cruising close by with its large blades cutting through the thick, sultry air, produced a sound similar to that of a slow-firing .50 caliber machine gun. A mini-gun being fired from two or three thousand feet high sounded almost like a cry from a wounded animal.

The mini-guns were visually impressive. Because of their rapid rate of fire, the tracers, which had five regular rounds between them, appeared so close together that they resembled an animated stream of fire. A two-or three-second burst from these amounted to two or three thousand rounds.

On post each individual organization, including the MPs, was responsible for pulling night guard duty. The 552nd had motor patrols all night and was responsible for overall base security, night or day. In the immediate MP company area, there were four bunkers spaced fifty yards apart, stretching east from the gate to the stream. These posts were each manned by four men. After 6:00 p.m., the only legitimate access to the whole compound was Gate One, the 552nd MP gate. All other gates were closed and guarded by the companies stationed in each sector.

The perimeter road ran east from our gate for about seventy-five yards to a dead-end at a small stream and concrete bridge. The area around this trickle of water made command nervous because it could be used as an enemy infiltration point. There was a wire gate there that was no longer in use. Many GIs returning from the red-light district would either climb over or under this gate as they reentered the post. Since they would not have a pass, they didn't want to be confronted by the MPs on duty at Gate One. They needn't have worried;

discipline at that gate was just as lax.

The guard bunker nearest the stream had two large floodlights mounted on poles for greater visibility. They shone directly under the bridge and were on every night for added security.

All of the bunkers were nearly the same size and shape—around ten-feet square. Each had a peaked roof covered with sandbags three deep. The bunkers were framed with heavy beams and 2x8 siding. A concrete slab was the floor. Sandbags, several rows deep, covered the walls outside. Inside were two bunks of planks attached to the walls. A guard team usually consisted of four men. Two men stayed awake at all times while the other two tried to sleep.

Even though I wasn't yet included on the roster, there was one very early morning when everyone was to work a special security detail. The Chiefs of Staff were meeting on our compound. I was loaned a rifle and an ammo magazine. Soon Jerry and I were sitting in one of fifteen jeeps on an access road across the highway, overlooking a deserted village called the Widow's Village. We were pointed south, away from the compound. Other units set up checkpoints on the highway. Armored vehicles from a local cav unit ranged from light and medium tanks to armored personnel carriers (APC). That made up the heavy stuff. We were stretched thirty to fifty yards apart for over a mile. There was also a full rifle company with the APCs. At first I had no idea what was going on, what to expect or what was expected of me. It had been a very long time since I had been rousted out of the sack before five in the morning. Being the new kids in the sandbox, Jerry and I asked the third member of our team, the guy who had driven us out, "What do our orders consist of here? What are we supposed to do?"

I didn't think it was a dumb thing to ask. The answer from this veteran of five months was, "How the hell should I know? Just keep a lookout and tell me if you see the lieutenant or sergeant driving this way," and he went back to sleep.

Jerry asked, as he looked over the M-60 machine gun, "Hey, Vic. Do you know how this thing works?"

I climbed in back and we both tried to figure it out. "Let's see," I mused, "lift this up; that opens the breech; now let's put in the first round of the belt like so, and then lock this down. I think that's it."

"I've never fired one of these, have you?" Jerry asked while we worked.

"No, not yet. Now where's the safety? Oh yeah, there it is and it's on!" I said.

"Hey, knock off the chatter. I'm trying to sleep!" came the grumpy complaint from our driver.

The detail lasted to noon, six hours. One of the guys in the APC next to us said, "Hey, we've heard about your mess hall. Why don't you two pile on and join us for lunch."

Jerry and I were dead-tired but the offer was too good to pass up. We climbed aboard their APC, and away we went. The only hitch was that we had to walk nearly three miles back to our company. Was it worth it? All I can say is, they served real food.

Our first sergeant had given the orientation on our first day, but aside from that he was really an unknown person. From time to time I would see him around the company area. He was not what I had expected, based on the two top sergeants I had known during basic training and AIT. On the surface he seemed to be well liked, and he got along with most of the men.

Late one morning my first full week in Nam, I was sitting in the club drinking a Coke and trying to understand the club's currency (called "chits"). Our club, like most on base, had mesh screen windows all around and halfway up the sides. The windows and doors were always left open, except during heavy rain or dust storms. Ironically, the club building was situated near the multi-holer latrine, and I suppose the thought might have been that after a few drinks, the guys wouldn't care.

As I sat there, Top strolled in for some coffee and met up with some of his enlisted underlings. He soon began playfully wrestling and grab-assing with them. Stopping for a moment, he took his dentures out, set them on the bar, and offered to fight anyone there. Looking over at me, he said, "How about you? Want to go a couple of rounds?"

Declining, I said jokingly, "No thanks, Top. You're too tough for me."

Something in his eyes told me his actions were more sinister than they appeared. The others had refused to take him on.

Seeing what I was drinking, he added with a menacing expression, "Why don't you try something stronger? Might make you a man." He turned back to the rest of the group and with a flailing gesture called out loudly, "This is the jerk who don't like loud music at night. Isn't that right, Private?"

Without saying anything further, he stuck his teeth back in his mouth and left the club. I couldn't believe that he was for real. One of the guys called over and said, "Hey, you! Whatever you do, don't get crossways with him. He's a bit squirrely."

Another soldier added, "But we aren't the ones who told you!"

Getting rid of body waste at a primitive military post is always a problem. Even though we were part of Headquarters Company, all facilities on post, with the exception of those for the higher-grade officers, were pretty rank. The installation five miles east of us had housing that resembled new apartments. Those units had flush toilets, hot and cold running water as well as some sort of sewer or septic system. Our latrine, by contrast, was an eight-holer out-house and an open urinal trough attached to the south end of the shower build-ing next door. Only twenty feet separated the hootches from the latrine.

Using the multi-holer really put a guy in harm's way. It was a favorite nesting place of spiders, both underneath and above the toilet seats, and there were some very large specimens. Given the odor and the spiders, no one took a book with them or stayed a second longer than necessary. My first visit made me wonder if I could "hold it" for a year.

The third or fourth morning, I woke up to one of the world's all-time worst, foul smells. It was about 6:00, and a lot of dark, acrid smoke wafted through my hootch. I put on my pants and boots and stepped outside into the smoke-filled sunlight. After walking past four hootches and the showers, I found the source of this horrible odor. At the rear of the outhouse were eight small doors and inside them were containers similar to old laundry tubs. Two Vietnamese men were pulling those containers out and away from the structure a few yards, pouring kerosene into each, and setting them on fire. While the tubs burned, the workers cleaned the building with sanitizing spray from a small tank, hosing it all down. This process was also intended to discourage the spiders, which it did for about fifteen minutes. These little "creepies" would be back in place before the tubs finished burning and the water dried.

The house girls who worked for the GI's ranged in age from eleven to sixteen years old. Some in their late teens or early twenties were married or widowed and had families. A few of the much older women, mama-sans as they were called, supervised the younger girls. In our company, there were more than twenty of these house girls. They did our laundry, polished our boots, and changed our bunks every two or three days. They also swept and scrubbed the concrete floors of our hootches—a service I quickly learned to appreciate—all for five dollars a month!

The civilian employees had to report in at the MP check station, a few yards inside our gate, to be checked for weapons. I met many of the men and women who worked on post and have never known better workers or a more gracious people. I enjoyed getting to know these gentle Vietnamese, and I didn't care for the derogatory names some GIs had for them.

Two weeks into my tour I was returning from a lunch of sandwiches and pop in the mess hall with a new friend, Bruce, when I saw one of the house girls running from the rear of the officers' and noncoms' hootch. She was crying hysterically, and it was obvious that she had been beaten and was very frightened. This girl worked in my hootch and was only thirteen years old. I called to her, but she kept running until she met some of the other girls and an older mama-san.

Tim Green, our master sergeant, followed her out the door almost immediately. Resting against the rail at the top of five stairs and smoking a cigarette, he smiled and said, "That slope knows who's boss now."

When I finally caught up with the child, an older girl who was about sixteen made it clear, in pretty good English, that they felt uncomfortable talking to me. They didn't trust anyone—and for good reason.

Bruce said to them in Vietnamese, "He and I are different. You can talk to us. You can trust us."

The Vietnamese all knew Bruce and seemed to like and trust him. After a few moments, several of the house girls did talk to us. What they told us was unbelievable. My new friend was aware of much of what had been going on, and that had already resulted in his being transferred out to field duty with the First Infantry Division MPs.

The older girl explained that the master sergeant had tried to seduce the younger girl, and failing that, he threatened her with a false report to the government that she was a VC collaborator or even a spy. When she protested, he hit her several times and tried to rape her. What most disturbed me about this, and other incidences, was that a quarter mile away was a red-light district where older girls voluntarily prostituted themselves.

Later that day, Bruce introduced me to a Cahn Sat, a South Vietnamese equivalent of our military police, and he explained that the problem was not uncommon. "Yes, it is true, and is very sad thing," he confirmed. "Some young girls who did not wish to sleep with GI go to Saigon. There they give a very quick trial and sent to prison, or more often, executed." These trials usually lasted from the bus or truck to the wall. Sometimes family members were included; and all because "*The Americans say so*."

I do not claim to have lived a totally virtuous life up till then, but what I heard was unbelievable. Most Vietnamese I met were quite religious. Because of this and because of family tradition, virginity before marriage was extremely important. Girls who may have been molested, even if technically still virgins were often ostracized and ridiculed.

Bruce had to go back to the field, and since I still hadn't been placed on the duty roster, I had plenty of time to consider this problem. Over the next day or two, I tried to be of some comfort to the girls, but because of their distrust I had to do so at arm's length. Unfortunately, I didn't feel there was anyone I could trust to discuss it with. I would have gone to our resident chaplain, but he was out of the country for two weeks.

One day, while I was walking up to the PX, still thinking about these girls and their treatment, a jeep pulled alongside and paced me for a few seconds. I was so preoccupied that I barely noticed it.

Then the driver yelled, "Okay soldier, you're under arrest for impersonating a private!"

Looking over, I was startled to see two MPs from the 720th. One of them looked familiar. "*BJ*—is that you?" I sputtered. What a surprise and relief to see a friend!

"Hey, come on, get in. My partner needs something from the PX."

It was great catching up on the past few weeks: on his leave home he had gotten married. I said I wished *her* well and we laughed. BJ introduced me to his friend, and I introduced them to our new outdoor canteen—a small eighteen-foot trailer. While the other man went inside the PX, BJ and I had some cold drinks in the shade of the canteen's canopy.

We had been leaning on the side of the trailer for a couple of minutes when BJ finally said, "Okay, what gives? What's wrong?"

"What do ya mean?"

"Shit, Mills, you look like my dawg gettin' caught comin' out of the chicken coop."

So I unloaded, explaining to BJ as much as I could about the house girl situation. It bothered him too. For a few minutes we didn't talk much. We sipped our drinks, and then he straightened up and with a little bit of a smile said, "Say, our CO back at Fort Gordon is our CO over at the 720th now. I bet he could help."

"Billy Joe, you might just be right. Captain Jake might be able to help."

After all, the three of us had been pretty tight back at Fort Gordon, and Jake definitely seemed to be an officer who went by the book.

BJ's partner returned just as their radio announced that their presence was requested elsewhere. They offered me a ride back to my company area, but I declined and sent them on their way. I went straight to our orderly room to see the first sergeant to request a jeep from our motor pool, explaining that I wanted to visit a good friend at the 720th. I didn't say anything about his being an officer. Top agreed and gave me the motor-pool form. Within fifteen minutes, I was on my way in a nice shiny, well-worn '59 Willys M-151 Jeep.

It took ten minutes to get to the 720th MP headquarters. After checking with the MP at the gate for directions, I found the orderly room and Captain Jake's office.

Only the company clerk was there. "Hi," I said. "My name is Mills, and if possible, I'd like to see your CO."

"Okay, I'll check to see if he's in. I just got back from chow," he responded, and disappeared into a back office.

While the clerk was gone I noticed a list of officers who were new arrivals. When he returned to his desk he informed me that the captain would see me in a few moments.

"Hey, that's great. He's my old CO from Gordon." The kid nodded. Then I said, "You know, I couldn't help but notice your list of officers. If it's not top secret, is there a JAG officer, Colonel Wilson, on the list?"

Mumbling names to himself as he searched down his sheet of paper, he finally acknowledged, "Yes! There he is," and he wrote down the Colonel's phone number at JAG. Stuffing the small piece of paper into my shirt pocket, I sat down to wait, but not for long.

Within five minutes Captain Jake came to the door of his office with a cigar clenched tightly between his teeth, saying in his gravelly voice, "Mills, it's good to see ya. Get your ass in here."

Snapping to attention and saluting, I said, "Good morning, sir. I appreciate your seeing me."

"So, what's on your mind?"

When I told him what was bothering me, he was a little surprised. He was also concerned that I hadn't been pulling duty yet.

"Concerning the housemaid problem, that's not right." Turning to his window he asked, "Have you reported this to anyone other than BJ and me?"

"No, sir, I haven't."

"Good! You leave it to me. I don't condone such treatment of civilian workers." Then he added, "I'm glad you came to me about this, Mills. I will look into it quietly and see what might be done. I'll be in touch with you in a few days."

Our visit lasted for only a few minutes. As I prepared to leave, I came to attention, saluted, and said, "Thank you again, Captain, for seeing me."

Driving back to the 552nd, I was feeling pretty good about things. However, as I approached the gate there were several of my unit's MPs standing around waiting for someone.

"Hi, who ya waitin' for?" I asked, my jeep coming to rest.

One of them reached inside my vehicle, turned off the ignition, and muttered, "You, asshole." Then he and one of the others pulled me out of the jeep and placed me in handcuffs. "The provost marshal wants to see you ASAP," another said as I was shoved and hoisted into the rear seat of their vehicle.

My mind was racing. I hadn't a clue what was going on, or what I had done that rated such treatment. Since I hadn't been put on duty yet, I certainly hadn't done anything wrong there.

As we headed for the provost marshal's office, all kinds of pictures went through my head, including one of me being shipped home in a rubber bag wrapped in a flag. When we arrived, getting out of the jeep was not easy. I was so shaky I could barely walk up the stairs. Nothing, prior to or after this incident, has ever matched the terror I was experiencing at that moment.

My CO, first sergeant, master sergeant and the provost marshal, a lieutenant colonel, were all waiting for me. I couldn't get over how fast all of this was happening, whatever it was. Once I was inside, the cuffs were removed. The only thing missing was a blindfold and a final smoke.

The cadre shouted a lot of obscenities at me while they hurled questions and accusations: "Why didn't you go through channels?" "You should have come to us." "You're not a team player!" Although not given much opportunity, I did my best to answer their questions. After a few minutes of intense grilling, I was told to sit down while they deliberated in the colonel's office.

As I started to sit down, that piece of paper in my shirt pocket crinkled. Remembering Colonel Wilson, I took it out and asked the clerk, "Please, would you dial this number for me?"

The clerk looked up and asked, "What the hell did you do?"

"I don't know. But I need to talk to this officer, now."

He dialed and handed the phone to me saying, "I don't want to know any more," and he disappeared into an adjoining stockroom.

I heard that familiar voice, "Colonel Wilson here."

"Hi, sir. This is Vic." Cutting off pleasantries, I exclaimed, "Sir, sorry, but I need help." Then I explained as much as I could about what was going on.

He broke in, "I'm on my way. Hang in there."

When he walked in the building ten minutes later, I started breathing again. His arrival coincided with the others returning from their meeting. To say they were surprised at meeting Colonel Wilson would be an understatement. This was the first time in the four months since meeting Wally that I ever saw him visibly angry. The noncoms and officers were about to be the recipients of his ire. Ordering them back into the provost's office, he unloaded on the officers and stared coldly at the two noncoms as he spoke. They all stood at attention. The clerk had returned from hiding and we looked on through the partially opened door.

"What-the-hell-did-you-do, Mills?" the clerk asked again.

"I tried to help a young girl."

Some of what Wally said had to do with him personally knowing me. He also pointed out that I had successfully completed all my training and he strongly suggested that I be put to work.

"I am convinced," Wally added, "this soldier has done nothing wrong. The mere fact he unintentionally went over the chain of command makes me wonder if perhaps he was correct in doing so." Colonel Wilson continued, "My office will investigate this soldier's claims. We're going to look into the cruel treatment of Vietnamese nationals by any unit on II Field Force, and especially by the 552nd. And we will find the officers and other personnel who have betrayed this man's trust."

This statement startled me, because up to that moment, it had not been a consideration. The possibility that anyone had intentionally set me up was hard for me to believe.

Colonel Wilson drove me back to my company area and asked, "Are you all right?"

Smiling slightly, I answered in a somewhat husky voice, "Sir, I'd rather be at thirty thousand feet in an airliner running out of fuel than to ever go through this again." Pausing for a moment, I added, "I'm fine; scared shitless, but fine. Thanks for helping out."

Nodding, he reminded me, "You be watchful; on guard. I'll be in touch." Thanking him again, I saluted, and he drove off.

It was just past 1 p.m. when Colonel Wilson dropped me off at my company. Apparently the officers took Wally's suggestion to heart, for within the hour I was on a one-man, ten-day roster working a shift and a half of guard duty. I was scheduled to work from 3:00 p.m. to 7:00 the next morning. For the initial four hours I would be alone. At least I was doing something.

I was finally issued my weapons, which included a .45 semiautomatic pistol and an M-14 rifle. The pistol was in good shape and easy to clean, but the rifle was another matter. It was so filthy and rusty that I had to break it down and clean it three times to get it into shape to test-fire a few rounds. After successfully test-firing it, I broke it down and cleaned it again.

After a quick shower and shave, and into clean fatigues, I gathered up my newly issued flack jacket and steel helmet, and headed for a one-man inspection, or guard mount.

The sergeant who had the honors was my squad leader, Sergeant Mitchell. As he looked over my weapons, the pistol first, he asked what I had done to rate such treatment, quickly adding that I didn't need to answer. Then, checking the rifle, he asked, "Will this damn thing fire? I thought all these were in the batch that was sent back to Saigon."

"It fires fine, Sergeant. I sent six rounds through it."

Handing it back to me, he said, "Well, at least you know how to clean it."

After dismissing me, he said, "If you want, pick up a sandwich and a soda from the company club. You'll be in Bunker Four—at the end of the perimeter road near the bridge and creek." Then he added, "If anyone questions you about the food while on duty, you tell 'em Sergeant Mitchell said it was all right."

Coming in from guard the next morning the temperature was already nearing 80 degrees. Those I worked with spoke little, and only as it pertained to work. While I was putting my gear away, I noticed that a small electric fan had been attached to my bunk, and that my boots had a nicer shine to them.

The house-girls never said anything about the trouble I had gotten into, but all the civilian workers seemed to know, and had their own ways of showing how they felt. For days after this, I found small gifts waiting for me: a set of ornamental ivory chopsticks, beautiful hand-painted silk scarves, and once in a while, food delicacies from someone's home. For a long time, the house girl I had helped wouldn't accept any money for her work, and I wasn't charged for clothing alterations or for haircuts. My laundry was no longer being done on post, but was taken to someone's home so it could be done "mo betta."

Even though I was still on the command's shit list, I was glad to be working. I continually watched my back and always checked my bunk and boots for snakes. Clearly, this company had a lot of problems. What made it all the worse was the vicious, corrupt behavior being condoned and practiced by command.

During my third week there, I experienced my first red alert. Late one night we raced for the bunkers and ditches along the south perimeter road. Our master sergeant, first sergeant, and captain were standing in the doorway of the company's bomb shelter. They were already drunk, and unable to function. Our leaders were nonexistent!

As time went on, a few of the guys began talking to me. I decided not to do any explaining about the trouble concerning the house girl. Many of them had felt the treatment of these girls was wrong but hadn't known what they could do about it.

There always seemed to be a game of touch football, a little baseball, or volleyball going on with those of us not on duty. Since I was still being ostracized by most of the hard core, I wasn't asked very often to join in. But when I was, it was a lot of fun.

I soon realized that my war in Vietnam had two fronts: one, the Viet Cong; and two, the 552nd MP command. When I was new in the military, I had trembled at the thought of anyone of rank or authority wanting to speak with me, regardless of the reason. But after three weeks with the 552nd, my timidity and fear were overlaid with anger. I had little respect for anyone with more than three chevrons on their sleeves or a lieutenant's bar on the collar.

Late one night while four of us were on guard duty, our lieutenant came out to the bunker. I didn't really know the man, but rumor had it that he was starting his third tour of duty in Nam and had been passed over for promotion at least twice. Apparently he had a reputation among his men for dealing in the black market. Part of the "good ol' boy's" network, he was popular with company command, but he was harsh with those who challenged him, and cruel and insensitive to the Vietnamese nationals, viewing them as less than human.

Anyway, he called me out of the bunker, asked why I was causing so much trouble and accused me of not being a team player. His comments surprised and angered me, because I had not been in trouble for at least a week, or since the incident with the house girl. Our conversation quickly became one-sided as I spelled things out using language that was completely foreign to me, but felt even he could understand.

"Sir, whatever is wrong in this screwed-up company was present long before I arrived. I am on a mission, and that is to survive. I know my job and will do it. I *am* a team player; but a team needs coaches and leaders. I have not seen evidence of either. If we are ever attacked, I think you and the rest of this command will probably get a lot of us poor bastards hurt or killed."

He leaned into me and growled, "You'd better watch your back, Mills," and stomped off. Prior to this, I wouldn't have had the guts to talk to anyone of rank in that way. Because of the conversation with the lieutenant, I doubled my own personal guard. I couldn't trust any of them.

Oddly enough, my older brother, Richard, inadvertently came to my rescue. While on leave, I had told him about the funny rumors that I was a stooge. As a joke, he sent me a letter using an envelope saved from his Air Force days, ten years earlier. It was addressed to "Major J. Blumberg." My name and service number were in parentheses just below, along with his old service number. The name Blumberg was a family joke concerning a childhood acquaintance of my mom's. When my brother's letter arrived, rumors flew fast and faster. Noncoms went out of their way to speak to me; the CO and lieutenant avoided me like the plague. A few days later I was out of the bunkers and on a regular rotation with the rest of the guys.

Some time later, I received an unsigned handwritten note on JAG stationery regarding the incident with the house girl. It stated, "Your ex-CO directly contacted command at the 552nd, warning them that you were going to cause trouble, and suggesting they take appropriate action." A few days later I was told Captain Jake lost his command and was sent elsewhere. Since the note in question was not signed, I assumed it came from Colonel Wilson.

One evening in the club, the lieutenant was showing off pictures of his wife (she was a real knock-out) and their two kids. He also talked regularly about a young Vietnamese woman he had led into a phony marriage ceremony on his first tour. She too was very attractive and didn't know about his American family. She was hoping to return with him to the States. I felt sorry for her because that was never going to happen. Anyway, they had twin boys, nearly eighteen months old, and she sometimes brought them on post for a visit. The lieutenant spoke quite coolly about his "in-country family" and how he could leave without a thought about them. "They're just slopes!" he explained. Not long after, the lieutenant received divorce papers from his American wife. Apparently she had found out about his *other family*.

SNAFU

A few days later BJ had a day off and stopped by my hootch. He asked if I thought his CO's departure was related to my trip to the provost. I showed him the note from JAG. We both found it hard to believe that the captain would have treated any soldier like that.

While we were sitting on my footlocker talking, the first sergeant came in wearing an unusually happy but evil grin. With some muttered expletives he handed me new temporary orders as he said, "Hey, Mills, get your gear ready. We're shipping your ass out to Di-An (Ze On) tomorrow."

At first I had no idea what he was talking about, but a kid who was sitting nearby filled me in after Top left. "You're headed for the Big Red One, the First Infantry MPs." Bruce was one of those sent from the 552nd. From what I had been told, the men sent there were generally considered troublemakers and social outcasts. Since the First Infantry MPs were always short on manpower, the 552nd had become their source of warm bodies, or cannon fodder.

Chapter 5
THE BIG RED ONE

"Hey, Kent, you ready to go? Jeep's here," I hollered.

"Yeah, I'll be right there." As he brought his stuff out he quipped, "Think he'd go without us?"

"Probably not!"

By late morning we were packed and ready to go. Kent Adams had been in-company less than a week and, like me, three weeks earlier, was fresh from Fort Gordon. Why he had been selected to join me in field duty was a curiosity.

The two of us walked up to the orderly room to meet the driver and the kid who had been five months TDY (Temporary Duty) with the Big Red One. He was rotating home. Talking with both men really helped to settle most of my fears. I had been scared shitless concerning my forced relocation to field duty. On one hand there was the fear of actually going into battle, and on the other hand I was leaving what, if only on the surface, appeared to be a haven of safety at II Field Force. There was a lot of spit and polish in the 552nd, but it seemed as if those in command were inept or incompetent. What would I find where I was going? Fortunately, according to Bruce, the First Infantry driver, and the kid returning, there truly was one big difference between the two outfits: leadership.

Kent and I continued to talk with the kid fresh from "the field" while we helped him carry his gear to a hootch. "Just remember," he added, "they have awfully good chow out there, good leaders—oh—and no bullshit. They'll back ya up."

"What a plan! Sounds like a good place to work," I said to Kent.

The driver brought the jeep through the company area to our hootches. There we loaded our gear, tied our footlockers down in the trailer, and were soon ready to go. The company clerk had placed a large canvas bag of mail, along with four cans of M-14 ammo, in the back of the jeep for the platoon.

It was nearly noon when we got underway. Driving through our company area, we made a turn around the last hootch and headed back onto the main road and toward the gate. Several house girls came out to wish us well. Some were crying, and they reached out to touch my arm as we passed by. Many others waved from the side of the road. One of the older girls grabbed Kent's right hand briefly. He just smiled at her.

Approaching the gate, the captain, lieutenant, and my two least favorite noncoms were all standing out in front of the orderly room. I nudged Kent, and we both stood up in the jeep and saluted our CO and said as we passed by, "Good afternoon, Sir." He had a doughnut in his left hand and a cup of coffee in his right, and because he was hung over, we caught him good; as he returned our salute he inadvertently dumped the contents of both hands. Laughing at his predicament, our driver shook his head and said, "Are those guys for real?"

After clearing the gate, Kent added, "What a sorry bunch of drunken bastards!" For an 18-year-old and for being so new in-country he was pretty observant. Clearly, he and I would get along just fine.

We had just turned onto the highway when I saw a 720th MP jeep approaching. I asked our driver to pull over. As I had guessed, BJ was in the other jeep. Making a U-turn, he pulled up alongside us. He looked at all the gear in our vehicle and in the trailer and said, "This is not good."

"I think going to Di-An and the Big Red One has to be an improvement over being here," I responded. Kent and BJ introduced themselves, and I added, "Kent's going too, although we haven't figured why."

Shaking his head, BJ added, "I just wanted to tell you to keep your damn head down out there. I heard a rumor that the VC are using real bullets this year."

"You know, Bev said nearly the same thing before she left. Must be something to that rumor," I said with a chuckle. "Hey, contact Colonel Wilson about my move. I couldn't reach him. Tell him I think 'business as usual' may resume with the house girl situation."

BJ assured me he would do so ASAP.

Until I witnessed firsthand some of the brutality leveled against the Vietnamese people and toward us GI's, I had been proud to be part of the military. I had believed the BS about the MPs being an elite group. I had been naive and ignorant.

As Kent and I bounced along en route to "the field" and what awaited us there, I began to grow up. Over the next few weeks, I would discover that the law enforcement personnel of II Field Force, from the provost marshal on down, were not respected and were widely looked on as laughingstocks.

The trip out to Di-An was pretty uneventful. I recognized a lot of the country as we drove through Bien Hoa. A few miles beyond, we came upon a South Vietnamese Army patrol that was on a "search and destroy" mission going on right alongside the highway. There had been a small skirmish a few minutes earlier, and they had captured three or four Viet Cong.

As we approached the patrol, our driver told us to be ready with our weapons. Kent got on the M-60, and I locked and loaded both of our M-14s, keeping the safeties on. A mile or so later the driver said, "Okay, you guys can relax a little, but don't go to sleep."

The narrow roadway was sometimes asphalt, sometimes oiled dirt, but mostly just dirt. On that day it was clogged with refugee traffic. Old women, bent under impossible loads, and young teen mothers led or carried Amer-Asian children, some nursing their babies as they walked. Others rode on bicycles or motorbikes, in Lambrettas, and in older cars. We averaged about fifteen miles per hour and had to endure several delays because of the traffic. It was unbelievably hot. Usually this trip was a two-hour breeze, but not that day. After three hours we were still barely halfway to Di-An.

Around 4:00 p.m., we stopped on the outskirts of a small village. In front of us sat a fairly good-sized, stucco building. It resembled a small French Mediterranean villa.

The driver said, "We're close to camp. It's less than an hour from here, but I'm hungry. How about you guys?"

We didn't need to be asked twice; morning chow had been a very long time ago, and none of us had had lunch. A sign on the front of the building read, "Welcome to the USO club." We unhooked the M-60 and carried it and our M-14s inside. This was my first time inside an actual USO club, and Kent and I were both ready to plant our buns in a chair that wasn't moving.

I'm not sure which we were happier to see, the young American women working there or a clean, functioning rest room. "Damn, it's even got hot water," Kent sang out. It was also equipped with several shower stalls, but unfortunately we couldn't take the time for that luxury.

The USO gave me my first good, American-style meal in weeks. Their menu wasn't very elaborate, but it was definitely more than I expected. The three of us settled on hamburgers, fries, and milk shakes. The girls sat and visited with us while we ate. What a godsend that USO club was!

We stayed at the club much too long and arrived at Di-An at 6:00 p.m. Bruce (who had helped me with the house girls) was the only person I recognized. He introduced us to several of the guys, commenting that our company hadn't mentioned whom they were sending. A message to Di-An had mentioned something about insubordination. Bruce had told his lieutenant that it had to be me, as no one else had ever made such a first impression. He also explained the things he had observed during his two-day visit back at the 552nd, which included the incident with the young girl.

As we worked to unload the jeep and trailer, a voice behind asked, "Which of you two likes gooks and mouthing off to sergeants and colonels?"

Being very tired and a little irked, I slowly put my load on the ground and turned, expecting a challenge. I glanced at Bruce, who had a slight smirk on his face. Then I saw the silver bar on the collar of one man and two rockers under the chevrons on the other, along with a bunch of silly-ass grins on those standing close by. I really felt stupid.

Coming to attention, I said, "Good evening, sir."

As I started to bring my right hand up to salute him, he caught it in his right hand, and after we shook hands, he said, "We don't salute much out here, Mills. It tends to shorten an officer's life expectancy drastically. Snipers, you know."

"Yes, sir," I responded, a little dumbfounded.

He introduced himself and his sergeant, with whom we also shook hands. Then he said, "Okay, stand easy," and repeated his question about gooks and mouthing off. I was still feeling a bit testy and wondered if I had once again managed to stick both boots in my mouth.

"Yes, sir, I do like these people. No, I was never insubordinate to anyone in command. And yes, I did complain about the beating of a house girl by our master sergeant at the 552nd."

The lieutenant then asked, "Is it true, Private, that you went in confidence to see your former commanding officer from AIT about this matter, and that this confidence was broken?"

Frankly, I was curious about how he knew all that. Bruce couldn't have told him, as he had returned to Di-An long before I had gotten into trouble.

Struggling for the right words, I finally answered, "Sir, as far as I know that is what happened, but it is hard for me to believe that the captain or any officer would do such a thing."

Looking at me as though his eyes could bore through me, he finally smiled and said, "Welcome to the First Infantry's Deuce Platoon, boys."

Then those from the 552nd and the others with the First Infantry introduced themselves as they helped with our gear. Some asked if I had really gotten into trouble for helping that girl. As we worked, the lieutenant explained, "I like most of the nationals too. The trouble is, out here, when it gets dark, it's difficult to know whose side some of them are on."

The informality really had me confused. I had never heard an officer or noncom address lowly privates in this way. On the other hand, I felt they accepted us as equals. I soon found that this was how the lieutenant and sergeant treated everyone in their command and, from what I heard and saw, most of the Vietnamese as well.

This was to be the place of my rebirth, my real training as a soldier. Here I would learn everything I needed to know about soldiering and staying alive; everything all the training back home didn't and couldn't teach.

Our quarters were right near the west main gate. These quarters were a conglomeration of tents and metal: canvas sides, metal and wood frames, and a galvanized roof. Having my bunk so close to the gate made me feel a little uneasy. If the enemy should attack from this side of the compound, we would be among the first to know. Fortunately, that never happened during the time I was there.

I had gotten used to having the services of house girls, but at Di-An those luxuries were history. We had to rough it and do our own chores: make and change our own bunks, clean the hootches, do our own laundry (or send it to the base laundry), and worst of all, we had to take turns burning the poop buckets.

This place was noisy, and it took me a few nights to get used to sleeping a few yards from the 105 and 155 howitzer batteries. I finally got too exhausted to stay awake. One morning as we were all getting up, I mentioned how nice it was to have slept all night without the batteries doing any firing, only to learn that they had fired nearly thirty rounds during the night!

The MPs in the First got most of the gravy jobs, which was to be expected. The 552nd got to clean up the mess the gravy made. On the whole, all of us from the 552nd were treated well by the brass and our fellow MPs. The officers and sergeants seemed to have a great deal of respect for their men and that extended to those of us on TDY. No one—absolutely no one—came between the lieutenant or sergeant and their men. Heaven help any officer or noncom from another company who might reprimand any of us of the Deuce! Rank made no difference; they'd pay a heavy price for interfering. If any of us should screw up, our immediate command personnel handled the problem. We might catch hell, but we never heard about it again. They were quick, they were fair, and the incident was over. On the other hand, if we were right in our actions, our leaders would back us all the way to the provost's desk. We would have followed these two men anytime, anywhere.

One of my first duties was to be part of a two-man detail working the west main gate. There we checked the vehicles entering or leaving the post and gave directions to keep the traffic moving. At night the gate was locked and the infantry took over guard duties. (They did a good job of it too.)

Occasionally, I got to do some on-post patrol work. This was usually accomplished with a partner from the First MP, and for good reason. Most of the men on post did not like any MPs very much, but those of us in the 552nd were often ignored. An MP wearing the "Big Red One" shoulder patch made a greater impression, so for the most part, we became their silent partners.

Working the gate was interesting—for about the first ten minutes. After that it became just plain dusty, dirty, and boring. The road coming into the post was dirt. Only for the first fifty yards inside the gate was the road oiled. Outside the gate for about a hundred yards the dirt was watered down once or twice a day. This was to help compact the surface, but it really didn't; the water evaporated almost immediately due to the heat.

A truck or jeep approaching the gate at just fifteen miles per hour created a dust cloud thicker than a San Francisco fog. It coated our sweat-drenched bodies even inside our mouths, noses and ears, in spite of the protective bandannas we usually wore. Even worse, it got into our weapons, though we kept them covered with a cloth or a poncho.

Many drivers relished every opportunity to give us a good dusting. To them it was just a game. One kid driving a deuce and a half (2-1/2-ton truck) made repeated trips through the gate just whipping up one dust storm after another. His sergeant was seated on his right. Both were laughing and yelling something about losing part of a non-existent load and how the kid was learning to drive the truck.

Purposeless driving like this had been the subject of complaints from those who manned the gates, and unfortunately this behavior was increasing. Even warnings from the post commander went unheeded. The perpetrators would just wait a few days and then start the dust storms again.

At first Bruce and I were teamed together, and it appeared that we were married to that gate. For several days two guys played the game of repeatedly going in and out of the gate. Later on they began doing it in shifts with another team. The dust problem had reached a crisis. Finally I had had enough, and I stopped both vehicles. Checking the drivers' authorization papers I found that neither of the two drivers had any authorization! With real pleasure I wrote them up. (This was one occasion when I really liked my job!)

Bruce hollered, "Hey, let me write up one of the guys."

"You've had months to do it," I answered. "Besides, I'm having too much fun."

Shortly after we stopped the first two trucks, more came to play, so we wrote them up too. Bruce called for backup and a duty officer, and then got busy writing as well. No one lost any stripes, but there were some fines and extra duty. The incident helped to clear the air around all of the gates on post.

Early one morning after I had been there about two weeks, Kent, Bruce, and Rob (who was also TDY from the 552nd) woke me up. I had been on post patrol until 2:00 a.m., and then the howitzers had been busy most of the night. It wasn't time to get up.

"We have a surprise for you," they told me.

I was too sleepy to even be curious, but they showed me a handwritten note from the sergeant instructing us to familiarize ourselves with various weapons and to do some target practice. I'd always liked target shooting, so I got up, had a quick shower and shave, and grabbed a quick breakfast.

Somewhat awake, wearing my pistol belt with my holstered .45, I carried my M-14 over to the jeep. We took three cans of ammo and an M-60 machine gun, which we attached to the tripod bolted to the floor of the jeep. We packed a grenade launcher, sixty rounds, and several boxes of ammo for our rifles and pistols. We also had something new, a Stevens pump-action, twelve-gauge shotgun which fired .00 buckshot. I had never fired a shotgun before and thought this could be fun. At the very least, we could make a lot of noise.

Bruce drove, and Kent and I were in the rear. Just outside the compound gate, Bruce looked back at me and said, "Hey, let's load up the 'sixty.' We're going into Charlie country."

Both Kent and I stood up, a tricky maneuver in the back of a moving jeep, and loaded the first round of the belt into the firing chamber. Just as we sat back down Bruce suggested, "Make sure the safety's on." As I reached for the handgrip to check on the safety, the swivel pin, which holds the gun steady, slipped out, and the muzzle began to rotate down toward the front of the jeep. Forgetting that the whole thing was bolted to the floor, my first thought was "Oh, no, it's falling!" I made a grab for it and accidentally hit the trigger, firing one round and creasing the center front edge of the hood just above the radiator.

Rob looked back at me and said jokingly, "Next time you might try to find a less desirable target than the vehicle we're riding in."

The mishap was pretty funny, but it had some serious overtones. Here I was in a war zone, and other than my rifle and pistol, I didn't know squat about basic weapons. Between basic training and AIT, I had had only a few minutes with the sixty. It was clear that I needed more practice, and that I needed a working familiarity with the other weapons as well. As it turned out, Kent had never fired anything other than a rifle and pistol.

We had traveled for several miles when Bruce turned off the main road onto a path little better than an oxcart trail. The land here was arid and flat; except for the humidity in the air, it resembled desert expanses in Colorado.

After two or three more miles the path began to climb for a short mile or so. We stopped in an area where the soil was reddish clay mixed with gravel. There was little foliage. Before it was cut down to build roads and bunkers, this had been a high mound. Now it was shaped more like a huge, empty bowl. The base was about two miles across.

Before selecting our targets, we did a quick recon of the area to be sure that neither friendlies nor VC were nearby. Then we checked in by radio, advising our company of where we were. As the crow flies, we were less than five miles from the post. Had it not been for the humidity and for the heat waves off the ground, we probably could have seen the base camp, but it seemed so desolate that I felt uneasy. Bruce reassured me that this area was regularly used for weapons practice. I asked him, "By us or by the VC?" Before waking me up, the guys had visited the mess hall to get cans for target practice.

They had gathered up several empty ones, everything from 5-gallon lard cans to 10-pound coffee cans, and they had an array of smaller ones as well. We placed the targets around the area, some for distance shooting and others fifty to seventy-five yards away. The farthest targets were over a quarter of a mile away. The course was egg-shaped, with the widest field of fire several hundred yards across. We practiced for over two hours, the first of many such practices. We had a blast, and it really paid off later—not only helping us do a better job, but helping us to survive.

The four of us gradually evolved into a team that worked well together. The Command at Di-An soon recognized this and utilized it. We continued to practice our shooting and continued to improve with all of our weapons until we were among the best.

Our favorite pistol targets were the old concrete telephone poles erected by the French during their occupation. They had been abandoned long ago, and only a few still stood in this remote area. They were about thirty feet high, shaped like elongated "I" beams—measuring about ten inches at the middle and widening to twenty inches at the top and bottom. Since they were spaced about a hundred feet apart, they made great targets. Using the .45s, we were eventually able to hit these targets five shots out of seven. We were even better with the M-14: seventeen rounds out of twenty at two hundred yards. Several times we all shot a perfect round.

About two weeks into my duty with the First Infantry, a few of us from both MP companies were selected to take a trip out into the country. We were to relieve a few people at an outpost near the Cambodian border and the infamous Black Widow Mountain. I didn't know anything about this place and wasn't eager to find out.

Bruce, Rob, another GI named Paul, and I made up the group from the 552nd. When we pulled out, a little past 8:00 a.m., it was still dark. Our destination was less than forty-five miles away, but we were restricted from traveling more than twenty miles per hour unless we were under fire. In addition, we had been instructed to stop at every village, hamlet, and town en route to help build better relations with their citizenry. Each stop took thirty minutes to an hour.

Along the way we also stopped at an obscure Army helicopter base to visit their PX. My ration card was of extreme interest to many of the guys from the First Infantry. The ration card was among the things the military had given us the day we landed in Nam. It limited the quantities of particular items soldiers could buy each month—things like soap products, cigarettes, and booze (the hard stuff). For each purchase the card would get a hole punched in it. If you used up your ration allowance, you'd have to wait until the next month for a new card. I had no idea that those little cards were so popular. In some cases, they were better than paychecks: we weren't allowed currency and were given only so much military scrip. Because I didn't smoke or drink, the ration card held little interest for me, so somewhere along the way—I don't remember how—I was talked into or tricked into making purchases for others. When I finally caught on, I refused to help.

We finally arrived at the outpost about chow time, although it was only 1600 hours. In the field, mealtime depended on daylight. The guys at the outpost spoke only "Army" nearly all the time, so we had to mentally reenlist before saying anything. They had a good field mess though, and we were allowed to eat before we unloaded our jeeps and trailers.

The outpost definitely did not resemble a Boy Scout camp. It was set in a clearing about the size of three square football fields, and it contained one six-man and one ten-man tent. The sergeant used one small tent for himself and his radio operator. This doubled as our operations tent. A short distance beyond the tents, the power generator groaned away twenty-four hours a day.

This far out, I really expected to find at least a first lieutenant or a many-rockered sergeant in command. Instead, a 20-year-old, E-5 buck sergeant ran the show. He methodically went over all our papers, especially the ones from the men of the 552nd. He already knew Bruce and Rob, but the 552nd still did not have a very good reputation.

A specialist fourth class showed us to our tent and we began unloading the vehicles. Since we were planning on being there for some time, we had brought along our footlockers. A couple of the guys who had been at the outpost for some time pitched in to help with unloading the jeeps and trailers. I finally asked one of the guys, "Hey, just where the hell are we, anyway?"

As we set an armload down in one of the tents, he said, "Come out here." I followed him out through the flap door. He stopped, pointed south, and asked, "See that large mound-like hill?"

Bruce and Rob had joined us, and we all answered in the affirmative.

"Well," the young soldier continued, "that's called Black Widow Mountain. It's about three miles from here and it's honeycombed with tunnels." Pausing for a moment, he continued, "We're just a few clicks from the Cambodian border and a main link with the Ho Chi Minh Trail. That mound of dirt is like a meeting point for the VC."

As we continued with the unloading, several other guys told how the Army of the Republic of Vietnam (ARVN) Air Force continually flew bombing, rocket, and strafing sorties against this fifteen-hundred-foot-high mound of dirt. Nothing the military had thrown at it had been able to destroy the tunnels or slow the insurgence.

Over the few weeks we were at the outpost, we watched many attempts by the South Vietnamese Air Force to work over that target. The ARVN pilots flew World War II planes: Corsairs and Mustangs. I enjoyed seeing these old war-birds at work.

This place was really isolated. At night, unless the moon was out, it was pitch-black. The evenings and mornings were glorious though, and the countryside was dotted with farms and rice paddies with all kinds of trees and vegetation. It was beautiful country.

At 5:30 we had the first morning call, and breakfast was ready by 6:00. The showers were primitive. There were two stalls and two sprinklers that I'm sure came off of a couple watering cans. The shower was open, the water was *cold*, and we were fast. After a quick dance in the shower, we stopped by one of three small 300-gallon water trailers to shave. Just like in the movies, we used our steel pots (helmets) as bathroom basins.

The two outhouses were not houses at all; each consisted of a toilet seat nicely attached to a piece of plywood, fastened to the top of a partially buried 50-gallon drum. The two facilities sat twenty feet apart, some forty yards from the tents and eating area. Except for eighteen-inch plywood sides, there were no walls. They offered a lot of fresh air but made good sniper targets. No one stayed very long, and needless to say, you took your weapons along when you had to visit. At least we didn't have to burn anything.

Although I liked the outpost, I was scared spitless most of the time I was there. We were deep in the heart of VC country, only a mile or two from the Cambodian border. Fortunately, while I was there Charlie never attacked the outpost. For the most part, it was quiet, and the weather didn't seem quite as hot and humid as it had been in Di-An or Long Bihn.

We also had a lot more work to do. The tents had to be cleaned out daily. Their platform floors were made of wood slats and sat about a foot above the ground. Every other day we'd have to raise the floor to check for snakes and rats. Each day we rolled up the sides of the tents to help keep them cooler and to let the air circulate.

During my first morning's chow, I heard about the outer perimeter defense, which was a grid about five miles square. The defense team consisted of tanks and armored personnel carriers (APCs) and about eight hundred men. We were mighty glad to have them around.

I couldn't believe how good the food was out in the bush. Occasionally the scrambled eggs were a light shade of green, but usually we could count on fresh, real food. Breakfast was no snack. It was good and there was plenty. Lunch was basic but also good, and dinner consisted of a meat plate with dessert. When we were on duty and late for a meal, the mess sergeant always made sure we got the best plate he could fix.

On our first morning there we toured the checkpoints with the sergeant and two other GIs who had been there for awhile. "The main job is to watch for contraband," the sergeant told us. "We are here to look for things out of place or not normal—for instance, too much rice for a small family or over-loaded vehicles which may contain smuggled weaponry."

We also learned that we were to check identification papers and look for discrepancies in appearances or locations. Several Vietnamese Cahn Sats (national policemen) worked with us. At times we wondered about the political leanings of a couple of these men. They never slept in our compound, and we were some distance from the nearest village through rough terrain.

It intrigued me that our M-14 rifles were so often the subject of conversation. Even men from the cav unit and from the First MPs offered to swap. We declined, wondering why we were getting these offers for the heavier, older weapon. We learned that the reason was the difference in firepower. It was clear that these young veterans respected the M-14. Later on, we let them fire our rifles a few times, and the four of us put on a little shooting exhibition of our own, which seemed to impress them.

We got along well with all the men in the cav unit. They were great guys who really knew their job and did it well. One of the tank commanders gave me my first and only lesson in how to drive a tank.

"What machinery," I commented. "Big and bulletproof."

One of the guys set me straight in a hurry, "You wouldn't think so if Charlie air mailed you a rocket." Then he added, "It sure would be nice if the Army would install air-conditioning."

We all laughed.

One morning Bruce, Paul, and I were working the checkpoint nearest to the compound, a couple hundred yards away. Traffic was practically nonexistent, and about halfway through the morning, Sarge sent Rob to pick up Paul to go help out at a busier location.

Since there had been only two vehicles all morning, Bruce and I had parked the jeep in the shade of a large tree. We took turns sitting in the jeep, trying to find that elusive cool breeze. It was my turn to relax, and I was sitting on the rear seat back resting against the spare tire, checking over our logbook. Bruce was walking back and forth on a cow-path twenty feet or so in front of the jeep smoking a cigarette. After a few minutes, I began to hear an odd hissing sound. Only moments before I had repositioned the jeep, so at first I figured it was letting off steam.

When the noise continued, I asked, "Hey Bruce, do you hear something hissing?"

Cocking his head he said, "No, I don't think so." Then a few seconds later as he walked back to the vehicle to get a drink, he stopped short and said in a quiet, almost frozen voice, "Vic, I think I just found your hisser." Bringing his rifle up he added, "Roll to your left, out of the jeep—*now!*"

Without hesitating I rolled, and from the corner of my eye I saw a cobra between the jeep and the tree, less than four feet from my head. It must have been close to twelve feet long. The area just below its head was flared out, and the body extended out to nearly the height of the machine gun mount. The snake quickly dropped to the ground. We were amazed at how fast it could travel. We both fired several rounds at it but missed. When we radioed the sergeant to explain why he and everyone else had heard about twenty rounds, we really got ribbed. With all our practice, we missed!

When we weren't on duty, we spent free time during the day writing letters or playing a little volleyball or football. A few of the guys besides me spent time with their Bibles.

My church printed a daily newspaper and sent it to me regularly. From that paper I was able to understand what was really going on in the war: actual, factual reporting. The other newspaper I received was a Seattle Sunday issue, which I had subscribed to shortly after arriving in-country. The difference between these two newspapers was night and day. It was fun to get the Sunday comics in the Seattle paper, but we found the reporting was far from accurate.

One of my tent-mates, Chief, a native American, asked if he could read my papers. I left them out for him and anyone else who wanted to read them. Late one afternoon, Chief came to evening chow holding up the Seattle paper, saying, "Hey, do you guys know that last Thursday we were all killed in a fiery battle?"

We looked at each another in surprise and laughed. Then we looked at the short United Press article and realized that it had been published nationally back home a full week earlier. The writer named our exact area, and except for a little target practice or people shooting at snakes, there hadn't been a shot fired. We were concerned that our families and friends would worry, so everyone got busy that evening with some short letters home. Our sergeant radioed to base and requested that any chopper flying close by our area drop in for a cup of coffee and a special mail pick-up. Bright and early the next morning we had three guests for breakfast, a chopper crew that stopped by.

The daily paper was far more accurate. In fact, during my fifteen months in Nam, the only reporters I met were from "my" newspaper. The guys preferred to read this paper, although they enjoyed the other paper's comics. I guess most people didn't care to read their own obituaries.

Chief was a great guy and a good MP, but he had a big drinking problem, which made him out-of-control angry. A couple of times a week he would slip out late at night to find a friend who would share a bottle with him, probably someone from the cav or infantry units around us. Every time Chief returned drunk, he would go through our tent throwing footlockers, rifles, and even bunks, sometimes with someone in them. Drunk or sober, he was very strong, and at 6 feet tall and weighing in at nearly 300 pounds, he was one bad dude. The military tried to regulate alcohol consumption, especially in the field, but their rules were rather ineffectual because the guys were permitted to buy booze at the PX.

Once I found a series of articles in my newspaper on Native Americans. The writer covered many of their problems, including alcohol abuse, and offered suggestions on how to find solutions. Not knowing for sure how Chief would take it, I left the articles open on my bunk. One morning after a particularly rough and rowdy night, he came to me and said, "I want to quit drinking. Can you help me?"

He caught me a little off guard, but I knew that Sarge was unhappy about his behavior and had arranged to send Chief back to Di-An for possible court action. I asked the young sergeant if Chief could be given one more chance since he did his job quite well. After much discussion, Sarge reluctantly agreed not to write him up. With some difficulty, I was able to send a message of urgency to the chaplain in Long Binh, asking if he would meet with Chief at Di-An. Chief flew back in the mail-and-supply chopper. The chaplain was waiting for him. When we returned to Di-An a few weeks later we found Chief a much-changed young man.

Not surprisingly, we didn't have much entertainment out near the border. At times we could pick up the armed forces radio out of Saigon, but the reception was pretty scratchy. So at night we did other things like play chess and cards. Rummy 500 was the only card game I knew, and it didn't require gambling. Such evening activity helped to keep us busy, but it was impossible to completely remove the stress of being so close to Cambodia, the Ho Chi Minh trail, and the mountain.

Another challenge was the mosquitoes. There were a lot of them and they were *big and hungry!* It seemed that they were thirstiest at night. Resembling a swarm of B-52s as they circled near the jeep headlight suspended at the top of the tent, they made an unmistakable, loud humming sound. The Army's bug spray was mostly DDT, which didn't slow down these flying meat-eaters; in fact, they seemed to thrive on it. Other than a rolled-up newspaper or a boot, nothing seemed to faze them.

While at the outpost, I began to realize the true value of the field radio and learned how to use it properly. Some parts of our messages were spelled out in code using the phonetic alphabet. For instance, if I stopped a vehicle (ox cart, small truck, etc.) with too much food and needed to report it to our sergeant, I might say, "*V*ictor *N*ovember (Vietnamese national) has too much food." If one of our names (for example, Smith) was part of the message, during transmission the radio operator would say, "I spell: *S*ierra, *M*ichael, *I*ndia, *T*ango, *H*otel."

As I was not a good speller, it was difficult to learn this new language. VC stood for Viet Cong, so we would say "*V*ictor *C*harlie" or "*C*harlie" on the radio. Any vital information was radioed to Di-An by our sergeant.

This work with the First Infantry Division, especially at the outpost, gave those of us from the 552nd some much needed *real* experience. There's a lot to be said for "on the job training," but going into combat is no time to be unprepared.

Bruce and I talked several times about the problems with the 552nd command. He, Rob, and others on field assignment understood all too well that if you weren't part of the drink-sex-and-stoned club, you were considered a liability, an outcast. You would be transferred to an active combat MP unit—in our case, the First Infantry. I knew of a few men who had requested and received their transfers to either an air-cav unit as door-gunners for choppers or to an armored unit, just to escape the 552nd's command personnel. These were men of good sense, willing to do their part. A lot of them got sent home wrapped in a flag.

We had rocked the boat and had been sent to the field, probably with the hope that we would be killed in combat. I wondered if this was typical of other units of the Army. Maybe it was in some places, but not at the Big Red One. Nearly all of us tried to transfer permanently to that unit, but we were told that we could not. In retrospect, I believe God's plan was to have us go back to the 552nd.

It's true that boredom was a problem in every unit. It created a lax mental attitude. I had to fight this enemy daily. It was hard to be brain-tough, to beat the monotony and not allow ourselves to be caught off our guard.

Several Cahn Sats worked with us throughout the district at different checkpoints. They served as interpreters and provided instant law enforcement. There was one Cahn Sat in particular none of us trusted. Our sergeant was well aware of this and had similar feelings. Over several weeks, not wanting to risk radio messages, he had sent handwritten messages back to Di-An via the chopper. Sarge had warned everyone to be alert and to exercise extreme caution when working with this man. We were given a free hand to deal with the situation we deemed necessary.

Trahn usually found some excuse to be late getting to the jeep or the checkpoint. In the third week Bruce and I were assigned with Trahn to the checkpoint closest to our compound, but Trahn was nowhere in sight. Sarge nodded for us to go and get set up.

The roads, really only cow or oxcart paths, were closed at night, and either an APC or tank would park at a checkpoint to guard them.

It only took us a few minutes to get into position as the mechanized guard rumbled away. Twenty minutes later Trahn came walking down the path toward us, smiling as always. Our checkpoint was my pet cobra's home, and we were pretending to look for it. The Cahn Sat handed us a message from the sergeant instructing us to do a second radio check; we knew this was a time-check as to how long it had taken Trahn to get to us.

When I called in, Sarge said, "You guys took too long getting set up." This meant it took Trahn too long to get there, and to be careful.

Business was brisk that morning. For an hour or so, Trahn did his job, checking nearly everything that came through. Gradually he became less and less thorough. Bruce and I discussed it a couple of times with him. At one point he lost his temper and yelled at us in Vietnamese, but after a few minutes he settled down and apologized.

A short time later, two villagers, a man and wife, came through on foot. They actually spoke a little English. The woman motioned toward Trahn and said quietly, "Very sorry for you and friend. This man, not good." Her husband gave a slight nod and they hurried away.

A few minutes later I went back to the jeep to make a notation in our logbook, which had somehow gotten stuck in between the rear seat cushions. Climbing in back to extricate the book I sat down to make my entry. Suddenly Bruce yelled, "Vic, cover me!"

I glanced up to see my partner sprinting forward, calling to Trahn, "Stop that truck! Trahn, stop him!" Bringing his M-14 up to a firing position, Bruce took aim at a Lambretta Trahn had just waved through. Trahn yelled something at Bruce in Vietnamese. This was not good.

When I stood up, I was at the butt-end of the machine gun. I watched as the Cahn Sat took his .38 from his holster and leveled it at Bruce about fifty feet in front of him. I couldn't use the M-60 because the tree blocked part of my field of fire, and my rifle was leaning against the left front fender of the jeep.

I hollered out, "Bruce, hit the dirt!" My partner instantly gave up his firing position and flattened out on the ground as Trahn fired one round at Bruce, barely missing him. I then pulled out my .45. Cocking the hammer, I jumped from the jeep, landing spread-eagle on the ground. Trahn was about sixty feet in front of me when I hollered in Vietnamese for him to drop his weapon. He abruptly turned toward the jeep and fired. The round ricocheted off the steel turret where I had been standing just moments before. Partially concealed by the tall grass and the left front tire, I yelled again at the Cahn Sat, this time in English, "Trahn drop your pistol!" Instead he looked down at me and moved his weapon to take another shot. I fired once, striking him in the right shoulder. I had never fully understood what a .45 round could do to a man, especially a small man. It flipped him like a rag doll.

Bruce, still flat on the ground, looked at me and nodded, then he quickly got to one knee, brought his rifle up and fired two quick rounds at the escaping Lambretta, now well over two hundred yards away. The shots split the vehicle's differential, collapsing the rear end.

Trahn was lying in some bushes and I rushed over to him. He was still breathing, just unconscious. I picked up his pistol and tucked it in my belt, then checked with my partner to see if he was hurt. He wasn't. Running back to the jeep, I then radioed for a medic and someone to cover the Lambretta and its driver. Help arrived quickly. Three men secured the Lambretta while others approached us with their weapons ready. Even some of the cav personnel showed up.

The medics worked on Trahn for a few minutes, and as they prepared to move him to the Cavalry unit's infirmary, one of the medics told our sergeant, "This Cahn Sat has a broken shoulder and collar bone, but he isn't seriously wounded."

Bruce and I were both fine, but with the adrenaline pumping through our bodies we were shaking so hard we could barely speak. The sergeant took us aside and, with a deep breath and a sigh, said, "I will never make fun of you guys from the 552nd again. You did one hell of a good job."

The sergeant told one of our guys to stay with the prisoner; then he went back to our area to make a radio report. He also requested a chopper to take Trahn back to Di-An for proper medical attention and questioning.

The Lambretta driver and one other of the Cahn Sats had long since disappeared. Searching the vehicle, we found large sacks of food with light weaponry and ammo hidden inside. Rocket launchers with ammo, additional rifles, and pistols had been concealed under a false floor and in the roof. It was ironic that most of the bags were marked "American Red Cross." There was also a mapped diagram of our deployment. It was scary to see how accurate it was.

Later I asked Bruce, "Did you intend to kill that Lambretta by shooting it in the ass?"

"I hit what I aim at," he said with a smile. "Unlike some snake hunter I know!" Lighting a cigarette he added, "You didn't do so bad yourself. Thanks for covering my butt. By the way, did you shoot to wound or to kill?"

I answered, "I'm not sure. The only thing going through my mind were the awful thoughts of having to write a note to your family, and of my ex-wife receiving all that life insurance money. I just couldn't see either happening."

Even though we were still shaking, we managed a much-needed laugh.

Our 1967 Thanksgiving Day dinner was super. A Chinook, a large helicopter transport with two huge overhead blades, landed on our grass helo-pad, and out came about ten members of the Army band. They lined up and played for about half an hour while our mess personnel set up our turkey dinner. Then, without a word, they all boarded the chopper and left. The Di-An mess hall put forth a supreme effort to bring such good chow out to the field. The armored units fared well too. The weekend of Thanksgiving our outpost was closed, and we were pulled back to Di-An. I had been there just short of five weeks.

Shortly after our return to Di-An, the Deuce Platoon com-center (radio) ceased working and a communication company from Saigon was flown in to take over until it was back to normal. Replacement radios, parts, and other equipment were not readily available, so we were temporarily forced to operate on a single band-frequency. With air-to-ground activities going on, that was one crowded channel! All the units were seriously handicapped by this setup. To make things worse, the new radio operators had not had any field or combat experience, and it showed. Some of our guys received minor injuries due to this major foul-up. On base, patrols were able to use walkie-talkies, but for those off base, the portable radios didn't do the job. Having to deal with the heavy radio traffic would have been difficult for any radio operator, but the guys in this particular unit were apathetic about the job.

Our lieutenant had volunteered to place an experienced MP in the radio center to assist with its operations and to make simple decisions. He pointed out that any major problems would still go directly to the desk sergeant or our duty officer. But the colonel turned the suggestion down.

All roads were regularly checked for mines—little wake-up calls from Charlie. Just fifty yards from the west gate (our gate), the ordinance people found a mine in a rock outcropping alongside the road. It had enough explosive power to cripple a tank or completely destroy an APC or a deuce and a half, including everything and everyone in it and near it.

The Army demolition experts used a specially reinforced deuce and a half. This brute was a minesweeper. The windshield and door glass had been replaced with thick steel and had a 4x20-inch slit cut out for the driver to see. A "magic wand" mine detector extended out from under the front of the truck. When on duty, top speed was kept to fifteen miles per hour.

A 3/4-ton truck—like a large jeep—that crawled along behind them supplied shotgun service. This vehicle was equipped with two dual .50 caliber machine guns mounted on turrets and one quad-M-60 (four machine guns) mounted toward the front. Six to ten riflemen went along for the ride.

The end of the minesweeper's route was at an airfield about twenty-five road miles out (probably closer to ten miles if it could have been traveled in a straight line) and usually took about two hours. This was a flat and winding stretch of dirt roadway.

A third vehicle followed about three miles back, staying in radio contact with the base. This was the jeep of MPs. We used a double-back maneuver in which we traveled at normal speeds for a mile or two, then did a U-turn and raced back a half mile and made another U-turn. We would repeat this maneuver until we all met at the airfield. On our return trip to base camp, we followed the same procedure.

It was my first run on this patrol, but three of our group had done it two or three times before. Kent had worked this road trip a lot during my stay at the outpost. Originally he had been assigned to do it again, but a switch was made at the last minute and Paul took his place. We didn't mind. Besides his skill as an Army cop, Paul was one hell of a mechanic. He could fix anything.

Kent was pleased about not going. "Take suntan lotion guys, and lots to drink. It's one hot *mother* out there," he warned.

We loaded the jeep with the necessary gear, including C-rations and water bags, two filled with water and one with ice and pop.

Before we left, we did our mandatory radio check. As our sergeant was talking with us, the com-center interrupted, "Get the hell off the air unless it's an emergency." Sarge just shook his head in disgust. Bruce asked him if we could have someone—anyone—from our group at the com-center.

Sarge said, "We'll try again before your first check-in time, but don't hold your breath."

Radio check-in times were to be every fifteen minutes. Unfortunately, this was not frequent enough to give us that safe, reassuring feeling. The com-center just wasn't able to handle any more traffic.

At first I thought of this duty as a joy ride. However, just as Kent had explained, it soon became a hot, sweaty, and dusty time of intense driving. As we passed through the gate, I locked and loaded the M-60. Bruce looked back and up at me with a grin and said, "Try not to shoot the damn jeep this time,

Mills!"

We all laughed, but Paul piped up and asked, "What the hell's he talking about?"

I replied, "It's a family joke."

After we got a ways out of camp, we test-fired all of our weapons to be sure the powder was dry. It was. And I didn't shoot the jeep.

Before our first scheduled com-check, we contacted the minesweeper's escort five miles ahead of us to let them know we were on the job. As of that moment, they hadn't encountered any problems or explosives. That was good news. Although the surface was hard-packed for most of the distance, it was sand and very dusty. This particular road was heavily traveled and very important for our base. At the airstrip we intersected another road. One part went west through Tay Lin and on to the old outpost near the Cambodian border; the other way headed southeast and straight into Saigon.

After only three miles, Bruce hollered at me to make our first radio check. "Home Base, Home Base, this is X-ray 2-3. Radio check. Over." Nothing. "Home Base, X-ray 2-3. Radio check. Over." Still nothing. "Hey, what do you suppose those guys are doin' back there?"

Bruce said, "Keep trying. I'm at mile number 3 and making our first U-turn. Radio it in even if they don't answer."

"Home Base, this is X-ray 2-3. We are at mile 3, U-turn, plus one mile. Next message fifteen minutes." Then, as a second thought, I called the trucks up front. "Garden Patch, you copy? Over."

"X-ray 2-3. This is Garden Patch. Good copy. We can't raise the base either. Over."

"Roger Garden Patch. Out."

By the time I got through playing with the radio, we were already making our next reverse turn. Bruce thought we might have gotten behind schedule and told us he was going to run four miles to the next stop. Three-and-a-half miles into that run we came to an abrupt stop.

Bruce said simply, "We need to check the radiator. The gauge reads hot."

That day's temperature would have been about 105 degrees in the shade, if you could have found any shade. The country was extremely open, dry, and barren. Everyone got a can of pop, and Paul opened the hood.

"Someone in the motor pool didn't tighten the radiator petcock. Looks like most of the water in the radiator has dribbled out," Paul quickly announced. "Fortunately, we stopped in time; I don't think we've damaged the engine." Paul told us to restart the motor and he slowly refilled the radiator from one of the water bags.

Sitting helplessly alongside the road makes for a dangerous situation. While Paul was tending the radiator, the rest of us watched, rifles in hand with the safeties off. I rested against the M-60. Bruce had taken Paul's M-14 from the jeep and placed it close to him. We were ready for action, but we also wanted to get out of there.

We notified the base of our temporary delay. At least they acknowledged us, but whoever was working in the com-center was not very bright or sympathetic.

"Don't call in unless you have an emergency," he warned us.

Since we couldn't reach the Auto Club, I for one thought our having to stop was an emergency. We looked at each other wondering just what constituted an emergency. We double-checked with the sweeper to make sure they monitored our delay.

"Roger, 2-3. You need us to come and assist?" they asked.

"Thanks, almost done. On our way in two minutes. Out," I responded. They were too far ahead to be of any help. It would have taken too much time.

After a few minutes of cooling the engine, Paul added a bit more water. "Hey, the needle's going down," Rob commented.

"Man, let's get the hell out of here. We're just sitting ducks," I quipped.

We all switched places. Rob took the wheel, Bruce the M-60, Paul the right front seat, and I sat on the left rear fender with my rifle cradled across my arms. The engine roared back to life, and we hit the road. It was good to feel a breeze again!

Rob floored the gas pedal and we blasted up the dirt road. From the cloud of dust we created, it must have looked like the whole battalion was on the move. After a fast five miles at nearly sixty miles per hour, Bruce suggested we slow to our normal speed in order to settle the dust cloud following us and do our double-back maneuvers.

Rob slowed down, and had just pulled off onto the soft shoulder of the road to make his U-turn, when a tremendous blast of fire, smoke, and dust engulfed the jeep. The vehicle began to roll slowly to the right, pitching upward like a wounded animal. It seemed as if everything shifted into slow motion. I found myself floating through the air and saw my three buddies slowly moving with me.

My first thought was "Help us, God." Whether through instinct or training, my right hand found my .45, and I fired several rounds fifty yards to the rear of us, although I was not consciously aware of danger in that direction. When I hit the ground, the slow motion ceased and life resumed its normal speed. I holstered my pistol and picked up my rifle, which was lying beside me. I flipped the selector switch to fully automatic. Dust was still settling around us, but through the haze, sixty to seventy yards to the rear, I could make out a large number of black pajamas running toward us. There were more in the ditch, and another smaller group south of the road heading for us as well.

I quickly squeezed off some short bursts at the Charlies in the ditch. Rob, who had started firing above me, yelled, "You got 'em, Vic. Keep it up. They've got grenades." The VC in the ditch quickly retreated a few yards while those on the road flattened out. Strange to say, only at that moment did I realize they were shooting at us. It seemed mighty dumb to all of us, but our standard operating procedure (S.O.P.) was to not engage the enemy first; we were to wait until they fired at us. Up until then I wasn't sure who had shot first. As my head cleared, I realized that we must have hit a small mine. That made the VC the aggressor; I felt vindicated.

The jeep had come to rest on its right side, burying the machine gun under several inches of soft sand and dirt along the shoulder of the road. Our M-60 could mean the difference between life and death for the four of us. Rob and Paul were trying to dig it out, but the weight of the jeep held it fast. As I loaded another magazine into my rifle, I realized that Bruce was sitting next to me. Both of us were exposed, leaning against the hot undercarriage of the jeep. Bruce held the barrel of his rifle against his chest, trying to jack another round into the chamber by pushing with his left boot against the rifle bolt—a dangerous maneuver if his foot slipped.

"What's wrong?" I asked.

"I think my right shoulder's busted," he said as he came up firing, using his left hand.

We surprised the VC by our ability to sustain fire. As Bruce continued shooting, I decided it would be better for both of us to be on the other side of the jeep with Paul and Rob. I took Bruce's rifle and we crawled around the front end of the jeep. When I straightened up, I saw half a dozen VC coming from the north of us about a hundred yards away. I brought Bruce's rifle up in one hand and mine in the other and began firing both of them from the hip as I leaned against the hood of the jeep. Several of the enemy immediately fell and the others pulled back, rejoining their comrades alongside the road. With all of our rifle practice, I had never been able to fire my weapon one-handed and hit anything. Now I fired two at a time, and rather successfully!

By digging with his hands and bayonet, Paul finally got the M-60 out and off the turret. Blowing through the breech to clear out the loose dirt and pulling the weeds and other debris from the muzzle, he gave us a questioning little shrug and rolled his eyes as if to ask, "Will it fire or blow up in our faces?" He reloaded the ammo belt, and ducking his head, he balanced the machine gun on the left rear fender above his head to point it toward the VC position. He flicked off the safety and squeezed the trigger, and it burped out thirty rounds. "What a marvelous sound," I yelled, and we all let out a loud cheer.

Except for an occasional round or two from our new neighbors up the street, it was quiet for a while. Rob and Paul tried the radio to see if it was still working. It seemed okay, but the antenna, which was attached below the right rear fender, was buried deep in sand. We tried to broadcast but only heard static.

Paul had an idea. "I'm going to remove the antenna and stretch the lead wire as far as it will go. I can wedge the antenna-base between the spare tire and tailgate, in an upright position." Quicker than it took him to explain it, Paul did it.

Evidently the sweeper and its escort had reached their objective, since we heard nothing more from them.

"We've got to try the base and get some help," I said.

Paul nodded as he picked up the handset. "Home Base, Home Base, this is X-ray 2-3. We need help. Over."

Nothing!

"Home Base, Home Base, this is X-ray 2-3. We are in a firefight. Need help. Over." No response.

He tried the sweeper and its escort again. No response there either.

Paul handed the mike to Bruce while we continued to watch and to reload our rifle magazines. We unearthed two cans of belt ammo for the sixty and more ammo bandoleers for the rifles. We worked as a team; we knew instinctively what to do, and we did it. In the lull, each of us took the opportunity to drink plenty of water.

A little over ten minutes had elapsed since we had been knocked off the road, though it seemed like hours. Bruce continued to call on the radio. "Home Base, Home Base, this is X-ray 2-3, do you read me? Over."

Finally, after several more tries, we got a response, "X-ray 2-3, this is Home Base. Stay the hell off the air unless it's an emergency."

It was a good thing that that man was not standing in front of us at that moment! Bruce explained our situation, but was cut off by the radio operator who responded saying, "A little engine overheating does not constitute an emergency. Home Base, out!"

After a few seconds of radio silence, another voice came over the radio asking our position again.

"All right," we thought, "they're sending help."

Just as we were answering, the VC cut loose again and it got a bit noisy and busy. The guys on the radio thought we were just playing cowboys, since the road had been reported as clean by the sweep team thirty minutes earlier. They thought it unlikely we had hit anything. The message ended with "Return to base ASAP, out!"

Paul took the handset and answered, "We can't, damn it! Jeep heavily damaged. Please send help or get our duty officer. Thirty-plus Victor Charlies. Over."

We held out hope that help was forthcoming, but after a few more seconds of radio silence, Home Base came back on the air. "X-ray 2-3, stay off the air and return to base. Out!"

Rob looked down at Bruce and at the radio and said, "Who is that sonofabitch, anyway?"

The term "cooked goose" kept coming to my mind. Fortunately, we had plenty of ammunition, food, and water. But it would be hours before the mine-sweeper crew would start their return trip.

The VC started moving in from two sides again. The main group was on our left and a second, smaller group, which we guessed to be nearly two hundred yards south, was trying to skirt around us to get on our right. I adjusted my M-14 back to semiautomatic, sighted, and fired three rounds.

"You got the distance, Vic!" Rob yelled as three VC hit the dirt. "You couldn't do that with an M-16," he added as he took aim and fired. "One more down."

Paul fired some bursts down the road from the machine gun while Rob and I continued to work on the VC out front. Soon, all retreated, only to regroup eighty yards east, and off to the side of the road. Then, after a minute or two of quiet, all hell broke loose as they quickly filled the road again, firing and yelling. Several incoming rounds whistled past us, while others ricocheted off the ground and jeep.

We responded with all we had to offer—an M-60 and four rifles. A few seconds into this mad firing I heard a new sound filtering through all the noise, coming from the right of our position. At first I was too busy to look. Then I recognized it: a chopper, firing short bursts from an automatic rifle. Even before I saw the bird I could see the dirt kicking up where his rounds hit the roadway near the VC's position. The chopper swooped to just inches off the road on its first pass. We could clearly see the muzzle of an M-16 sticking out the door. The pilot climbed his bird to about a thousand feet, made a 180-degree turn, and came in for another pass, firing more short bursts. He dove again and again as we continued shooting. On one pass a skid lightly made contact with the soil.

The Viet Cong virtually melted into the countryside, probably thinking our reinforcements and more choppers weren't far behind. Our *new* friend made a quick recon above us to see if there were any other enemy troops in the area then came down to within twenty yards of us across the road, trying not to kick up too much dust. There he hovered a couple of feet off the ground and waved at us as if asking if we were okay. We waved back. I held up my two hands to make a "T" as in "time out," asking if he could hold fast for a few minutes. The pilot acknowledged that he understood and would stand by.

We checked with Paul to see if he thought the jeep would run. He made a short inspection and some adjustments then said, "Let's see if we can put her on all fours."

Using leverage from the bent machine-gun turret, we pushed and grunted and finally flipped the jeep back onto its four wheels. Both rear tires had been flattened by the blast, and most of the driveline to the rear end had been knocked out.

"The front end is still intact," Paul announced. "The rear wheels should track okay." The engine had lost some of its oil, with perhaps two quarts remaining in the crankcase. To help slow the oil leakage, Paul had individually wrapped small strips of cloth around three or four live cartridges and plugged the larger holes in the oil pan with them. He used twigs and grass in the others. The moment of truth came as Paul kicked the starter. The engine slowly turned over; we could hear some clanking inside the block, but it wouldn't start. There was also a strong acid odor. "Battery acid," someone said.

Looking around at the three of us, Paul solemnly said, "If anyone knows some strong prayers, this would be a good time to use them."

Looking at him I answered, "I've used all of mine. Let's get out of here. Besides, I don't think there's much we can tell God about this he hasn't already heard."

With a chorus of "Amen," Paul hit the starter again.

"Smoke's coming through the broken tail pipe," I yelled.

"That's good."

He hit the starter again and puffs of bluish-white smoke belched out. The starter turned the engine over a little faster. The engine sputtered; more smoke blew out of the exhaust. Then the engine began to rumble a little. Finally the motor began to run, at first with a dreadful knocking sound, then more quietly with a series of muffled clunks.

Paul slipped the transfer case into the four-wheel-drive position. "Hey, it went in!" he said, sounding a bit surprised.

Gently shifting into first gear, he slowly let out the clutch. The jeep moved forward. Grinning broadly, Paul yelled, "Thank God it's a Kaiser jeep!"

We waved okay to our new friend in the chopper, made a wobbly U-turn, and headed for the base. The vehicle shook terribly, but considering the damage, it was running quite well. We passed several wounded or dead VC, but didn't stop to check. The chopper pilot followed us for a few miles, then flew past us waving his hand. He rocked his bird and was gone.

We picked up a little more speed, the rear tires flapping away with bits and pieces of rubber flying off. There was nothing we could do about it. As long as the rims stayed intact, this would have to do. Because the mounting for the machine gun was so bent, we took turns holding the sixty. All our weapons had the safeties off as we kept a wary eye out for any sign of the enemy.

Most of the jeeps and light duty trucks were lined with sandbags to help protect the occupants from grenades or other small explosives. We threw out the remaining sandbags and lessened the weight by three hundred pounds. I was extremely grateful for every mile we traveled. The noise from the engine grew louder; it was starting to overheat again. I took the handset. We could hear other units using the same frequency.

I keyed the mike and said, "Home Base, Home Base, this is X-ray 2-3. Over." There was no response. "Home Base, this is X-ray 2-3. Over."

I repeated the effort several more times, but got no answer. Finally I told the guys, "I'm going to change to the Deuce frequency. Maybe our radio center is working now."

"Go for it," they agreed.

"Delta Papa, Delta Papa, this is X-ray 2-3. Over."

Nothing!

I repeated, "Delta Papa, Delta Papa, this is X-ray 2-3. Over."

While I was calling, Rob and Bruce rechecked the radio connections. "X-ray 2-3, X-ray 2-3, this is Delta Papa. I read you five by five. Over." This was a voice we recognized.

"Hey, Sarge, is that you? Man, is it good to hear your voice!"

He asked how the trip went and why we weren't using the base frequency as instructed. Bruce took the handset and, in brief Army lingo mixed with some expletives, he explained that we had hit a mine, had been blown off the road, and had been engaged in a firefight.

"That's a roger, Sarge. A forty-five-minute firefight, and assistance was denied."

Sarge began to ask a lot of questions: "Are any of you hurt? What's the condition of your vehicle? What's your location?"

Bruce told him that he thought his shoulder might be broken, but other than that we were all okay; "The jeep is heavily damaged but is still running. I put our location at around three miles out."

We could tell from the sergeant's voice that his anger was building. He was silent for a few moments. "X-ray 2-3, we have a tow truck en route and two escort Mike Papas (MPs). Over."

By this time, the gate was in view. We had only about two more miles to go. I took the handset, "Delta Papa, X-ray 2-3. Cancel escort. Gate in view. Over." Sarge acknowledged the message.

I asked Bruce how he was doing. He said, "I'm fine."

I had used his belt to make a sling for him. "You know, it looks like your shoulder's not broken, just dislocated," I told him. That seemed to encourage him a little., I knew that he was still in a lot of pain, but he was more angry than hurt, and it was not just anger at the VC.

As we came closer to the gate, Bruce took the handset, "Delta Papa, X-ray 2-3. Request drive to base com-center. Over."

Moments later the lieutenant came on the air, "That's a big ten-two-four.

Out." That meant, "Okay."

All of us *really* wanted to meet whoever had been operating the radio. That guy was thigh high in fertilized rice paddy water.

Our jeep was barely able to maintain a speed of fifteen miles per hour. Smoking and knocking, it was now running on only two of its four cylinders. Paul slipped the tranny into second gear as we passed through the entrance to the base. The MP gate guards just stared at us. I figured a combat unit like the Big Red One must see sights like this and worse all the time. They just hadn't ever seen an MP jeep from the 552nd all shot to hell. A couple hundred yards more was all that was needed to reach the communication center; the jeep clanked and rumbled along, trailing a cloud of smoke. As we closed in on the com-center, the poor beast wheezed its last bit of life and coasted to a halt a few feet from the front steps of the building. We must have been quite a spectacle.

The canvas and wood structure that housed the com-center resembled a small Australian farmhouse. It had a wide porch across the front with a few steps leading up to it. Like most of the buildings at Di-An, it was built a little off the ground to keep it above the heavy monsoon rains.

Our sergeant and lieutenant had driven up behind us and they hurried over to witness this exchange and to learn what had gone wrong.

A young corporal stood at the top of the steps observing us. Our vehicle probably looked like the Army's version of olive green Swiss cheese. The two rear tire casings were long gone, and the bent rims were clearly visible. Looking at how filthy we were, he asked in a spiritless voice, "Are you guys hurt?"

Without answering his question, I inquired, "Do you know who has been the radio operator over the past couple hours?"

"I had that duty."

"Wrong answer!" Bruce muttered as he slowly climbed out of the jeep.

I asked him another question. "Tell me, Corporal, who was making most of the decisions concerning radio traffic during that time?"

Moving slowly from the pain, Bruce made his way to the first of five steps as the young corporal answered arrogantly, "I did. I did it all. I am the NCO in charge."

"Wrong answer, again," Rob observed wryly.

Reaching the last step, Bruce finally asked the corporal, "Do you recognize the call sign X-ray 2-3?"

"Yes," he answered with a slight chuckle, "the Deuce Platoon, and especially you guys from the 552nd. Even in the communication company we've heard about you guys. You're all just a bunch of fuck-ups—you never do anything serious." Then, with a look of disdain, he added, "Yeah, I've heard all about you clowns."

Bruce pointed to the jeep and asked, "You sonofabitch, does that look like we've been clowning?" Before the young noncom could answer, Bruce used his good left hand to deliver a tremendous roundhouse blow, striking the corporal squarely in the mouth. The effort nearly took Bruce off his own feet. The young noncom landed hard on his backside and rolled right up against the wall of the building.

Looking up at our lieutenant and sergeant, he yelled, "You saw that, you saw him hit me. I'm a noncom. I'm a corporal. You saw him hit me!"

The lieutenant looked at him sprawled out on the porch and just smiled. "Son, I believe you just tripped over your tongue."

Leaving our jeep to the tow truck, we put our gear in Sarge's jeep and crowded into the back. We dropped Bruce off at the infirmary, and the rest of us went to our hootch to clean up.

A captain from First Infantry G-2 (Army Intelligence) Headquarters asked if he could talk with us for a few minutes before we got cleaned up. The few minutes turned into more than an hour. By that time, Bruce had rejoined us. Our lieutenant finally intervened, and the interview came to an end.

As the meeting broke up, the lieutenant said, "After you guys get cleaned up, I'd like a short report from each of you. I'd especially like you to include specifics concerning the attack and the radio communication."

Both he and the sergeant apologized, and Sarge summed it up by saying, "There can be no excuse for what took place today at the com-center. You did a great job."

The shower really felt good. I couldn't believe how much muddy water poured off me.

The medics snapped Bruce's shoulder back into place, applied a more professional sling, and placed him on a few days of light duty.

"How ya feeling?" one of the others in the platoon asked.

"My left hand hurts more than my shoulder now," he answered, and smiled, "but it hurts sooo gooood."

It bothered me that I might have actually killed someone. There was much to think about concerning our assignment—the initial overheating of the engine and the time it took to refill the radiator—was that enough time for the VC to plant a mine? What if we hadn't broken down? Would we still have hit the mine and been attacked? As I continued to think about it, I realized that none of us had set out to find someone to hurt, and I certainly wasn't going to feel guilty that we had defended ourselves, or that we were still alive. My concerns finally dissipated.

The next morning, about 0800, the four of us were in the mess hall eating breakfast. We had been given the day off. Kent, on break from patrol, was drinking coffee with us as we described to him some of the previous day's adventure. Because of the hour, we had the hall to ourselves. As we ate, we worked on the reports the lieutenant had requested. No one had slept very well that night, and I guess we looked it. Kent glanced up and saw Sarge, the lieutenant, and a major walking toward us. The major, at the lieutenant's request, took a table a couple of rows away. The others, looking very somber, came over and sat down with us.

"Hi, guys," the lieutenant greeted us.

"Good morning, sir; Sarge," we all said in unison.

"We have some bad news for you," Sarge began.

Kent asked, "Excuse me, sir, but should I leave?"

"No, this may concern you as well," Sarge explained.

The lieutenant added, "It could have been you or any one of us out there yesterday."

Our two leaders were clearly pissed off, and what they told us was unbelievable. "The major is here to present the four of you with court-martial papers."

"What for?" we asked.

"There are some people in command who are trying to cover their butts," began the lieutenant. "They're charging you with purposely destroying government property, falsifying messages, using improper radio procedures, *and,*" he added, wincing during a painful pause, "dereliction of duty."

We took a deep breath as Sarge added, "They also wanted to hold the four of you in the stockade pending trial. Get this—so you wouldn't go AWOL."

We all looked at each other and asked, "Where the hell would we go?"

Taking another deep breath, I said, "What are the charges again?"

"Basically it boils down to: falsifying radio messages; purposely damaging government property, namely one M-151 jeep; and not finishing your assigned mission."

This plainly disturbed our sergeant and lieutenant. The lieutenant added, "Both the sergeant and I have gone to the mat to put you on light duty to keep you out of the stockade. Naturally, you'll be confined to our area when not on duty."

"*Naturally,*" one of the guys whispered.

We were happy for their concern and help. Both of them were walking a fine line by supporting us in this way.

Sarge added, "The 552nd will have a field day with you guys on this, especially since it was one of their vehicles that was destroyed."

They told us that just after we limped into the compound, a platoon was sent to the place where we reported that the alleged battle had taken place. They found where we had gone off the road, some spent cartridges and pop cans, but they found no physical evidence of an explosion. No one could find any sign that the VC had recently been in that area, dead or alive. There wasn't a single drop of blood anywhere nor were there any empty AK-47 cartridge casings. All they found were our spent cartridges around where the jeep had been.

I asked if there was any explanation for the obvious scorch marks on the jeep's left side and undercarriage. They looked at each other, then at us, and shook their heads as the lieutenant made a quick notation.

I felt numb. We all did.

"This is unbelievable," we kept saying.

As far as we were concerned, someone at command had screwed up, and his butt was about to be burned. He was looking for a way out, and we were it.

The lieutenant lowered his voice and looked directly at Kent as he said very slowly and deliberately to all of us, "They hope to limit your choice of council from their own list here within I-Corps." Without saying any more, he winked at Kent and motioned for him to leave, saying, "Now, Private Adams, you are dismissed."

A bit confused over the abruptness, Kent gave a quick, "Yes sir," and headed out the door.

The major, who had been waiting a few tables away, was then invited over. He introduced himself and handed us each a copy of the court-martial papers.

Once outside, it took Kent just minutes to understand what the lieutenant had been trying to tell him. "How could they limit the use of an attorney?" he asked himself. The answer was, legally they couldn't! That was what the lieutenant wanted Kent to know. He jumped into his jeep and headed for the com-center's telephone.

At the other end of the line, Kent heard, "Yes, this is Colonel Wilson. Who's calling?"

Kent had remembered the colonel's name from our conversation with BJ nearly two months earlier when we were leaving the 552nd.

Wally listened intently as Kent explained what was going on, and within the hour he had contacted our lieutenant to get the particulars.

Defense council didn't waste any time. Wally flew over the next morning and interviewed the four of us. Part of the concern was why there had not been any evidence of the Viet Cong's presence after the skirmish.

As we were finishing up, Chief walked in, overhearing most of what was going on. He explained, "Colonel, sir, the VC could have planted that mine two minutes after the minesweeper and its escort passed that location." Then he added, "And, as far as the VC being able to clean up a fire-shoot scene, they're as good as my people were a hundred years ago in America."

A week later we had a preliminary hearing. We just sat there listening, dripping wet with perspiration, as much from the emotional turmoil as from the heat and humidity. It was close to 2:00 when Colonel Wilson's aide came into the small courtroom. Walking quickly to our table, he leaned down and whispered something in Wally's ear. Immediately Wally jumped to his feet and excitedly interrupted the prosecutor, who was laying the groundwork for his part of the proceedings. Addressing the President of the Court, he said, "Sir, my apologies to the court, but something of great interest to these proceedings has just been brought to my attention. May we have a ten-minute recess, sir?"

Recess was granted, and the four of us went with Wally and his aide into a small room where a young warrant officer, a pilot, smoked a cigarette. As soon as we walked in, the pilot jumped to attention, saluted Wally, and gave his name, rank, and job description. Then he handed over a rather thick file folder.

"You see, sir," the pilot explained to Wally, "I fly photo recon taking pictures of various areas the brass wants to know about."

By chance, or in answer to our prayers, the pilot had checked the bulletin board that morning at the Air Base in Bien Hoa where he was stationed. He came across the notice of our trial.

"I rarely check the board, as my orders always come from Saigon," the pilot explained.

He put times, dates, and places together and figured out that we were the ones he had helped on the day in question. As we listened, I wondered where all this was leading. Wally suddenly became as giddy as a new bridegroom. On the day of our misadventure, the chopper pilot had been on a photo recon mission ten miles south of where the attack had taken place. Finishing his job, he started for his air base. Inadvertently, he switched on his ground receiver. The pilot heard repeated requests for assistance.

The pilot explained, "Hell, from what I could hear, someone was in trouble but was being stonewalled." He went on and said, "Since I was just a few minutes away from them, I decided to check out the distress call. I climbed to six thousand feet and headed my bird over."

It wasn't until he was well on his way home from helping us that he discovered his camera had been left on, merrily snapping away frame after frame every two or three seconds.

From the pilot's file, Wally pulled out sixty beautiful black-and-white glossies of the fight scene. There were several shots from about thirty-five hundred feet as the chopper approached our position from the west. Time, date, and altitude automatically identified each picture. He also had photos of the four of us firing our weapons at a very visible enemy. A few other shots showed us looking at our overturned jeep in bewilderment as he hovered across the road from us. As the pilot reviewed some of the photos with Wally, he added, "I have no idea how they were able to drive that vehicle back to base."

"Heads are going to roll," Wally exclaimed gleefully. "We got 'em now. Let's go."

The pilot was asked to accompany us into the courtroom while Wally presented the photos to the court for evaluation. Having the warrant officer handy would be helpful should there be any questions. As soon as the judges and the prosecutor saw the pictures, their faces turned crimson.

Clearing his throat, the President of the Court said, "In view of these new findings, this case is dismissed. The court's apologies to these four young soldiers." Then he turned to the pilot and added, "And the court thanks you as well for bringing this information to our attention."

As the court officers got up to leave the room, we stood up at attention. We, of course, were elated. The sergeant and lieutenant, who were in the courtroom, immediately went out and arranged for a barbecue for all of us, including the pilot and Wally. Festivities went on well into the evening. We ate steaks like we hadn't seen since leaving the States. I was told they had been "commandeered" from the general's mess.

Privately, we thanked Wally, his aide, and the warrant officer. Chief was happy about the good news. I was surprised how much moral support we had received from all the members of the Deuce Platoon. The young sergeant from the outpost told us, "You guys did a first-rate, First Infantry job. Welcome to the Big Red One." We finally belonged.

This court thing was a close call, perhaps even closer than the VC encounter because it came from our own people. It's difficult for soldiers to be alert if they constantly have to watch out for danger coming from their own side.

Things happened rather quickly to people in the communications company. The corporal became an instant PFC; two sergeants and a lieutenant were severely reprimanded; another was demoted; and their captain was reassigned. As for us, we went back to work with a much better feeling about the Army and life in general.

While we were going through our adventure, there had been growing talk of some big buildup and push coming from the North Vietnamese. Army Intelligence (G-2) was vague, however. About ten days before Christmas, we were told to report back to II Field Force. Nearly all of us tried to transfer out of the 552nd and into the First Infantry MPs, but we couldn't.

The commanding officer of the Big Red One, with recommendations from the lieutenant, and the sergeant of the Deuce Platoon notified all of us guys TDY, of the brigade's intention to award us with various medals, as in the Silver Star and the Bronze Star. Unfortunately, when the requests were sent to our CO at the 552nd, he refused them.

A First Infantry colonel was incredulous and couldn't believe our captain would do such a thing. The Deuce Platoon, however, did give us a big party, our last steak barbecue. They presented each of us with a plaque inscribed with our names and dates. It said simply, "A job well done." What we learned from everyone at the Big Red One was invaluable. I will always be grateful to all of them. I remain convinced that the knowledge we gained during our stay with them saved many lives.

On the sixteenth of December, we started back to the 552nd—five jeeps, three trailers, and fifteen much-improved soldiers.

Inscription reads:
TO PFC MILLS
552 M.P. CO. FOR A
JOB WELL DONE WHILE ATTACHED
TO THE DEUCE PLATOON 1ST MP CO.

Chapter 6
USING ALL WE LEARNED

Over the ten weeks spent with the First Infantry, Bruce, Rob, Kent, Paul, and I became very close, pulling much of our duty together, sometimes as a group, sometimes in pairs. Whenever one of us was sent into a hotbox situation, the remaining four would surely show up. We were a team; we had become known by the Deuce Platoon of the First Infantry as *The Five.*

"Boy, that was one hell of a party last night," Bruce mused as he loaded his gear with one hand and held his head with the other.

"They do know how to throw a shindig, that's for sure," Paul added.

Bruce hoisted the last bit of gear and equipment into one of the trailers, and as I tied it all down he confirmed, "Shit, this drinking could ruin my Mormon upbringing."

The three of us broke out laughing and Bruce stopped what he was doing and asked, "And what's so damn funny?"

"Hell, you are," I answered. "You and your two cans of beer."

"Personally," Kent chirped, "I think it was the 5-pound steak he ate."

Sarge, the lieutenant, and a few of the guys came to see us off. They had been a great bunch to work with. As we started the engines, someone stood up in back and hollered, "Head 'em up, move 'em out!" We all finished the refrain, "Rawhide!"

I overheard Sarge say to the lieutenant, "You know, sir, if shit hits the fan with a major push from up north, these boys won't have a chance—not the way all of II Force is run. These are good men."

"Well, you're right about the problems in their unit," the lieutenant agreed. "But these guys ain't boys. They have First Infantry blood in them, and if anything, these fifteen men from the 552nd will make the difference because of what they know and how to use it." As they both waved, the officer added, "No, they aren't boys. They're soldiers from the Big Red One."

It was 3:00 in the afternoon, a bit late leaving for Long Binh. We had expected a two-hour ride back to the 552nd. The locals were scared and sure that the VC were coming soon, in force. Most refugees wanted to get closer to Saigon for better protection. With the sudden increase of refugee traffic, we only got as far as the USO club that afternoon. As we secured our gear, we saw part of a cav unit camped nearby.

Inside the USO we were introduced to the same group of girls Kent and I had met on our trip out to Di-An. It was a treat to see those friendly American faces again!

"Very few of you guys have stopped in over the past week," one of the girls told us, "but a few days ago, an armored cav unit set up a bivouac area practically at our back door."

"It's nice to have them there," another girl added, "but we're still a little nervous."

Not knowing what was really going on made things seem worse than they were, and the rumor mill had fanned the flame of uncertainties, adding to everyone's fear and stress.

It was starting to get dark, and we still had a long way to go. The roads were jammed with traffic and getting worse. With that in mind, I suggested that it might be better to avoid traveling at night. We decided that we should either camp out with the cav unit (they usually didn't like Army cops either) or sleep on the floor of the USO. We chose the latter. The girls were happy and relieved to have us stay, especially since the husband and wife who managed the club were away and not due back until late the next day. We didn't even have to ask for anything to eat; the girls already had the cooking started.

Before chow, Bruce, Kent, and I went over and introduced ourselves to the cav's first sergeant. We wanted to secure our vehicles with them for the night, and we offered our services to the cavs to bolster their guard. Their watch commander seemed pleased to have the extra manpower, even for one night. Some of the infantrymen attached to the cav unit wanted to trade their M-16s for our M-14s. We declined, although it was interesting how we kept running into offers like that. From our time in the field, we understood why. The M-14 was one tough shooter.

Back at the USO we took advantage of the hot showers. Even though we limited ourselves to less than five minutes each to conserve hot water, the showers were wonderful. For the first time in many weeks, I felt almost clean. Our original plan had been to throw some bedding on the downstairs floor, but the girls wouldn't hear of it. We used real beds, or close to real—actually they were thick, soft mattresses on pull-down wall bunks. Not everyone could have the luxury of a bunk because there were fifteen of us, so some of the guys elected to sleep on the floor. The girls doubled up in their dorm rooms, except for two who were very scared. They brought some of their bedding downstairs and slept on two of the sofas. I think having five or six guys on walking guard or sleeping nearby helped to put all the girls at ease.

Some nervous GI from the cavs accidentally discharged a couple of rounds from his .50 caliber machine gun during the wee hours. Other than that, the night was uneventful. Morning came with a glorious sunrise along with a great breakfast. Definitely not Army chow. The girls knocked themselves out preparing this feast, and it tasted great!

We had repacked our gear in the trailers long before we ate. The cavalry sergeant and the captain thanked us for our help during our stay as they topped off our gas tanks. The USO girls also thanked us with hugs and kisses, and we were back on the road by 8:00 a.m.

The traffic of the previous afternoon seemed to have evaporated, so we made good time for a short distance. As we approached Bien Hoa and the Air Base, we changed radio frequency over to the 552's band and called in to report our location and ETA (estimated time of arrival). Traffic had gotten gradually heavier, and eventually it came to a crawl as we entered Bien Hoa. At 10:30 a.m. we drove through the gates of the 552nd. We parked in line on the company road near the orderly room. Our vehicles looked like hell, as did we.

Everything was dusty and dirty. Our fatigues were well worn.

Rob, Bruce, and I went to report in. The first sergeant and the master sergeant were talking when we walked in. The two stared at us for a minute then Top said with his evil laugh, "Hell, we heard you guys were on your way to Leavenworth."

"It was a bad rap. They had nuttin' on us," joked Rob.

But Top was not amused and added, "You were supposed to have returned yesterday. What took ya so long?"

"We radioed what was going on, Top," I said, "All the roads in and around Di-An and on into Bien Hoa were jammed with refugees. We decided not to risk traveling by night."

Top interrupted, "Just excuses. You assholes wouldn't know a refugee if one stuck a finger in your eye."

"No, Sarge, I'd definitely recognize that, all right," I challenged.

Adding his two cents, Bruce said, "We missed you too, Top."

It was obvious Top wasn't fooling as he added, "You're troublemakers; all you guys from the field. Nothin' but smart-ass troublemakers."

Hearing that we were back, the CO came out from his office. Top told us to wait outside. After greeting the captain, we returned to our vehicles.

Looking at those three men, I couldn't help but wonder how they ever got into such positions of responsibility and command. Somewhere in the back of my mind, though, I still entertained the hope that if and when the chips were ever down, they would come through.

During basic training and in AIT, like any other recruit, I was a bit intimidated by DIs and officers. Later on I figured out that all the yelling and harassment of the recruits had a purpose. It was to help make us strong under pressure. At the 552nd there was a lot of harassment too, but it was not the same. In the 552nd it was vicious and directed at anyone who might threaten all the illegal and inappropriate activities that went on there. It had been different at the Big Red One. There we had learned to live by one important principle: *Understand and know all orders, written or verbal, as well or better than those who issue them.* This rule was to become our common defense against the drunken insanity of the 552nd MP command and the whole compound.

As we waited by our jeeps, a few of the house girls and other civilian employees stopped by to visit. They were obviously glad to see us. I had missed their gentle, modest ways. I noticed that only a handful of Vietnamese workers, half of the normal number, were around.

One of the girls told us, "VC come very soon. Many families go away."

After a few minutes, Top and the CO came out, and Top hollered, "Fall in for inspection."

Did we hear him correctly? We couldn't believe it. Most command personnel would never do this to a group returning from the field. Unfortunately, we had heard right. As we stood there in disbelief, all of us tried to keep from showing our frustration and anger.

Then I hollered, "You heard the first sergeant. Form up! Clear your weapons. Get ready for inspection."

Bruce quickly added, "On the double. Let's play this silly-ass game and show 'em how the First Infantry, *real Army,* does it!"

Within a few seconds we were lined up and standing at attention, our M-14s at our sides. The sixties, still mounted on the jeeps, were ready as well. Bruce was at the far end of the column and marched back to where the captain and first sergeant were standing.

Stopping in front of the CO, Bruce came to attention. Snapping and holding a salute, he said, "Sir, platoon ready for inspection." We waited. It was well over 100 degrees. We stood at attention in a perfectly straight line, our dirty uniforms tattered from weeks of work in the field and wet with sweat; and we waited.

The captain seemed slightly embarrassed and irritated at our readiness and was probably a little put out with the first sergeant. He finally returned Bruce's salute and, turning to Top, he said, "You asked for this. You do it," and he went back inside.

Top was hoping to catch us with our "dirty britches down." He took his position in front of me. I snapped my rifle to port and slid the bolt back to lock. Top took the weapon, almost dropping it, and glowering at me, he looked inside the breach and the barrel, then handed it back. Repeating this with several men, he finally retreated in disgust, dismissing the troops with a comment to check in with the supply clerk. All the guys wanted to cheer, but Paul and Kent kept them quiet. We had made our point.

Top was really pissed off. What he hadn't known or expected was that all of the weapons had been cleaned the night before. He had only two negative comments: one about our dirty vehicles and, second, our uniforms. We were a mess—no argument there—but we had worked hard to get that way too!

I was not glad to be back, and everyone else voiced similar sentiments. After several weeks of being treated with respect and dignity, we felt that the command's attitude here was total BS. If a combat situation arose, this was not where any of us wanted to be.

The platoon unloaded the jeeps and trailers, found their hootches, and checked the vehicles into the motor pool. After a shower and a change of clothes, we headed for the canteen for lunch and a quick visit to the PX. We eventually made it to the supply room for new fatigues, boots, and other gear.

Our supply sergeant was actually a specialist 5th class. He said his name was Norman, and he didn't like to be referred to as a sergeant. Nevertheless, we affectionately and respectfully called him Sarge. Although he pretended to complain, I think he liked the gesture. He knew his supply room and every other one in-country. If he didn't have what we needed, he was not above going outside of channels to get it. Nothing was too hard for him to find. He thought of it as an art.

"Hi Sarge," I started. "I need a new rifle stock. My old one is held together with duct tape."

When I showed it to Norm he said, "I don't have any on hand, but I'll look around." Two days later, I found a long box on my footlocker. I guessed right off that it wasn't roses; it had Army ID numbers all over it. One part of the ID specified "M-14." "It must be my new rifle stock," I mentioned to one of the guys. When I opened the box, it was just like getting a Christmas present.

This stock was sure different from my old one. I really liked the way the weapon handled. Definitely no one else would have one like it. I hurried over to show it to Bruce and some of the other guys. The supply sergeant was on his way out of their hootch as I started in.

"Hey, Sarge," I called, "this is a great stock. Thanks!"

He glanced at it, smirked a little, and with a wink said, "I've never seen it before."

My rifle was now an assault-style weapon, complete with a pistol-grip and a folding handle under the barrel.

Our lieutenant was walking past and saw it, and tried to confiscate it. "A mere private cannot legally have such a weapon," he squawked. "This is intended for an officer."

That was a bunch of bull, of course, but the lieutenant suggested we trade weapons anyway. He had an M-2 carbine. Norman intervened, "Sir, it isn't possible to trade or reassign weapons."

That wasn't quite true, but it sure sounded good. He went on to explain, "We don't have any more stocks, sir, and I have no idea where this one came from."

Much to my surprise, the person who came to my defense was my old squad leader, Sergeant Mitchell.

"Lieutenant," began Mitchell, "there is no regulation that says a PFC can't have such a stock, sir, but if you really want to trade, perhaps you can take his place on the front line when the shooting starts."

The officer stammered a little, then walked away as Mitchell muttered to himself, "Gawd, what an asshole."

It was part of our responsibility as MPs to provide ongoing security for dignitaries visiting the II Field Force compound. An officer's rank determined how and where he would arrive, and what security would be used. Gate Three was the main entrance to all headquarters facilities, TOC and the Provost Marshal's office. Directly across from the gate was the Widow's Village and a helo-pad used by some higher-ranking officers.

A short time after our return from the field, I was cutting through the area from the PX, heading for the south perimeter road. I was off duty and was walking back to the company area. When I got to the gate, I stopped to chat for a moment with the kid standing guard; his was a lonely, boring job. As we talked, a jeep came through, taking a colonel back to his waiting chopper.

Three of our MP patrols were stationed there at the LZ (landing zone) for security, and I knew that Bruce and Kent were among them. My buddy on gate duty informed me that an MP, whose name I recognized from AIT, was the gunner on the chopper, serving as part of the 716th MP out of Saigon. I decided to hurry over to the helo-pad to say a quick "hello" to the guy before he had to leave. I dashed across the highway in time to join the others who were already visiting with Boomer. It was great to see him again.

When the officer, his aide, and the pilot climbed aboard the "Huey," Boomer clambered on to take his position. The whine of the jet engine filled our ears, and the huge blade and tail rotor slowly began to turn. To avoid being blinded by the dust and stung by the gravel, we all moved several yards away.

"You know, Bruce," I yelled over the nearly deafening sound of blades and jet, "I don't think I have ever heard one of these birds make such a racket. What's the problem?"

"I dunno," Bruce called back. "Boomer says it's going in for a 'major' as soon as they get back to Saigon."

Boomer began waving to us as the bird crisply lifted off the ground. I retreated several more yards, slowly heading toward Gate Three, and had just turned to give my friend one more wave when something suddenly went terribly wrong. The pilot had taken the chopper up about a thousand feet when a shaft somehow came up from the engine, shearing off one blade. Just as time had slowed when we hit the mine, everything seemed to go in slow motion until impact. We could not believe what was happening.

The ship made a horrible, crashing, screeching sound as it hit the ground and the jet engine came to a grinding halt. A small fire broke out, but there was no explosion. I ran toward the site; the guys in the jeeps were all momentarily motionless. When I got to the nearest vehicle, I picked up the handset to call for medical aid; then two of us grabbed fire extinguishers and sprayed down the wreckage. Although it was only seconds, it felt like hours before help arrived. We all stepped back when the medics moved in, but there was nothing anyone could do. Everyone aboard had died. The doctor told us that probably the end had been so quick that there was no pain.

Soldiers in Nam were always alert to the possibility of enemy contact and the danger of aircraft being brought down by ground fire. That was combat—expected. In combat a man could fight. But death from a mechanical failure somehow shocked us. It made us feel helpless. Unfortunately, as fliers told me, it was all too common.

Christmas and New Year's celebrations came and went without a hitch. My only problem was having to start 1968 in Vietnam instead of around a nice warm, crackling fire in Seattle. It would have been nice to be watching snow falling and enjoying the Rose Bowl with a warm, cozy lady. At least the date for my departure was now in the same calendar year, although it was still many months away.

There had been no enemy contact or action in our sector before or during the holidays. Our area didn't normally have much combat activity, but G-2 said this was slow even for us. The U.S. had stopped bombing as of January 1st in the hope that they could convince the North Vietnamese to sit down at the bargaining table to work out a cease-fire.

The predicted big push from the North Vietnamese did not materialize, and eventually things got back to normal. The civilian employees were allowed to return to their jobs, and we ran our routine patrols into Bien Hoa and the surrounding villages and towns, checking the bars and cathouses for GIs in the wrong places.

Bruce, Rob, Kent, and I often wondered what the traffic was like back at the outpost, but none of us wanted to volunteer to find out. Our CO, the first sergeant, still viewed us as incompetent and did not believe we had been assigned to such a post.

A few days after I returned to the unit, Top managed to find a really nice job for me. He assigned me to ride shotgun on the post garbage truck, which was contracted through the Vietnamese government. If it hadn't been for the smell and slimy goo and grit, it wouldn't have been a bad detail. The truck made the rounds twice a week. We covered every company, garbage can, and dumpster on post. Then I would ride with them to the garbage dump, my Stevens pump shotgun in my right hand.

A couple weeks prior to the garbage detail, I had learned about several families living at the dump. They slept in makeshift shelters of cardboard shipping boxes that they had tied together. Many of the young mothers were barely fourteen years old, victims of the war and of our soldiers.

On my second day of hauling garbage, I spotted two children who seemed to be on their own. I guessed the little girl was no older than four, and her brother must have been about twenty months old. I spent a few minutes with them and was impressed with how friendly they were; they were so starved for affection.

On my day off, a couple of friends and I went to the PX and purchased some essential food items. We took the stuff to the dump to give to the two kids and to the other families. (Of course this was against the rules.) We also found a young mother whose own child had died of malnutrition and who was willing to take care of the two children. She warmed to them quickly.

There were huge rats at the dump, some about the size of a house cat. They were extremely aggressive and quick, and could those things jump! Whenever they saw the garbage truck enter the area, the rats would scurry around excitedly, as if preparing for a meal.

It had become the practice of many of the guys to stop off the highway and fire a few rounds from their pistols into the dump, sometimes going in closer looking for rats. This worried me once I knew there were families living there, but my objections fell on deaf ears.

The day after our food delivery to the families, I filled in on patrol for Kent's partner, who was ill. Most of the guys in the 552nd were good soldiers and MPs, but there were also the screw-ups: the "good ol' boys." The two other patrols were manned by guys in that good ol' boys' club. Early that evening there was an opportunity for Kent and me to stop by the dump. Four men from the other two patrols had already arrived, and we could see tracers from their .45's flying against the evening sky.

"Hey, knock it off," I protested as we pulled up. "There are little kids living down there!"

"Tough shit, Mills. They're just slopes. Don't mean anything to us," one of them called back. "If they mean so much to you," he added, "why don't you and your friend just take a little ride on into all the garbage? You like garbage, don't you, Mills? We won't shoot ya—*maybe*." Laughing, he and another man slapped another clip in their pistols and prepared to shoot some more.

"Kent, let's go on down," I said. I got out of my seat, placed my butt on the dashboard and faced to the rear. Picking up my rifle I yelled out, "One thing you bastards oughta know by now," and jacked a round into the chamber, "*I shoot back!*"

Kent hollered, *"Me too!"* Then he turned to me and said, "Let's go see if anyone's been hurt." Then gesturing to the others he added, "Aren't you concerned about the possibility of those bozos blowing your, ah, *our* heads off, though?"

"I used to be," I told him, "but not anymore."

The two of us headed down and cruised through the dump. We were relieved to see that no one had been injured. No more shots were fired that night.

One day, after I had been working the garbage truck detail for a couple of weeks, we arrived at the dump and saw the rats scurrying around as usual. As the driver prepared to dump his load, a rat came out from nowhere and began attacking the right front tire of our truck. At one point it actually hung onto the sidewall by its teeth. This rat didn't squeak, it screeched. The driver went nuts and began yelling frantically in Vietnamese as he rolled up his window and closed the door. Even for a rat this was very strange behavior; the beast acted as if it might go after us, jumping up and down in a frenzy.

I was outside the cab perched on the running board, holding onto the right door when the rodent started coming toward me. It jumped two or three feet into the air, flipping and emitting an awful sound. A fearful a shiver went down my spine. I leveled my weapon at it, pushed the safety to off, and blew the rodent to rat heaven.

On our way back to the compound, I thought about the rodent's strange behavior. Getting off at the gate to sign off on the driver's logbook, I happened to see one of the guys from the field working a motor patrol.

"Hey, Johnson, I need a quick ride to the post infirmary. Can you help?"

I wanted to describe this incident to the doctors there. Johnson was a little less than reluctant, mostly because I smelled so bad, but he finally gave me a ride with the understanding that I had to walk back.

I spoke at first to a captain, a doctor who was new in-country, and eventually ended up talking to all four doctors at our infirmary.

"Mills," one of the MDs began, "could you locate the remains of that rat?

"Yes, sir. I can take you to the exact spot." (That was probably all there was left to see.)

They called our desk sergeant for two, two-man patrols armed with shotguns to accompany us. I rode with the medics and located the place where I had killed the rat. They took over from there, telling everyone to be alert for other rats or for any other animals in the area, and to be extremely cautious.

For the next few days, the dump was off-limits for everyone. All of the families that had been living there had to be moved. Some of the people, including infants, had several rat bites and showed them to the doctors. The Vietnamese Army medical staff was notified of the possibility of rabies at the dump. All of the people were tested and were treated for the disease as a precaution.

The tests proved that the rat I had killed was rabid, but fortunately none of the people were infected. The medical staff called in a napalm strike. The ground was burned twenty-four inches deep. Everyone kept a lookout for other animals exhibiting strange behavior, but none were found or reported.

I was given a verbal commendation from the medical staff and the II Field Force commanding officer for being alert. My CO and Top commended me too, although they were pissed off because I had failed to go through channels and hadn't reported in with them first. Roger, our company clerk, unexpectedly came to my defense and said, "Actually, sir, Mills did come here first, but both you and Top were off post at Long Binh, and I couldn't locate the lieutenant." Reluctantly they had to accept this explanation.

Later, when thanking him, I asked Roger why he had put himself in possible jeopardy with Top and the CO.

"I think if I hadn't," he began, "all you TDY guys would've been pulling guard duty at the dump every night for the remainder of your tours. Besides, since they weren't here, they wouldn't have known whether you checked in or not. To hell with them!"

It was conceivable that these men were capable of any vindictive action. Roger was probably closer to right than I wanted to believe. Bruce knew Top better than most of us, and said that the captain always went along with whatever Top suggested.

I was rewarded for my efforts by not having to work the garbage truck detail anymore. Not having to ride that smelly old truck couldn't have come too soon to suit me. I was losing friends!

Shortly after the site was burned and bulldozed, the dump reopened. None of the locals returned to it. Several of us helped to move many of them into the deserted village across from our compound. Even though the village, known as the Widow's Village, held some security concerns for headquarters and G-2, we were given the okay to use one small section for housing. The vacant shacks were far better than the sewn-together cardboard boxes the people had been living in at the dump. The move not only gave these few people a better place to live, it also lent us some very grateful eyes and ears.

As these families settled in, we began delivering small amounts of food (milk, canned meats, etc.) to them. Company Command regularly chewed us out for this, but we kept on helping just the same.

A few days after the rat died, and much to my surprise, I was assigned to be Sergeant Mitchell's driver for the night. Guard Mount (duty inspection) was held at 2:30 in the afternoon. After inspection, we headed for the motor pool to check out our vehicles. Unless it was raining, patrol jeeps had the canvas top removed so an M-60 could be mounted in the cab. The supervisor's jeep kept the top.

Throughout most of the shift, Mitchell and I spoke only about the business at hand. I conducted a few routine stops, wrote a ticket or two, and gave some warnings. Because the headlight dimmer switch on our vehicle kept smoking, we stopped by the motor pool and changed jeeps.

About three-quarters of the way through our shift, we took a break for coffee and doughnuts at the 199th Choppers mess hall. Mitchell knew the mess sergeant. As we sat there Sarge asked if he could see my rifle. He was curious about my new stock and wanted a closer look at it. After removing the magazine and clearing my weapon, I handed it to him.

"I wanted to thank you for bucking the lieutenant the other day. His carbine was not my idea of a weapon of choice."

"That's all right," he said quietly. He continued to admire the assault stock and then spoke in the same low voice. "I was wrong about you and the others from the field," referring to the men from the Deuce Platoon. "I may never like you personally, but as far as I'm concerned, you're a good team player and a good leader. And that goes for your friends too. You guys took a lot of unnecessary shit and kept working."

I almost fell out of my chair.

"This is a great stock. How in the hell does Norm find these things?"

He handed me my weapon, and I thought about his remarks while I slowly replaced the magazine and the two of us went back on patrol

"X-ray 9 to Mike Papa One. Over."

"That's Bruce and Rob calling," I said.

"Mike Papa One. Over," Sarge radioed back.

"Hey, Sarge, we've just returned from checking the tower. All our company lights are on. Com-center doesn't respond to calls. Over."

All military installations throughout Long Binh were under a yellow alert, which meant blackout status, one notch away from a general red alert.

We had just finished checking the 199th helo-pad area at the far northeast corner of their compound, and Sarge said, "Do a 180 Mills. I want to see."

From over two miles away we could see our company lights burning brightly. Mitchell tried to reach the desk by radio, "Slick Pole Tango, this is Mike Papa One. Over."

After several tries, there was still no response. Sarge told me to get there as fast as possible and mumbled something under his breath. We weren't to use headlights, only our blackout lights, but Sarge said, "Turn 'em on, Mills—reds and siren. If Charlie don't know where the hell we are by now, he never will."

The compound floodlights lit up the night sky like a small city. They also made an easy target for enemy rockets. Coming around the corner from the east perimeter road onto our company road was like driving into the midday sun. I wasn't sure if what I was seeing was real. There was Top—smashed out of his mind—supervising a sandbag-filling detail. He had everyone who was not on duty standing in formation; even our radioman was there. Our acting desk sergeant, a Specialist 4th Class, was trying to reason with Top, but to no avail. Any vestige of respect I had had for the first sergeant permanently evaporated at that moment. A lot of the other guys felt the same. Top was no longer top dog of the good ol' boys' club.

Both the first sergeant and his friend the master sergeant had been getting more and more into the booze. So had the captain. This was especially troubling because of the increase in alerts. Army Intelligence had been reporting additional VC activity in sectors around us. There was indeed a push coming from the north, and some areas were already experiencing stepped-up activity with snipers.

I slid the jeep to a halt opposite of Top, who stood weaving back and forth. Bruce drove in from the other direction, and Rob jumped out at the gate to add more security there.

Sergeant Mitchell asked, "Mills, you got your cuffs handy?"

"Yes, Sarge, I do."

With vehemence he said, "You know what to do with them."

I grabbed Top by his belt and shoved him against a hootch to keep him off balance which, given his drunken state, was not hard to do. I put his right arm behind his back and locked one end of the handcuffs onto his wrist; then I brought his left arm back and cuffed that wrist.

Mitchell quickly ordered, "Someone, anyone, go kill those damn floodlights."

Almost instantly we resorted to flashlights. Our radio operator ran back to his radio like a scalded cat, and the acting desk sergeant was close behind.

Top was in bad shape and he continued to yell and curse at everyone. I had Bruce hold him while I retrieved my rifle from the jeep. We had heard several pops coming from across the highway, and a few rounds zinged over our heads.

Mitchell told the rest of the men, "You guys get some sleep, but keep your weapons ready and sleep in your fatigues."

Top, still yelling orders, mostly at Mitchell, roared, "You bastard! Do you know how much trouble you're in?"

Turning to the first sergeant, Mitchell said coolly, "Shut the hell up, or I'll shoot ya right now."

I think he would have too—he was that angry. Top had not only endangered the safety of the immediate company area, but he had compromised the security for all of headquarters compound and its Tactical Operation Center. This was serious.

The first sergeant quieted, mumbling incoherently, but still struggling a little as we moved him toward our MP station and a holding cell. As we approached the front door of the MP station behind the first guard bunker, twenty yards from the gate, about thirty rounds came at us from across the highway. Sparks flew as the rounds hit the compacted dirt of our company road and ricocheted off the orderly room. The shooter was about one hundred yards out. I pushed Top to the ground to protect him, put my knee in his back and dropped my M-14 to a firing position. Bruce went spread-eagle alongside some sandbags. He and I had seen the flash of the sniper's weapon. I clicked off the safety and fired, emptying my magazine. Tracers tore through the night to the exact spot where I had seen the muzzle flashes. That new rifle stock was really slick. Rob and Bruce added a few rounds of their own while I reloaded. Mitchell was impressed with how fast we responded.

"Good shooting, guys," he said.

We wondered why the people in the bunker hadn't responded with their sixty. We soon found out that of the three, two had been filling sandbags and the other had been in a semi-drunken sleep. Mitchell was livid. He ordered immediate replacement for the third man.

I don't know if the three of us hit anyone with our rifle fire, but the night quickly returned to a quiet tension.

After we got Top into a cell for the night, we searched around camp to locate the master sergeant and the CO. Walking between the two rows of hootches in the pitch-black was unnerving, and I was glad we had flashlights. A man returning from the latrine asked about all the shooting. Mitchell told him it was over, but to be ready.

"Have you seen the CO or Sergeant Green?" Mitchell asked. The man nodded and pointed to their bunker.

The bunker, or bomb shelter, was dome-shaped with two or three layers of sandbags covering the entire structure and doorway. We slowly opened the door to see a low-burning Coleman gas lantern. In that dim light we could see two trembling figures standing near the center of the bunker. They were dressed only in their shorts and T-shirts. One of them held a bottle of whiskey and the other a .45.

Mitchell and I looked at their scared faces a few moments. No one said a word; no one had to. Then we slowly backed out, closing the door. Sergeant Mitchell was nearly off the scale with anger. I think he had believed, as most of us did, that even though the company had been run a bit loosely, if and when fighting came, there would be some degree of leadership from these men.

After a little talk, Bruce, Rob, and I suggested to Sergeant Mitchell that it might be a good idea for us to check the other company area bunkers along southern perimeter and east to the bridge. It was obvious that a lot of people had heard the shooting, and we figured explanations could ease things, and keep some nervous kid from shooting some poor SOB returning from the local cathouse.

Bruce added, "You know, Sarge, it might be a good idea for you to make an in-person inspection of TOC, the guard tower, and the rest of the post perimeter."

The TOC was in the dead center of the compound, just behind the II Field Force Headquarters building. The tower was off the compound and directly across from the 199th Choppers.

As we walked back to our vehicles, Mitchell had cooled off some. He had a puzzled expression on his face as he looked at us. Finally he said, "You guys really did work the outpost and get into a firefight or two while at Di-An, didn't you?"

This caught us a bit off guard, and before we could respond, he added, "The whole court-martial thing was a cover-up?"

We gave a simple "Yes." I don't know what had prompted his questions other than the fact that he had probably believed the "bull" about the quality of men the company had sent to the field. In his five or six years of Army service, this was Mitchell's first taste of combat. Now he had witnessed firsthand how three of those from Di-An performed. What was more important was that now he knew he could depend on us, crisis or not, to do our jobs.

As we continued to walk to our jeeps, Sarge added, "At first I thought you were screw ups like everyone said, but you guys are all right. Now, let's get back to work."

Sarge listened to suggestions we made, including one about not using the field phones in the bunkers and tower until the lines could be physically inspected. He got on the radio and requested that patrol number three meet us in front of the headquarters building in fifteen minutes and added that they should stay alert. Then we headed toward our guard posts and the bridge.

We had just talked to the guys in the second and third bunkers, and we were moving our two jeeps slowly on to the next, when we noticed a dark figure. He was silhouetted by the floodlights from the bridge some distance behind him and was calmly walking toward us. Sarge and I were in the lead, and I turned on the headlights for a moment. Turning the lights back to black-out, I took out my flashlight and walked up to the soldier and began to question him. Sarge was right behind me. One of the men came out of the bunker to see what was going on. The man we stopped had crossed in front of the last two bunkers without being challenged. Sarge wanted to know why.

"What the hell are you guys doing out here?" he asked. "How could this individual scale a ten-foot wire fence and walk calmly up the road in the middle of the night during a yellow alert, and not be stopped?"

Sarge was beginning to see what most of the other companies in the area had known for some time concerning the 552nd. After chewing out the rest of the guard detail, he turned to one of them and said, "Take this AWOL to the office and write his ass up."

He relented a little when he learned from the guard that neither the duty officer (everyone's least favorite lieutenant) nor the sergeant of the guard (no one knew who that was) had been by to check on these posts all night. There had been a request by field phone from two of the bunkers for the sergeant of the guard. No one had come.

Calmer again, Sarge explained, "You guys are trained soldiers and MPs. You heard the shooting. The front gate was fired on, so stay ready and be alert. Act like soldiers who want to go home!"

It was nearly 1:00 a.m. when we got back in our jeeps and started out for headquarters to meet the third patrol. They had tried calling us a few minutes earlier but everyone had been told to keep off the air unless it was a "code five-one" emergency. Before Sarge could pick up our handset, our radioman jumped down their throats.

When we got to the intersection of our gate and the company road, Mitchell suddenly told me to turn right, and he motioned for Bruce and Rob to wait at the gate. We stopped at the last hootch. Grabbing his flashlight, he jumped over the sandbags at the entrance and disappeared into the darkness. A moment or two later, a dim overhead light came on, and a man emerged from the hootch with Mitchell. It was Smith, his carbine in one hand and his holster and belt draped over his shoulder. He had been promoted to sergeant just days earlier.

The two talked for a few minutes. Evidently Mitchell was having Smith double up to help supervise guard duty and the desk. (Master Sergeant Green, who was shivering in the shelter, was one of the men missing that night.) Smith had been the only man in his hootch. He had been sound asleep through the whole incident, his head buried under two pillows.

Mitchell explained that the first sergeant was in the lockup sleeping off too much booze, and that the CO and master sergeant were quaking in their bomb shelter. He added that no one had seen the lieutenant since early afternoon. Smith shook his head and slipped on his shirt, stopping briefly to tie his boots and buckle on his .45. Then he started up the boardwalk to take over his dual posts. Smith was a good man who worked and played hard. He knew his job and was well liked and respected by all of the guys.

I drove Mitchell back to meet Bruce and Rob, and we all continued on to headquarters. We were running a bit late. The guys in the other patrol were sleeping and hadn't even heard us drive up. During all of the excitement they had been visiting one of the many clubs on post and had had a couple of beers. Both activities were definite no-nos!

Sarge sent Rob and Bruce to the tower to fill in the guys there, and Mitchell and I went to check on some of our perimeter defenses. We stopped midway between Gate Four and Gate Five. A kid on bunker duty was standing outside his bunker.

"Who goes there?" the kid called out.

"Sergeant Mitchell, MP patrol sergeant, and my driver," Sarge stated. "Call your duty officer or sergeant of the guard. I need to brief one or both."

The soldier disappeared into the small two-man bunker where his partner, who had overheard the order, was already on the landline. In a few minutes, the soldier reappeared and said, "Sergeant, the lieutenant is asleep, but someone is trying to locate our sergeant." Then he said, "We saw your lights, then heard some shooting and saw lots of tracers going out from near your gate. Is everything okay?"

These two men were doing their jobs well. "Everything's fine, soldier," Mitchell assured him. "Just stay alert. You'll be okay."

We were about to leave after several minutes of waiting when a man walked up and introduced himself as the sergeant in charge of the guard detail. Mitchell asked if his lieutenant was ill, and the response was, "No, just tired."

"Tell your lieutenant about the alert status and let him know that the main gate has been fired on." Then he added, "His sleeping on duty will be reported."

From there, Mitchell and I went to the tower. We had recently started using a night-vision scope, and it got a lot of use that night. Our group was familiar with it since we had worked with a similar one during our stay at the First Infantry outpost. Using the scope, we watched for any sign of troop movement, taking turns to avoid eyestrain. Sarge told those on duty to continue watching and to use the radio, not the landline.

All seemed quiet, and Mitchell turned to the four men on duty in the tower. "It is possible that the firing on the gate was an isolated incident, but I want you all to stay alert. I'll see you in a couple of hours, at breakfast."

It was nearly dawn when Sergeant Mitchell and I resumed our patrol. He had the desk check with all units and bunkers. Everyone checked in okay. No one had had any questionable sightings. Bruce and Rob had gone back to post patrol a few minutes before we arrived at the tower, and I called to have them let us in at Gate Five. Once we were on post again, our first stop was the Tactical Operations Center, where most of the field intelligence and planning took place. Sarge explained to them what had happened. There had been no reports from G-2 of enemy troop movements during the night. We took one more turn around the post and met up again with Bruce and Rob at the 199th.

"Have you guys seen the other patrol the past hour or so?" Sarge asked.

Rob looked at Bruce, shrugged and then answered, "They parked their jeep in the motor pool some time before we came on post from the tower."

Too tired to fume anymore, Mitchell just sighed and shook his head in disgust.

"Rob saw the sixty was still on the jeep," Bruce explained, "so we secured it."

This did not please the sergeant either. Lighting a cigarette, he thanked us for a good night's work. "Let's get a cup of coffee," he suggested.

We left our vehicles and walked into the 199th mess hall. The cooks were getting things started for the day, and one of them motioned for us to come in. "Coffee's done," he announced.

We had had a busy night. And I knew of two MPs who would be wishing they had not been born after Mitchell got through with them. We were curious what would happen to our *fearless* leaders, but we didn't ask. It was obvious that the 552nd MP Company was in dire need of a strong shot of basic training.

We were really tired having been on duty for thirteen hours. We had been going strong most of the shift, while the guys in the bunkers and tower had been able to trade off for some sack time.

"You three guys, close up shop for the night," Sarge began. "Mills, you ride back with them. I'll bring the jeep in shortly."

We finished our coffee and doughnuts, thanked the mess cook, and waved to Mitchell as we headed for the motor pool. By the time I had secured all my gear, cleaned my rifle, and given an oily rubdown to my pistol, the sun was almost ready to peek over the horizon. The instant I finished my cleanup, I headed for the mattress, and my eyelids locked shut before my head reached the pillow.

I began to regain consciousness when my sea of tranquillity suddenly became violent. Someone was calling my name—*loudly*.

"Gee, I know that name," my subconscious said.

Then a small hand began pulling at me, and I reluctantly opened one eye. A bright light was shining all around me. I tried to sit up but banged my head on the overhead bunk. I mumbled a couple of swear words. When I finally focused, I saw Lin, my little housemaid.

Paul and Kent had been shaking my bunk, and Lin was saying, "Bic, Bic, must go now, Sergeant Top come now. Very mad!"

"What the hell's going on? What time is it?" My voice sounded like a foghorn.

"It's 1:30 in the afternoon, and Top is after two hides—yours and Bruce's," was the response.

I asked if Mitchell was around, and they answered in the negative. "Whoops! Too late," one of my friends muttered as he spotted Top.

The first sergeant swaggered into the hootch looking a lot better than he had the night before. "Mills, you sonofabitch, I'm going to have you and your friend court-martialed. I'll nail your heads to my wall."

"Gee, Top, that has already been tried," I replied calmly, "and it hasn't been done yet." Smiling, I added, "But there are at least 250 men you put in danger last night who will testify at *your* court-martial."

There was one thing I had little tolerance for, and that was a drunk, even a sober drunk. I had finally reached the point where I no longer felt threatened by the first sergeant, the master sergeant, or even the CO. As the first sergeant raved on, I grabbed a towel and my shaving kit and started for the door. Top took a wild swing at me, missing my face by inches as I ducked. Dropping everything, I grabbed him, twisted his right arm behind him, and threw him up against a wall locker. Locking my left arm tightly around his throat and windpipe I growled, "You ass! I hate drunks! Because of you, every man in this company—hell, nearly every man on this post—was put in danger last night." Taking a big breath, I continued, "If you ever come at me again, I'll put you in a body bag!"

Kent and Paul added that they were witnesses to the first sergeant's attempted assault.

Lin looked frightened. As I passed her, I put a hand on her face and said, "It's okay, Lin. It's okay. You can go back to work now." She handed me my things and smiled her innocent 13-year-old smile, and I headed for the showers.

Now that all of us were back from the First Infantry, the first sergeant really had it hard. And because of the new VC buildup, he could no longer threaten some poor, unsuspecting, green kid with field duty. To save his own ass, Top desperately needed to nail all of us on something, anything; but shortly after his ranting attack, Top backed off. His popularity in the good ol' boys' club was gone. And because of the behavior of the CO and the master sergeant the previous night, they were right behind Top. Things were changing!

A good friend of Sergeant Mitchell's tracked me down in my hootch a day after the incident with Top to say that he had heard Mitchell having a long talk with our CO.

"This is in confidence, but you need to know this." He went on to explain as Bruce joined us, "Mitchell didn't actually make any threats, but he did promise that if the three of them—the master sergeant, first sergeant, and captain—didn't get themselves straightened out and get things back on track, he would personally bring charges against them." The kid continued, "Mitchell said the charges would range from cowardice, to being drunk on duty, to dereliction of duty, and more."

Master Sergeant Green and Top were due to retire out of the service within a few months, and Captain Gordon was in line for promotion. Ordinarily a court-martial would have been in order, but it never happened. I have no idea why. In any case, any one of those charges would not look good on a resume, even if the person reading it was an antiwar sympathizer.

Apparently Mitchell also explained to the CO, and later on to Top, that Bruce and I had been responsible for keeping Top from getting his head "blown off" the night before.

Part of our MP patrol work was to routinely drive into the Widow's Village. Except for the few young families we had moved in, the village was deserted. Other Vietnamese were not allowed to live there. This area was a mile or so long and a quarter of a mile wide. A rail line separated it from the garbage dump to the west. There was a very suspicious refrigeration and ice plant to the east. This ice plant was directly across from Gate One and was where I believe the shooting had originated the night we played games with Top.

A few of the men who had been at Di-An and who worked the night patrols were also more than a little suspicious of some of the buildings. They were sure they had spotted glints of light coming from two or three of these shacks during night patrols. I had not personally seen any of the lights, but the guys who reported them had been part of the Big Red One duty, and I trusted them.

Several of us had a meeting with Sergeant Mitchell and told him about the sightings. He took our report to Top and the captain. For the following two nights, the tower guard concentrated their night-vision scope on a particular grid in the village and reported definite activity.

We worked out a plan similar to one the First Infantry had used successfully a few times. Mitchell liked our idea and took it to G-2 and base command. We needed some backup, and I suggested that we call on a few of our friends with the 720th MP—BJ and three others I knew from Fort Gordon.

Our plan was simple. Usually three times a week we road-raced our jeeps on the village roads. These races were great fun, and because no one ever got hurt and none of the vehicles were ever damaged, no one seemed to mind. Our plan was to use one of these races as a trap. We would run it later in the afternoon than usual and continue on into the early evening. We needed all the yelling and commotion that usually went along with this event. We would concentrate the race on the roads closest to the shacks in question. Instead of three jeeps, we would use six to play a kind of "pea and shell" game to create confusion. The 720th came through, lending us BJ and friends.

Our friends at the 199th Airborne were quite pleased to be invited as well, and they brought a couple of their choppers, gunships, to the party. The birds were stationed two miles south of the highway on the village boundary. The railroad that separated the village from the garbage dump created a high berm along the north-south boundary, well within the vision of our guys in the tower. The berm, the surrounding trees, and the noise from the jeeps and all our yelling would help to muffle and blend most of the sounds from the choppers as they hovered just off the ground, below the berm.

We planned to have four men and an extra machine gun assigned to the tower. Four more of our men with two M-60s would set up out of sight on the berm, one weapon on each side of the railbed. This would put them about twenty feet above the tracks for clear visibility of foot traffic, should any VC try to escape in that direction. The whole area would be well covered.

Everything went off without a hitch. We had several good races, and we caught Charlie with his drawers down. We netted nine captives, three from up north, and loaded their cache onto a 3/4-ton truck. It was an incredible haul: AK-47s, crates of rocket launchers with rockets, and hundreds of boxes and bags of rice. Best of all, not a shot was fired. We literally caught them coming out of their tunnels. They actually seemed glad to be caught, and they willingly showed G-2 other hiding places on a map of the area.

The next evening we were in our company club, waiting for the night's movie, when Sergeant Mitchell and a captain from Army Intelligence joined us. Two of our guys were drinking the Army's version of low-octane beer while the rest of us were quaffing Pepsi and Dr. Pepper. We were really a wild bunch. It quickly became clear that this was a "non-briefing" debriefing—unofficial. Interestingly, three of us (Rob, Bruce, and I) had the highest security clearances of anyone in our company, including our CO and the provost marshal.

The captain asked how we suspected the possibility of a VC weapon cache.

We told him a little about our experiences with the First Infantry. Apparently our answers were general and vague enough. By the time the movie started, the officer had left, but not before he showed us something that made our spines tingle. It seemed that the VC had put bounties or "wanted" posters out on specific GIs, and especially MPs. They particularly targeted those who had operated out of Di-An near the forward outpost. We were surprised to find several of our names on that list. It was an eerie feeling!

During the next two weeks, we had several red alerts. Many nights the whole company took turns guarding and sleeping along the sides of a ditch six inches deep with smelly, stagnant water and flocks of bloodthirsty mosquitoes. Several times I woke up in the morning with my lip the size of a Ping-Pong ball from the kiss of one of these flying buzzards. Some nights, after we had put in a full twelve-plus hours of patrol, the siren would call us to perimeter duty again. We would go running out of our hootches wearing only shorts, grabbing clothes, boots, and weapons on our way. A couple of times we were told to bring our gas masks—a scary prospect.

A few days before the Tet Offensive of 1968, several members of the old Deuce Platoon were talking about our defenses. There was plenty of concern about the setup at our company area and the whole base. When we realized the severity of the problem, Bruce and I went to have a talk with Sergeant Mitchell. Early in the morning, we knocked loudly on his door many times before we finally woke him. In a shaky, sleepy voice, he told us to come in.

"Sarge, good morning," I began. "We're really sorry to have to tell you this right now."

Bruce butted in, " . . . but you really gotta take a look at our company area defenses."

"Man, I'm beat," growled Mitchell, as he sat on the edge of his bunk. "Won't this wait for a few hours?" Looking at his watch he grumbled, "Only two hours, guys. I've had a total of four hours of sleep in two days."

"Sarge, I'll take the heat," I started again, "but this is serious! Give us just ten minutes."

I guess the urgency in the tone of our voices woke him up the rest of the way. Top had given a new guy, a corporal who had transferred in from Germany, the responsibility of setting up the perimeter defenses for our company and for most of the compound.

We took Mitchell on a little hike, just in our company area. As we walked by some of the gun emplacements still being built, he said he had thought something was wrong early on, but he hadn't been sure what it was.

The corporal had set up the machine-gun pits in direct line with where our riflemen would be. The short explanation we gave was, "We would be shooting ourselves in the head." This setup had been duplicated around much of the II Field Force compound.

Then it finally sank in. Sarge exclaimed, "Holy shit! Where the hell is that kid?" Rubbing his face and eyes in disbelief at what he was seeing, he said, "You know, the whole district goes on full alert for at least the next three days beginning today at 1700 hours." Taking a deep breath, he added, "*Sonofabitch! What a hell of a mess. If it wasn't so stupid, it'd almost be funny.*"

"Whenever any of us questioned the corporal," began Bruce, "he would get angry and tell us to take it up with the first sergeant—that *he* had approved it."

"Well," started Mitchell again, "Top probably never saw this layout. Even he would never go for this." Under his breath he added, "He wouldn't be anywhere near the fighting anyway."

Turning to what was now a group of several men, he asked, "Think you guys can fix this?"

Looking around at each other, we answered in the affirmative.

"What do you need?"

Thinking for a moment I said, "Get us some of the guys from the construction company."

Then Bruce added, "Get Smitty (Sergeant Smith) and the rest of the Deuce Platoon, and we'll have it done before 5:00. It won't be pretty, but it will do the job."

Sarge didn't blink. We had stopped walking. Standing outside the rear of Smith's hootch. Mitchell hollered, "*Smith!* Get out here!"

Waking from only four hours of sleep himself, Smith half stumbled through the door and said, "Hi guys, what's up?"

Mitchell took him on a brief survey of our area and explained that nearly all of the II Field Force compound was like this.

Scratching his head, Smith commented, "You know, Mitch, I've looked at this damn thing all week. I knew there was something wrong, but I couldn't put my finger on it."

Mitchell said, "Smitty, work with these guys; do whatever it takes to make this right. And do it fast." Then he added, "Oh, and take the corporal with you and introduce him to some hard work and *Army* tactics. I'm going back to bed for a few hours."

Top was steamed about Mitchell's interference, but there wasn't time to go through channels. When Mitchell and Smith showed Top the layout, Top had to agree and shrugged, saying, "I can't believe this. I'm leaving it up to you to get it repaired."

We set up several work groups with ten to fifty men each. Cooperation came from every company on base. The construction guys were great and pitched right in. I think everyone felt quite relieved. This was hard and fast work. What should have taken days to build took only hours. Our work wasn't fancy or pretty, but at least we were now shooting in the right direction and not at each other. It was interesting that when the corporal saw his mistakes, he went into high gear—working with all of us, shirt off, shovel in hand. We couldn't ask for more than that.

When the alert siren sounded a little past 5:15 that evening, every MP vehicle capable of running more than twenty-five miles per hour was on patrol. We covered the compound and village area across the highway. Some jeeps carried two M-60s—one mounted in the jeep and the other resting on the hood. There was even a .50 caliber machine gun set up in the open field thirty yards inside the gate and directly across from our orderly room. I manned that gun awhile, but never had to fire it.

Nearly dawn of my second night, while assigned to the big machine gun, I was reported as sleeping. It was a natural assumption, but not a correct one. Around 7:00 that morning, I woke up in the field hospital. A couple of the TDY guys had found me semi-conscious. I had eaten in the mess hall again. Over the next three days, several others in our company also ended up in the hospital. The mess hall had used poorly washed or unwashed pans and dishes. After all the emergencies were over, one of our medical officers finally got busy and had the mess hall cleaned up. Five days later, I was rehydrated and back at work, resolved to never visit the mess hall again.

Several times during my tour, and especially during two particular weeks, Generals Westmoreland and Haig visited II Field Force and our Tactical Operations Center for high level talks. Whenever this took place, we provided security. A cav unit would set up defensive positions across the highway from our headquarters company with all guns pointing at the empty village. With the reported VC buildup, there was also a canopy of gunships flying overhead.

After returning from Di-An, I saw my friend Jerry and worked on a few patrols and in the bunkers with him from time to time. He was a good MP, but he wasn't one to make waves; he played the game according to the rules Top and his cronies had made. This was probably the smart thing to do, and I could not fault him for it. In a way, I wished I could have done the "smart thing" myself, but I probably wouldn't have survived Vietnam if I had. It was my objecting that got me sent to the First Infantry. It's funny how Providence works things out for us.

During one of the visits from Westmoreland, I was working Gate Three, the route which went directly to headquarters. The general's motorcade was going west on the perimeter road toward my post, and I thought it peculiar he hadn't entered the compound at the gate I was guarding. I received a message from the desk sergeant via the field phone and also from two guys on motor patrol that an ambulance needed to enter through my gate to get to our infirmary, the closest medical help. A soldier had appendicitis. I saw the ambulance as it approached my gate, red lights flashing and siren blaring. I stopped the general's column for about two minutes.

As soon as the ambulance cleared the gate I blew my whistle and directed the general's motorcade to proceed. A colonel, who was an aide to the general's staff, jumped out of a staff car, walked over to me, and proceeded to chew my ass out for holding up the general's column.

Coming to attention I said, "Colonel, we usually don't salute officers while in the field. Do wish me to salute you, sir?" Looking surprised, he answered in the negative. I simply replied, "Good morning, sir, may I help you?"

Looking at my nametag, he asked, "*Private First Class Mills*, do you have any idea who are in these vehicles?"

I said that I did and named both Generals Westmoreland and Haig.

He asked, "Why the hell did you stop us then?"

I answered, "It's standard operating procedure, sir. 'Unless under fire or imminent possibility of same, all emergency vehicles displaying lights and siren shall be given the right of way.' This order is countersigned by the general, sir."

The colonel didn't buy my answer. I was used to Oak Leaves and Birds, but I was concerned when I saw General Westmoreland walk calmly over to us. I was still standing at attention as the general looked right at me and said, "You see, Dick, someone does read those damn notices." He shook my hand while I shook in my boots, and he said, "Good job, soldier. I'm glad you're on our team."

For some time there had been running reports of a large North Vietnamese buildup infiltrating various areas in the south. One of these areas was the old outpost we had gone to from Di-An. Because it was so close to the Ho Chi Minh Trail, a large buildup had been rumored even before we returned from Di-An. Although alerts were kept to a minimum, they increased everyone's awareness and improved the work ethic. One day Bruce, Rob and I, and two others were working the tower. We got a call on the field phone asking if we could see someone climbing the base of a gravel hill about three-quarters of a mile away from us. We searched the area with our field glasses.

Suddenly I hollered to Bruce, "That must be him!"

Bruce's binoculars were stronger than mine, and he said, "Yeah, I see him." Then he said, "Oh, shit. Hey, you've got to see this. It's just a kid."

Swapping glasses, I took another look.

Bruce asked, "Do you see what he's carrying?"

"Yes, looks like a camera case."

"That's what I thought," Bruce responded.

Rob had been looking a few hundred yards southeast of where Bruce and I had been looking, and he said calmly, "There's a platoon of Marines closing in on him."

"All they'll do is shoot him. He can't be more than twelve years old," I said.

We were so intent on what we were doing and in relaying the information to our people, we hadn't realized that a major from G-2 had joined us. He signaled the other guys not to alert us to his presence. Looking through his glasses, he commented, "He'll be dead in four or five minutes."

Realizing the major was there, someone else hollered, "Attention."

But the officer said, "Can it! You're working." I couldn't help but like an officer like that. Then he said again, "Yes, he'll be dead in less than five minutes."

"Sir, wouldn't you rather be able to talk to him?" Bruce asked.

He looked at us and said, "Very much, but right now it doesn't seem possible."

We suggested that we could try to stop him from our position if the major could keep the Marines from firing on him. The major said that the target was way out of range for an M-16.

We agreed, but Bruce pointed to our rifles and said, "Not for the M-14." Pointing to the pistol grip stock of mine he added, "We can stop him, sir." The officer told us that he didn't think he'd be able to contact the Marines in time, but he would try. He nodded to his aide who quickly climbed down from the tower to get to the radio in their jeep.

"Bruce, mark the target for me," I said calmly.

I took a toothpick-sliver of wood and wedged it into the peep sight on my rifle. "Here's where all that target practice had better pay off," I mumbled. Bruce and Rob grunted in agreement. As I worked on the sight, Bruce and Rob continued to track the young Vietnamese boy. I repositioned a few sandbags for a little higher shooting platform and carefully brought my weapon up. I knew the round, or projectile, would be nearly spent, and I silently whispered a prayer not to kill the boy, but just to stop him for capture so the ground force wouldn't fire on him.

This far away, the kid looked like a moving speck against the hill of loose gravel. Using my makeshift gun sight, I lined up the top of the toothpick with the front bead on the barrel, trying to place a shot about ten feet ahead of the target. I took a deep breath and let it out slowly. The tip of my right index finger tightened on the trigger.

"Bang!" One round fired.

"High about ten feet and to the right, two feet," read Bruce. "Drop a half-inch lower in your sight picture," he said softly.

The boy was getting close to the top of the berm. Resting against the sandbags, I sighted again.

"Bang!" The second round fired.

"You got him!" Bruce and the major yelled at the same time.

I asked, "Can you see where he's hit?"

After a few seconds Rob answered, "Yes, yes! The right hip pocket."

I quietly sighed and said, "Thank God!"

The major slapped me on the back, saying, "If I hadn't seen it with my own eyes, I wouldn't have believed a shot like that was possible. Great shooting Private! Great shooting!"

Within a few seconds, the ground troops were picking up the wounded boy. His case held two cameras, a 35mm and a black-and-white Polaroid. There were almost twenty-five pictures from the Polaroid and several rolls of used 35 mm film, which we were sure the major would order developed, courtesy of the U.S. Army.

As we had guessed, the boy had been forced into helping the local VC. They had kidnapped and threatened to kill all the members of his family, one at a time. This was not an unusual story. The North Vietnamese military were well known for using brutality with little or no provocation. The boy's family was rescued, and he told us where some of the local VC and sympathizers could be found. Except for his wound, the boy was not harmed—not by his government or by our military. Regardless of their age, most such kids ended up being executed on the spot. We were happy for him.

From the middle of January to the end of February, we had our hands full. The busiest time was from January 28th to the 5th of February. Before the 28th, we had gone in and out of red alerts, sometimes hourly. At night we were always on alert. Without fail, just about the time the all clear sounded, a sapper would hit our munitions or fuel depot—or another one close by—and blow it to hell, and we'd start the alert all over.

One recollection I have of this was early one morning, around 3:00 a.m. I had just gotten into bed and suddenly sat up to see a bright orange ball of fire. It was our fuel depot two or three miles away. I yelled, *"Hit the floor!"* and rolled out of my bunk, grabbing two handfuls of concrete as the concussion hit. The blast pushed the wall in nearly eight inches, right above where it had been bolted to the concrete. It knocked over every wall locker on that side, and the impact also popped most of the foundation bolts and buckled the roof. We spent the rest of the early morning hours in our mosquito-infested ditches.

Even though we missed the main Tet assault force, the Viet Cong made their presence felt all around us. They seemed to be focusing mostly on cities and larger towns, which had air and communications installations. From the DMZ south, these targets were hit hard. Our compound and the main Long Binh compound were both hit to prevent us from sending any help to Saigon. During the fighting in Saigon, I lost several friends from my AIT group.

Shortly after the main battles, while we were still on heightened alert status, the 552nd was asked to supply security for the Tactical Operation Center at the Bien Hoa Air Base. This center was a backup to ours. I had just made specialist fourth class, and because I was the oldest man in the group, I was selected to play acting sergeant.

The Bien Hoa Air Base compound perimeter at the TOC included an L-shaped, two-story building with a courtyard. A couple of years earlier this had been a posh hotel. The architecture was French Mediterranean, and in spite of war damage, it still looked very beautiful. There was a large, circular, gravel driveway and what used to be a fountain and fishpond. The driveway led through a large, iron gate; a wide, tree-lined boulevard was just beyond. Everything seemed elegant, even in those times. The grounds butted the air base's perimeter wire. There were a number of floodlights, which could illuminate the buildings and courtyard, although we didn't use these lights much at night and not at all during alerts.

The gate had a parapet with two twelve-foot high towers, one on each side of the driveway. We used them for guard stations during daylight hours. At night the gate was locked, and we retreated to TOC's inner-perimeter, maintaining tight security from there.

Our general orders allowed no one to be in either of the compound areas without written authorization from the office of General Westmoreland or General Haig. This order couldn't have been clearer; it was only five lines. It read, in part: "If a person enters the compound without proper authorization, and does not comply when he is ordered by security to vacate the area, you are to fire on him."

The center was thirty feet underground and built entirely of steel and concrete. The main area inside included a map room and communication center. It had walls nearly two feet thick, and its dome was covered with dirt and sandbags. There were two entrances; one came out near the airfield and the other on the courtyard side. We patrolled both sides but concentrated on the courtyard side. This was especially important at night when it got really dark. When there was no moon, it was a like looking into a deep well.

We set up two six-man teams. I was the acting NCO of one, and Bruce of the other. We both answered either to Sergeant Mitchell or to our (usually misplaced) lieutenant. Our group of five, and most of the TDY guys, worked together once more. In the beginning, we assisted the 720th MPs by rotating five or six of our group to complement their men. Eventually we took over.

One evening around 7:00, shortly after having been relieved by the other shift, we started back to our company area. This was a very spooky drive at best, and it took about thirty minutes. We seldom saw any other units or citizens. Several miles of straining to see into the near darkness and beyond our headlights made us jumpy, and our adrenaline ran high. About halfway into the trip, we entered a village and saw a soldier standing at attention alongside the road. He was carrying his M-16 at port arms. This area was off-limits to all military personnel, but occasionally our MP patrols would find a GI or two visiting the girls. The GIs would get cited and given a ride back to the cooler.

This particular night Rob was driving, Bruce was in the right front seat, and I was in back. We stopped right in front of this kid and waited for a few seconds; he didn't move. I slowly rolled out of the back seat into a crouch. The man made no sound nor did he respond to my repeated orders to place his rifle on the ground. He simply stood there.

After a few moments, Bruce got out and I handed him my rifle, saying softly, "Watch him!" and started moving toward the soldier. When I got closer, it was obvious the man was high on something. Moving very slowly and talking softly, I took his rifle and quickly but carefully handcuffed him. I leaned him against the hood of the jeep and did a very quick pat down for weapons. Not finding any, I got him loaded into the rear seat of the jeep, where I could hold him in. Then we got the hell out of there. This was VC territory after dark, and none of us wanted to sit there as a target.

"We'll find out who he is when we turn him over to the desk sergeant," I suggested.

Having no pass, being high on drugs, in an off-limits district with the region full of VC during a yellow alert was a dangerous situation for anyone. I couldn't understand why he was still alive. We may have saved this man's life, but probably not his Army career. Once we were on our way, I called in to give our location, ETA (estimated time of arrival), and to say that we had a "Golf India" (GI) prisoner with us.

"X-ray 1-4, say again. You have a Golf-India in cuffs?" They couldn't believe it either.

"This is X-ray 1-4. That's affirmative. ETA ten minutes. Over."

A short time later we were at our lockup, and I took the cuffs off the kid. A more thorough search of the prisoner produced some hashish. As we took his belt and bootlaces, I took a long slow look at our prisoner, and said firmly, "Smitty, get the medics down here on the double. We have a serious problem here."

The man hadn't moved or twitched for nearly an hour and his breathing had become very labored. Smith called the infirmary. A doctor arrived in less than three minutes. Not waiting for the ambulance, he quickly rushed the kid to the field hospital with the help of an MP patrol. Because of the doctor's quick response, the soldier was okay. The doctor told us later that the man had actually been choking but that he had been too drugged to help himself.

It was great to learn that Sergeants Mitchell and Smith would be sharing overall responsibility for security at the Tactical Operation Center in Bien Hoa. We had twelve-hour shifts. When our cots finally arrived, we placed them outside TOC. We rotated turns for sleeping so that everyone got some sack time. Three men had to be working at all times. Smith and Mitchell usually checked with us by radio and occasionally in person. During every guard mount, or inspection, we heard the same lecture about standing orders, general orders, standard operating procedures, and what our expected responses should be. One night our ability to follow these orders and instructions was put to the acid test.

My group started at 6:00 p.m. As usual I checked the log notes from the previous shift to see if there had been any trouble. There hadn't been, so I dispersed the men. About 11:00, after overseeing the guard for five hours, I took my rest break. I had been asleep for about half an hour when one of my team, a new man, woke me and said, "There's some trouble with an officer. He's demanding entrance. Rob wants you to come up front."

The officer identified himself as a full bird colonel and said he had been

SNAFU

sent by General Haig's staff on special orders. He wouldn't produce his ID card and couldn't produce any written orders to back up his claim.

A truck had damaged the gate entrance a few days earlier, and we had placed a simple sawhorse across the driveway as a barricade to help keep out unauthorized motor traffic. We knew quite well that if Charlie or anyone else really wanted in, the barricade was certainly no deterrent, but neither was the locked gate.

Rob quickly filled me in, saying that the officer and his aide had removed the barricade and had come rolling in with headlights on, demanding entrance to the center.

I turned and spoke to the colonel, who was standing about one hundred feet away with his aide, "Sir, you need to produce your ID, password, and a signed copy of the written orders from the general's staff."

"My orders were given to me orally, and I have no intention of showing my ID card to any of you."

Their jeep was still idling with its lights on. "Colonel, we are with the 552nd MP Company. I am the Acting Sergeant for this detail. Please turn the lights off and leave."

He refused.

"Sir, due to our alert status, you and your aide are not in compliance with the standing orders. You are also jeopardizing the security of our position. I request that the headlights be turned off immediately and you and your driver leave the area."

"You go to hell," he said, which I took as a refusal.

I turned to one of our men and said loudly, "Private Lopez, shoot out those lights." As the private started to bring up his weapon, the colonel's aide jumped back into the jeep, hit the light switch, and killed the ignition.

Just to cover my butt, I called the center and spoke to the duty officer, a major, "Excuse me, sir. Acting Sergeant Mills. Are you expecting a colonel and aide from command tonight?" He answered in the negative.

Turning back toward the pathway I said, "I'm sorry, Colonel, but according to the officer on duty inside, no one is expecting you." There was a pause, and then I added, "Sir, I am going to send out a man to check both of your IDs. It may be possible that you're at the wrong location."

"No Private is going to check my ID. Now move aside, I'm coming in," was his foolish retort.

It was a clear night with a bright half-moon, and with occasional flashes of light from the airfield flares, it was easy to see forms.

"According to my orders, Colonel, if you come any closer I will be forced to fire on you and your aide." I felt confident that this was a pretty clear-cut statement based on an equally clear-cut set of orders.

He yelled back, "You wouldn't dare!"

"Sir, wrong answer!"

Then he added, "Just who the hell do you think you are? I am a colonel in the U.S. Army. And what are you, a PFC or maybe a Spec 4?"

We all were getting a little tired of this game, and I told him, "I am Acting Sergeant, Specialist Fourth Class Mills with the 552nd MP Company, at Second Field Force, sir. And I'm the one who's going to turn his M-14 loose on you, if you don't leave—*now!*"

Rob had suggested we arrest him, but I said, "It would split our manpower, as we'd have to keep him all night."

During much of this exchange, the aide, who had identified himself as a captain, was pulling on the senior officer's sleeve saying, "I think we should go, sir. I really do think they will shoot us."

"They wouldn't dare open fire on us," the colonel said to his aide, again taking a few steps toward us.

At that moment, scenes of being in Fort Leavenworth passed through my mind like a bad movie. I was going to be in deep shit regardless of what I did.

If I let this clown into TOC, I'd be court-martialed, and if I shot the bastard I'd probably be court-martialed as well. I was in a lose-lose predicament

I brought my M-14 up and ordered him again, "Sir, you are to halt and not proceed any farther. You are ordered to leave this compound immediately."

The colonel kept inching his way forward, and all the while his aide kept tugging at his sleeve. I slipped off the safety.

Rob leaned over and said, "Hey man, are you sure about this?"

"No," I answered, "but how does prison sound to you?"

Rob brought up his weapon too. My weapon was on full automatic. Again I ordered, "Sir, please stop." But the colonel ignored me. With my rifle resting on the sandbags, I pointed it low, a couple yards ahead of his feet, and squeezed the trigger. The reverberation and echo were tremendous as a dozen or so rounds kicked up gravel around his boots and laces, showering his legs with sparks and debris. There was quite a light show for a couple of seconds. His aide was already in the jeep, and the colonel was now running to join him. "*You sonofabitch*, I'll see you court-martialed for this! I'll have you all court-martialed! You nearly killed me!" he yelled repeatedly as they drove out of the compound. Actually, I was a little nervous until he said something about a court-martial. After all, that had been tried already.

The major inside the center heard the commotion and buzzed me on the intercom to see if there was trouble. I explained what had happened and that it was now over. About ten minutes later, he and a master sergeant came out bringing us hot coffee and doughnuts.

"If anyone wonders, there are only three of us down here right now," the master sergeant said as he placed the tray on the sandbags. "I know you're not supposed to have this on duty, but we sure won't tell."

"It's a stupid rule for out here anyway," added the major. "Besides, it's hard to stay awake." With a wink, he added, "Unless you're shooting at colonels."

They asked us about the two intruders, and I explained what had happened. As they started back inside, the master sergeant looked Rob and me in the eyes and smiled, "You won't be visiting Fort Leavenworth—not over this."

Rob and I just looked at each other. How did he know what we had been thinking? Maybe the sergeant had been in a similar jam himself.

Then with a slight chuckle the sergeant added, "But if you do, we'll come and visit," and he disappeared behind the heavy door.

Rob turned to the rest of our group, and said, "Now that's real comforting." Taking a sip of coffee and a bite from a doughnut, Rob added, "You know they're a lot like the sarge and lieutenant back at Di-An. These are good guys too."

I had to agree. And the coffee and doughnuts were a nice touch.

The next morning, our relief showed up right on time at 6:00. They knew nothing about the incident the night before, so I briefed them about it. When we got back to base, all of us were immediately called into the orderly room where our CO, noncoms, and a new lieutenant were waiting to question us. I was surprised but glad to see Colonel Wilson there as well.

Mitchell came in a few seconds after we arrived and asked, "What the hell did you guys do last night? Did you really fire on a colonel, Mills?"

Rob answered, "Yes, we did!"

Moving in front of Rob, I made it clear that I had made the decision and had done the shooting. As I handed my report and log to Mitchell, I explained why.

While we stood at ease and answered questions, the clerk came in with four sheets of paper. He gave two to Mitchell and two to the CO. Then they huddled in the corner with Colonel Wilson for a minute or two. The CO approached us saying, "The colonel wanted to file formal charges against you both. However," the captain continued, "we have a report from Major Kirkland and Master Sergeant Kennedy, who manned the center last night, that backs up everything you have reported."

Wilson then took over, "Evidently the major and the master sergeant teletyped their report about the incident to Haig's command late last night, and now Haig's aide wants to know if you two wish to bring charges against the colonel."

I glanced at Rob and the others of the guard for a few seconds, then to the captain. I said, "Sir, do you mean those two men were part of the general's staff?"

The captain answered in the affirmative.

Then Rob said, "Sir, I have a question. What happens to him and to his aide if we don't file charges? His aide was really wanting to catch the train to Hoboken, sir."

The captain nodded and asked Wilson to explain. Wally said, "His commander will bring disciplinary charges against the colonel for a whole lot of violations. It will cost him any chance for promotion as well as a large fine, and he will probably go through a reevaluation hearing. His aide will not be charged." Wally paused for a moment, and added, "For all intents and purposes the colonel's career is over."

"I'm happy with that, sir," responded Rob. The rest of the group and I nodded in agreement.

Mitchell added, "There's something else from command. This is a personal note from General Haig's office—I think from the general himself. `Great job. It must have been very difficult for all of you boys. Keep up the good work.'"

We were dismissed, and we headed for chow. It was nearly 0800 and very warm. The interview had taken almost an hour. I grabbed half a glass of milk and a stale roll and headed for my hootch and some sleep. We were going to do this all over again in about nine hours.

Another situation arose during the Tet offensive, one of the few times our compound was actually under attack. It began without warning. Army Intelligence hadn't given us any word of imminent VC activity in our sector. For several days, the alert status had vacillated between red and yellow. Our security detachment at the Bien Hoa TOC had been canceled and the Air Force had taken it over. This gave us more coverage at II Field Force.

When we weren't on alert status, the MPs manned gates. With all the active alerts, our day and night patrols, had been stepped up. We had closed and barricaded all gates with the exception of Gate One. Gate Five was for use only by MP vehicles going to and from the tower. Adding more patrols had left us a little shorthanded for regular guard duty, and our company had requested and received assistance from the other companies on the compound. Consequently, we were able to double the manpower at bunkers near all gates to more effectively guard against enemy assault.

One day about noon, the base sirens sounded, taking us from a yellow to red alert status. Bruce and five others were working the tower, and Paul and I were on post patrol. Our job on patrol was to secure the gates. When we arrived at Gate Five, we met the two soldiers from the quartermaster company who were pulling guard duty there. An hour earlier, they had called their compound and reported to their company about a few rounds fired by a sniper. This information had not been forwarded to our desk sergeant, nor had their company seen fit to look into the matter. Their corporal was a guy who looked and acted like a 15-year-old. He went against standing orders, wearing no steel helmet or flack jacket, and he did not have a weapon. The two guys were telling us about him just as he walked up.

"Corporal," I asked, "are you in charge of this detail?"

"What if I am? What business is it of yours?"

With that, I glanced over at my partner who just shook his head slowly. Controlling my building anger I asked, "Why didn't you call the MP desk on the field phone, as required by standing orders?"

The corporal answered, "Our orders are to report directly to our lieutenant, who in turn sends me to investigate."

Pointing to the field phone, Paul said, "In the future, call the MP desk sergeant first. This order is law."

Right then, a half dozen loud pops came from the direction of the village. Paul and I had been sitting in the jeep, but quickly ran to the small guard shack, and the five of us all crouched down. These shacks were perhaps three feet square and were open from the waist up. They were really meant for only one man. Sandbags were stacked all around with a double row at the opening.

We remained crouching as thirty to forty more rounds came at us. Most were high; some went through the roof. Several new openings appeared in the sandbags, and one round hit our jeep's left rear tire. One of us had tripped over the wires and disabled the field phone, so I sprinted the ten yards to the jeep and quickly backed it up so we could use the radio.

Paul grabbed the radio handset even before I brought the jeep to a halt, and I retrieved our rifles. While Paul was on the radio, two more bursts came at us. There was more than one shooter because the last rifle reports were closer. Crouching down behind the sandbags, I looked at the guards' weapons, M-2 carbines, and saw empty slots where the ammo magazines should go.

"Okay guys, let's lock and load," I told them, thinking they had their ammo magazines in their pockets or belts.

"Sorry, but we're not allowed to carry any ammunition," one of the guards announced.

We just stared at the young NCO, who in turn shrugged as we all hugged the ground. The corporal explained to us that they were required to call their duty officer with any request for ammo. Paul and I were dumbfounded! Next to the war itself, this was the stupidest thing we had ever heard.

I asked the three of them, "How fast can you guys run? You've got less than ten seconds to get back to your company area."

As they got up, Paul took the corporal by the arm and yanked him back to his knees. Nose to nose he growled, "The next time you or anyone else from your company reports for guard duty, come armed!" Then the three of them ran like crazy, leaving their two useless carbines behind.

We were east from the 199th helo pad by about fifty yards. Some of the guys who were on guard duty with them saw and overheard much of this conversation and couldn't believe it either.

"Hey, coppers," two hollered. "You need some bodies over there?" They waved two M-60s in the air and chanted, "We have bullets. We have bullets." We motioned for the men to come down.

While they were on their way, Bruce called from the tower telling us that about two hundred VC were moving through the village toward us. We couldn't see them because of the higher ground, the tall grass, and the old deserted shacks.

"If you place your fire about floor level with the shacks," Bruce said, "you could sting a few and discourage the rest."

While the 199th were setting up their .60s, five other GIs from a different company made themselves comfortable in the ditch at the far corner of the gate. They brought a .50 caliber machine gun, M-16s, and one more M-60. "What's the target?" everyone asked.

"They are coming in groups using the huts as shields," I explained. "Aim a few inches above the floor." Using my M-14, I sent five bursts across the floor of a few huts and the open grassy area between them. "Right along there would be fine."

Then we all let loose with rifle fire, three M-60s, and the .50 caliber.

After a couple of minutes, Paul held up his hand to stop. With the handset up to one ear and a finger in the other, he turned to me and said, "Bruce says 'the kitchen got too hot' and that we should elevate our sights about a foot." We gave Charlie another blast. That was the end of this skirmish, and we all relaxed a little.

One of the men from the air unit asked, "Hey Mills, did we hear right, that those three guys came out here on guard duty with no ammo?"

"Yeah, Butch, you heard right. The corporal was really something." Butch was a buck sergeant, and looking around I asked, "Will it cut you thin to stay here for awhile?"

"Hell no! This is as good a place as any."

So we were well covered. Our friends with the .50 caliber (do those guns ever shake the ground!) and M-60s said they would withdraw a few yards back to their bunker. After rewiring the field phone, we called the desk and filled them in, mostly about the guard personnel. We informed the desk we were trading vehicles, and then waddled our wounded jeep back to the motor pool.

Two days later, the quartermaster company was again assigned to guard duty at Gate Five, and the same two men were there. This time they were properly armed but according to them, only their lieutenant or sergeant could give them permission to fire, regardless of the situation. I found that kind of thinking frightening, but more the norm than the exception around II Field Force.

Rob and Bruce were on patrol, and I introduced them to the two gate guards. No one could believe the story Paul and I had told about the weapons and no ammo.

"We want to make it clear that orders to shoot or not shoot rest with the MPs," Bruce began. "Also, if there are VC across the highway from your position, don't ask, just shoot. We would really appreciate it. The whole compound would appreciate it. That's why you guys are here."

Then Rob added, "If your command personnel gives you any static, you come see us. Our orders to you are from command in Saigon. You're here to protect this gate, and that's hard to do if you're waiting for some idiot to come out of hiding to tell you it's okay to shoot!"

"It'd be too late by then," I quipped.

The two guards meant well, but they were very scared and confused. I think we helped to ease their fear. As a result of working with us, they had better instructions, and they also brought M-14s with ammo. Each picked up his weapon, inserted a magazine, and loaded the first round. They put the safeties on and laid their weapons on the sandbags. Opening the two cans of Coke we gave them, they just grinned at us. They would do!

While there, we got to meet their lieutenant, and boy, was he a lulu! He nearly got us all creamed. Charlie opened up on them just after the tower guard changed. The guys at the tower were short on sixty ammo, and we had told them of two or three extra cans we had. We were only a quarter of a mile away, but to get to us, they would have to drive to Gate Five under fire. It was imperative that we give them immediate access through the gate, and we would need to provide cover fire.

The boys in the 199th had opened up with their "sixties" west of us. Then from behind our position, we heard the familiar refrain that only a .50 caliber machine gun could sing. It was a sweet song!

The two gate guards left their weapons in the shack and nearly buried themselves in the grass a few feet away. I told them, "Get over here and start firing."

But their lieutenant, who was huddling with them, said, "*No!* This is not our fight."

Since we were on open ground, I took the M-60 and ammo off the jeep and set it up in the shack. The guys coming from the tower in the jeep were catching hell. Bruce and Rob had inadvertently left their rifles in our jeep when they ran and took cover in the perimeter ditch to be ready to open the gate. Everything was happening so fast. I had already fired half a belt through the sixty. I looked at the two young guards who were hiding in the grass. I slid their rifles to them, one at a time, yelling, "Use them now!" They finally did.

All the time, their DO (Duty Officer) kept raving and repeating to his two men, "This is not our responsibility, not our fight. Stop shooting!"

I ran to our jeep, grabbed the first two rifles I could reach and tossed them to Bruce and Rob, who immediately began shooting. Back in the shack, I took hold of the machine gun once more and laid down another barrage of cover fire as the guys from the tower came roaring down the road. The gate swung open just in time, and the jeep careened through and then flew past us. Two of the four passengers jumped off.

"Where's that ammo?" they asked.

"It's in the back of our jeep," I hollered.

The two MPs grabbed the ammo as their driver continued another twenty-five yards or so. Spinning his vehicle around in a 180-degree turn, he banged the tranny back into first gear. He came thundering back toward the gate under full throttle, with all four wheels grasping at the gravel road for traction. The jeep hit second gear, and as it sped by us, the two men threw the ammo cans and themselves into the back. The vehicle pitched and rolled, the tires screeching as they met the asphalt roadway. One of the men grabbed the sixty and instantly had it belching fire. The driver held his M-14 across his lap, firing out the left side as he drove, and the fourth man clung, spread out over the hood, still firing his weapon.

The way all of us worked together and what we were able to accomplish was a gift from the Big Red One, the First Infantry Division. All but a couple of the men involved in this had been TDY to Di-An. We, as a team, pulled it off.

Within five minutes, quiet took over once more. As we continued watching, we reloaded our magazines and made ready for more activity. The gate was now closed and secured. After surveying our position, I tapped Bruce on the shoulder and pointed to the lieutenant. He was still on his knees curled up in a ball, sobbing and saying over and over, "You can't shoot. You can't shoot.

It's not our job."

Rob held up his right hand, and holding his index finger a quarter of an inch from his thumb, he said, "And to think I came that close to shooting him."

Bruce looked at the lieutenant intently while reloading a magazine and said, "It might have been more merciful if you had."

We called the tower to see how they were doing. They reported that the enemy was pulling back beyond the gravel hill. Several gunships from the 199th had taken over and were engaging the VC force.

As the calm continued and the choppers landed, command told us the worst was over.

I told our two young friends, "You guys did well. Reload your magazines." Then motioning to their lieutenant, I suggested, "Take him back to your company doctor and tell *him* what went on here. Tell everyone else that he bumped his head pretty hard." Looking at the others, I said again, "He hit his head." Then I added, "He's going to remember this day and dream about it for a very long time. It will be his personal hell; no one will have to remind him of it."

The two nodded and slowly got up. They gently helped the man to his feet and started toward their company area.

"We'll keep it quiet," they agreed in shaky voices.

"Hey, get some ammo and report back here, ASAP." I called after them. "You're still on duty."

As Bruce watched them leave, he shouted, "Guys." They stopped and looked back. He gave them two thumbs up. "You can come to our party any time." With big smiles, they nodded and hurried on their way.

The back of the Tet Offensive had been broken. We had lost a lot of people in the south, but the Viet Cong had lost an incredible number of men.

A week or so later, the base commander called an awards assembly in front of the headquarters building. Several men on base and in our company had earned the Bronze Star or the Silver Star, and one, a Purple Heart. No one had been shot or wounded, but apparently some clown had tripped over his own feet and gotten skinned up. The first sergeant and master sergeant were among the heroes awarded metals. Mitchell received one too, but he earned his. Not one of us who had served with the First Infantry was awarded anything.

Mitchell corralled all fifteen of us a little later and told us that, in his opinion, we deserved better, since we had been instrumental in reinstating post security and had been in the thick of battle.

Several weeks later, as things slowly got back to normal, I was on duty at our main gate when two deuce-and-a-half trucks rolled onto the base and parked in the clearing across from the orderly room. Four men got out of the vehicle and began walking toward the PX. I hollered at them to come back, but they kept walking, either ignoring me or not hearing me. One of our patrols heard me and said they'd bring them back. A few minutes later, the four walked up to me and in a surly manner asked what I wanted.

"You have left two open trucks full of VC bodies" I told them, "Don't you guys have any canvas tarps with you?"

They acknowledged that they did, but when I told them to cover the bodies, they started to argue. Fortunately, one nice thing about being an MP was that arguments were generally short and usually settled in my favor.

I calmly reiterated my point, "With all the civilian nationals working on this post, there may be a spy or VC sympathizer." Pointing to their load I said, "Covering the truck beds is not only proper and decent, it also may keep one of Charlie's friends from dropping a grenade down someone's shorts in retaliation for seeing their dead comrades or relatives."

I mentioned the fact that most VC had strong feelings about their cause.

Though their field tactics were brutal, they were still soldiers. I knew how I would feel if our guys were treated in such a shabby way (of course, they had been). I would hope for a little dignity. Finally I pointed out that because of the sun and heat, the odor was another problem. At that point the four soldiers agreed.

Originally, I had only given them thirty minutes to make their purchases and clear the post. However, after they tied their tarps on as requested, I added an additional forty minutes. I knew it would take them half an hour to walk to the PX and back. They cut their time pretty close; it was exactly one hour when they drove out the gate with their load. That must have been one hellish detail.

Chapter 7
SURVIVING THE ELEMENTS

If I could choose one descriptive word for Vietnam, it might be "extreme"—extreme in dust, heat, humidity, rain, mosquitoes, and discomfort. I can't speak for the extremes and horrors of jungle duty because that wasn't part of my experience; but I know many men who lived and fought there, and their reports are gruesome.

The roads varied with the weather, from hard-packed dirt to very fine dust several inches deep. When jeeps and trucks rolled through on dusty roads they created clouds of dust just like talcum powder. It billowed out from under the tires like rooster tails from speedboats. When working a checkpoint we would often wear bandannas to cover our mouths and noses, but the cloths didn't help much. The dust coated us with a gritty film, even in our mouths and on our teeth. Sometimes our mouths were so dry it was impossible to spit.

We were soaked with sweat day and night. My arms blistered so much from the sun's intense heat that I often rolled down my sleeves, ignoring the dress code that specified wearing them rolled up. Depending on the duty, we often wore bush hats to protect our ears and faces from sunburn and blisters. Only at night during the rainy season would the temperature drop down to the sixties.

Water was another big problem. To me, purified drinking water tasted the way scorched blood smells. Just rinsing my mouth was nauseating. In self-defense, I mainly drank pop. Care packages from home often contained jars of tap water and canned whole milk along with instant coffee. I tried to make the milk and water last, but usually finished them off within a day or two.

Since we couldn't safely eat in our mess hall, packages from home were a lifeline to all of us. Quite often they contained a variety of canned staples, including meats, vegetables, and fruits. These rated even higher than the usual cakes and cookies, although we liked those too. Friends created a little storage area of goodies that could be shared by a small group. On one occasion, a soldier's 6-year-old kid sister, unbeknownst to their mother, added a half-gallon carton of ice cream to one of his care packages. Man, what a mess! We all laughed till our sides ached.

It was difficult dealing with the extremes in weather. I have never experienced rain like that of Vietnam, although Georgia's came close. At times it rained so hard we couldn't see fifty feet in front of us. The high humidity coupled with the rain caused vapors to form and rise from the earth to become clouds as we watched.

Sometimes it seemed as if we could see the rust form on our weapons. That was one of the hardest things to cope with. Once, during a particularly hard rain, I was on guard duty in one of the bunkers. My partners and I had wrapped all our weapons and ammo in our ponchos to protect them from the weather. At 6:00 that evening, we re-oiled and wiped down all the weapons, then wrapped them up and went to eat. When we returned just thirty minutes later, they were turning red with rust. The best antidote we found for this problem was the army's insecticide. The military's bug spray was not successful as a bug killer, but it did great as a weapons lubricant and rust inhibitor. The "bug juice" prevented rust from forming well into morning.

The spiders and mosquitoes were another problem, and they worked as a team. Not only did spiders attack our posteriors in the multi-holer latrine, but they would also drop down from the rafters in our hootches while we slept. Some spiders had bodies larger than a silver dollar. At night the mosquitoes plagued us. Because we usually slept in shorts with only a sheet on top of us, we were pretty vulnerable. When we awoke in the morning, it was not unusual to find two or three spiders and mosquitoes squashed on the bedding and several large welts on our bodies.

It was in Vietnam that I met the spider monkey. Some of the guys bought them as pets, and the animals turned out to be very useful to have around. They were named "spider" not because of their appearance, but because spiders were their favorite food. The monkeys would swing through the rafters gathering and eating these delicacies. The only place the monkeys wouldn't visit was the latrine area. They didn't like that place any more than we did.

Army aerosol bug spray hardly affected the mosquitoes and the spiders. If we sprayed them with maybe a whole can, we could drown them, but that was all. One of my sisters was faithfully sending me a package about every two weeks. When she heard about these "battles of the bugs," she included a new brand of bug spray with my usual box of staples and treats. I gave it a good test. That night while we were playing cards, a swarm of these hungry carnivores was working the room. I gave a short blast of spray into the cloud of mosquitoes, and almost instantly they came spiraling downward.

With a cheer from everyone there, I went after the spiders with equally good results. By morning, our hootch was clear. Our resident monkey tended to leave messes, and we almost preferred the spiders to cleaning up after him. We gave the monkey away and kept the spray.

Snakes presented a deadly serious problem, especially out in the jungle areas. Other than the cobra incident, I had had little contact with snakes. While at the outpost I saw perhaps a half dozen. One humorous, but potentially dangerous, occurrence happened shortly after Tet. I came in from bunker guard duty one night for dinner break and stopped in the hootch for my utensils and some canned food. I planned to heat my dinner in the mess hall. There were three men in the hootch. Two were sleeping, and my
Chicano friend was sitting up on his bunk writing letters. He was using the light from his small lamp. Since he was off duty, he wore only his shorts, T-shirt, and thongs.

Our guys had adopted a puppy, which was not quite "hootch-broken." An empty wicker chair sat underneath the overhead light. I walked down the aisle to my footlocker, moving the chair out of my way as I went. Where the chair had been, I saw a small curled pile of puppy poop. I made some silly comment to my friend and left. After dinner, I returned to my locker and noticed that my letter-writing friend had moved from his bunk to the wicker chair where the overhead light was better. I also noticed that either the poop or the chair had moved. I asked the kid if he had moved the chair. He said, "No." Quietly, I told him to get up very slowly, and he did so. I eased the chair back, and in a few seconds the "poop" slowly uncurled, stretched out, and moved back into the shadows under the chair to escape the light. I had my rifle with me, so as my friend moved the chair, mumbling something in Spanish (roughly translated "I'm one lucky sonofabitch!"), I placed the barrel just behind the snake's head and pinned it down. As it squirmed we tried to ascertain the species. The kid quickly found the book that the military had issued to us on snakes in Vietnam. He found a picture that looked just like the snake we had captured. A bite by this little critter gave you less than ten seconds to live. The natives referred to it as a "two-step." We quickly dispatched the snake. After this, everybody became more conscientious about checking boots and bedding. (And we got rid of the puppy too!)

As guys rotated home (or out of our unit), we took in replacements. Many of them arrived during hostilities, and they were immediately pressed into guard duty—really just an extension of their advanced training in the States. A few men who came from duty in Europe wanted nothing to do with Vietnam.

Warren Norton came directly from Germany, where he had served three years of his five-year hitch. We were surprised that he had risen only to specialist fourth class. In Nam, a soldier who was on the ball would usually make this rank in a few months.

Those of us who cared about survival soon learned to stay away from this man. After a week, none of us, including many men from the "good ol' boys" club, wanted to serve with him. Besides his problem with drugs and his habit of drinking before, during, and after duty, Norton was very outspoken about which side of the war we should be supporting, which wasn't the side we were currently fighting for. Whether in a bunker or on patrol you were never quite sure how this man would react. None of us felt we could turn our back or depend on him in a tight situation.

He made friends with very few of the men. His one real buddy was a kid from Tennessee who had been in-country just a month longer than me. These two clowns knew that I was among the minority who chose not to drink, take drugs, or touch the Vietnamese women. They never missed a chance to harass me. I had good reasons for my abstinences. I didn't drink because I needed to be alert to any emergency, and I had never used drugs. Simply put, I wanted to be in complete control of myself. As far as the women went, I could wait. I wasn't a prude. But the U.S. Military hospital in Japan was full of GIs with incurable cases of sexually transmitted diseases. I didn't need any problem like that. In short, regardless of what anyone else thought about the war in Nam, I planned to go home in one piece, walking and functioning under my own power. Was I different? I don't think so. I found more GIs who felt the way I did than those who didn't.

I must admit that most of the time I was not very tactful when speaking to these two guys about their drinking and drugs. Because we were in the same hootch, I became their target of choice. I often found my bunk torn apart, the mattress outside in the grass, foot and wall lockers broken into, and all my things scattered around. They were hoping I would fight. No chance! Norton was about 6 feet, 5 inches tall and weighed nearly 250 pounds. The other guy was more my size, but it was a little like "hit my friend, hit me." At 5 feet, 11 inches in boots, and weighing only about 170 pounds, I was no match for trading blows with the bigger man.

Because many of the guys had flatly refused to work with either one of these men, Mitchell was well aware of the problem and their antagonism. He had intervened once or twice, but with no lasting effects. Norton and his friend thought that I had complained about them, but this was not the case. Mitchell was not blind.

One rainy night I had just finished fourteen hours of patrol, and was beat. It had been a particularly busy night. All I wanted was a quick shower and my bunk. As I walked into the hootch, I found my bedding all over the floor and my foot and wall lockers dumped. What a mess! I was almost too tired to care, but with the help of my young Chicano snake-charmer friend, I set about picking up my things and remaking the bed. Drunk and grinning, Norton and his friend were making comments about how sloppy my area was and that I should do better. I continued with what I was doing, suggesting they sober up and grow up.

I clicked my padlock shut, and was putting the finishing touches on my bunk, when both men walked over and stood behind me. I remember saying something like, "Why don't you guys stop before some one gets hurt."

Most of my gear had been secured, and as I leaned down to pick up something off my bed, Norton hit me hard in the small of my back, knocking the wind out of me. Trying to catch my breath, I remembered the threats he had made about "crushing my head like a grape." Out of the corner of my eye, I saw the other guy coming in for his licks. They hit me twice more in the ribs and once in the face. By now I was on my knees, half-lying across my bunk.

For some time, it had been my habit of sleeping with my nightstick and .45 under my pillow, instinctively placing them there after each shift. I had just placed them moments earlier. I shoved my hand under my pillow, pulled out my nightstick, and struck back at Norton, hitting him on the right side of his head and ear. As Norton was going down, the other guy came at me again. I countered with a nightstick to his groin, folding him up like a wet copy of *Stars and Stripes*. Norton, back on his feet, charged for me and ran right into the muzzle of my .45, and I placed it hard just under his chin.

I was angry, and I said in a hoarse voice, "Okay, you two bastards, it's over! This stops now!"

Then I recited to Norton what he already knew about the safety mechanisms built into the Colt .45 automatic. "Now—as long as there is enough pressure held against a person's body, it won't go off even with the trigger held back." He tried to speak, but I said, "Shut up and listen!"

I pulled the hammer back until it clicked into the cocked position. He suddenly looked very pale and nearly sober.

"I have the trigger tight," I said. "If *you* lose the tension," I continued to explain, "you'll lose the top of your head. Understand?" He grunted in the affirmative.

His friend slowly began to unfold off the floor and quickly confirmed the fact that I was holding the trigger tight. Norton was visibly shaken.

"Just in case you have any doubts about my weapon being loaded—anyone who knows me knows that I always keep a round in the chamber." I added a little more pressure under his chin, which was now bleeding, and asked, "Shall I demonstrate, Norton?" And I received a strong negative response. "Now, you two assholes are going to accompany me outside and up to the CO's hootch. Do you both understand this order?" Again I received an affirmative reply. My tactics seemed to be working quite well.

My Chicano friend had long since run to get help and had found both Smith and Mitchell coming from the mess hall. The three of them and several others heard the commotion and came running toward the hootch. We all met up outside. Bruce and Rob came flying out of their hootch and were now walking beside me telling me not to lose my cool. I simply responded, "It's too late."

Mitchell said, "Mills, why don't you put the gun down."

" No," I answered. "Let's all just keep walking. I'm in perfect control. I'm a little pissed off, but I'm feeling okay."

When we reached the officers' and NCOs' hootch, I spoke to Norton's friend. "Come around and open the door, but be sure to stay in front of us." A few feet down the hall, I pushed open the captain's door with my boot and we calmly walked into his room. He had been entertaining one of the company's prostitutes. Shaking like a leaf, I said, "Captain, I am placing these two men in your custody." I continued to press the muzzle of my .45 hard under Norton's chin; a lot more blood was now dripping down onto the pistol frame and my hand. My head and face were also bleeding.

The captain slowly stood up. "What the hell's going on here, Mills?"

I explained briefly what the past few weeks had been like with these two, on and off duty, and said, "Sir, I will not trade blows with Norton. He's too damn big. Besides, there were two of them against one of me."

Mitchell managed to get inside the small room, and he confirmed what I had said.

Then I finally removed the pistol and carefully lowered the hammer. Norton took a deep breath.

Turning to the captain, I said, "No one, who wants to go home in one piece, can trust either one of these two. They've been drunk and on drugs, on and off duty." Taking a breath, I added, "So as long as they are on post I'll carry my .45 with me, and if I ever see either of them with a weapon, I'll shoot 'em on the spot."

Captain Gordon gave me a very puzzled look, then asked me to wait outside. He told Mitchell and Smith to remain, along with Norton and his friend. I don't know what they talked about, but when the two sergeants came out, Norton and his friend were given a night in our MP cage to cool off and sober up.

I had been sitting on the back steps of the captain's hootch, waiting for either Mitchell or Smith to come out so I could find out what charges the captain might bring against me. I was shaking so hard I could barely speak. Mitchell came out and sat down next to me. Bruce and Rob stood by, leaning against the wet sandbags at the bottom of the steps. It had stopped raining.

I asked, "Do you want my pistol now, Sarge?"

"What the hell for?" he snorted. "It's not even loaded." He was right, but no one, including Norton, had known it.

The next day about noon, Bruce, Rob, and several others found me in my hootch and said, "Hey, tough guy, pack up your gear. You're coming with us." And I watched my footlocker heading out the door. I was being transferred to their hootch. It was a great change. These were people I trusted. Besides that, my friends had set up a club with air conditioning, cold drinks, a coffee maker, and their own food. Most of them were men who had served with the First Infantry, and they had learned well.

Norton and his friend didn't lose any rank, but they were disciplined and lost some pay. The only assignment they were given was night-guard duty. I had no further run-ins with them and saw them only once from a distance. They stayed with the 552nd for just another month, then transferred out separately.

Rob did have a fracas with Norton's friend one night when someone from one of the bunkers called for assistance. Rob was on motor patrol and was just leaving our MP station when the call came in via the field phone. Smith was the desk sergeant, and he called, "Hey Rob, check out this problem for me. I can't make any sense of it."

Since it was only a hundred feet away, Rob walked to the bunker. As he approached, he heard a lot of loud talking and swearing. Inside the bunker Rob found three guards trying to restrain Norton's friend. The man was absolutely out of control, yelling about how he was going out to find the VC and make friends.

When he saw Rob in his MP garb, he really flew into a rage, ranting about

Rob being the enemy. He broke away from the others and charged Rob with a bayonet. Rob simply brought his rifle up and neatly placed the butt plate across the guy's forehead. He went out cold. Rob picked up the field phone and reported the situation to Smith, who in turn called the medics to pick up the man.

A few days later, Smith reported that the doctors thought the kid had experienced a flashback from some unknown drug. They weren't sure whether he would ever recover. They sent him to an Army hospital in Japan, and we never heard about him again.

Around the end of February or the first of March, activities slowed down to the usual routine. We maintained a tougher watch, which included setting up checkpoints for the first time since before I arrived. We pulled some duty with the 720th MPs, helping out at their checkpoint near the intersection across from the 90th Replacement. The next checkpoint was about three miles west near the tower and Gate Five. A lot of weapons and foodstuffs were still being smuggled in from the north, and it was our job to intercept all of the supplies we could find.

Late one night, a couple of enemy rockets slammed into the 90th Replacement, killing and injuring several men waiting for their flight home. The buildings were so damaged there were no accommodations for new men arriving in-country. For some time afterwards, new soldiers were sent directly to their assigned units.

Our company was given the loan of a new arrival, a 20-year-old 1st lieutenant named Richter. This officer was not a happy man, a condition that probably dated back to a severe case of diaper rash. He was not MP-trained, but he seemed to think he had all the answers even without hearing any of the questions. He wouldn't take suggestions from anyone under him, including sergeants. This all came to a head one very warm and busy afternoon.

The traffic through our checkpoint was unusually heavy. We checked everything from motorbikes and Lambrettas to old cars and trucks. Army Intelligence had alerted all units to be particularly watchful for small arms and medium-sized weapons coming south—things such as rocket launchers and mortars. I was working the checkpoint nearest the tower with Rob, Bruce, and Kent. Two experienced Cahn Sats were assigned with us, but the green lieutenant didn't trust any of us. He didn't believe we should stop every vehicle, and since we had a lot of vehicles backed up, he started to let several through with nothing more than a cursory glance.

A small Japanese pickup truck carrying two occupants rolled into the checkpoint, and Richter passed it through. We could tell by a quick look that this vehicle was not right. The bed of the truck appeared to be nearly empty, but the vehicle sat low on its springs and the tires appeared to be low. For an empty truck, the motor labored much too hard. Bruce, Rob, and one of the Cahn Sats started yelling at the driver to stop, but he tried all the harder to accelerate.

Kent was on a slight embankment near our perimeter fence. He immediately went prone, and I hit the dirt on the opposite shoulder of the road.

I called to him, "Can you see to hit the left front tire?" He answered in the affirmative. "Good," I told him, "I'll shoot for the right tire, on three."

We took careful aim and I slowly called out, "One, two, three." With simultaneous reports from our M-14s, the truck's front end collapsed. I missed the tire, hitting the right hub and wheel bearing instead. The truck rolled off the road and into the ditch.

During the ruckus, the lieutenant was having an absolute fit. He kept yelling, "Who's in command? Stop firing!"

Mitchell and two other men took the truck occupants into custody. When they checked the pickup, they found rockets and mortars hidden in the cab, under the hood, and beneath the truck bed under a false floor. Sarge went up to the lieutenant who was still screaming at us. Rob sarcastically said to the sergeant, "It was so darn noisy, no one could hear him clearly. Hell, we thought he was yelling 'Start firing! Start firing!'"

Sarge reported to the lieutenant on their findings, and added, "Sir, if you hope to survive your tour of duty and avoid a lot of trouble, I strongly suggest you listen to these troops."

The young lieutenant started in on Mitchell saying, "Sergeant, there are people who have witnessed this insubordination." However, he soon found out that no one had heard anything. A major from G-2, whom we all knew and respected, had parked his jeep inside the fence at Gate Five. Observing this whole exchange from start to finish, he was quite impressed by our alertness and ability in stopping the truck. He called the lieutenant over to him. We couldn't hear anything that was being said, but it was a very animated, one-sided conversation. The major locked Richter's heels and quietly dressed him down. When our new officer came back to the checkpoint, he said nothing more.

Shortly after this incident, the weather began to change. We were moving toward the end of the Southeast Asian summer and heading into autumn. It was hard to tell the difference except that it seemed to rain a little more often. The temperature dropped slightly, but seldom went below 90 degrees. At least the rains helped to control the dust, and we liked that.

During the Tet offensive, most of the families who had moved from the garbage dump into the vacated village had now taken over and moved into an old, bombed-out Buddhist temple near the center of the village. One of our house girls told us about the move. We found nearly thirty men, women, and children living in and around the temple. When we finally convinced them that most of the heavy fighting was over, all of the men who had families with them packed up to move elsewhere.

The two South Vietnamese policemen who had worked with us on our checkpoints lived in a town just a couple of miles away. They told us that they wanted to help with the kids and young mothers who chose to remain in the temple. We had hoped to do some repairs to the temple for the young mothers and their children. The two Cahn Sats found some discarded building materials—sheets of corrugated steel siding, plywood, and some used lumber. Because the roof was almost gone, we began our work there.

One of the reasons the temple repair project began was due to my desire to adopt the two Amer-Asian children I had found roaming the dump. Most of the people who lived at the dump suffered from malnutrition. The little girl had learned to speak only a few words—mostly about food, water, and sleep—but she instinctively took care of her little brother. With their parents gone, they had been on their own until we moved them in with the young mother.

In our efforts to remodel the temple, we started to recruit help from some of the other men on post. One was a sergeant from the construction company, whose crew had been instrumental in helping to fix the post defenses prior to the Tet Offensive. He had a drinking problem—a big drinking problem. His name was Dan, and he was getting close to losing his stripes—again. To get his help, we bent a few rules. We had stopped him for driving under the influence, but he seemed sober enough to understand our proposition. We told him that we would give him just a verbal warning, that I would drive his vehicle back, with him, to his company area if he would help us rebuild the old temple. It's funny how people can change. Dan agreed and we soon had three, sometimes five men from his company helping us. Over the next three weeks, his drinking went from almost constant to nearly nothing.

The temple never looked better, though it no longer looked like a temple. With our help and help from some ARVN soldiers, Dan and his crew rebuilt the temple from the ground up, including a completely new interior. The remodeled building had fifteen separate rooms: sleeping areas, a mezzanine floor, a cooking and eating area, a classroom that doubled as a family room, and a separate laundry area. The floor was concrete. Next to the new privy, the guys erected a salvaged 100-gallon water tank and installed three or four shower stalls.

I think the men from the construction crew really enjoyed working on this project. They made some friends among us MPs, and it helped keep all of them out of trouble during their free time. Dan's lieutenant was so pleased that his men were not drinking, fighting, or wrecking equipment that he came to look the job over. Then he went to see our CO, Captain Gordon, to compliment him.

The talk with Gordon didn't help much, but the construction guys had told their families back home about the project. The families started sending care packages for the orphans. Dan's wife sent some of their son's old baby clothes. Other packages contained food, clothing, small tennis shoes, books, and toys.

From time to time, when other MP companies in the region found a young mother (or a grandmother) with toddlers or babies, the MPs would tell them about our temple project. If these families were interested, room was made for them. Transporting the women and children was illegal, but some GIs were still willing to help.

Some of our new draftees had come to us courtesy of the "Gray Bar Hotel"—jail. In several cases, men with jail records had found their way into the MPs. This was like having a tarantula stand guard inside the cricket cage.

Jamal was a GI with a criminal record. He was from New York City. He boasted about the young girls he had raped; he wasn't just sure how many. During his sentencing he had been given the choice of five to seven years in prison or a three-year hitch in the Army. On the surface, he actually seemed to be a nice enough guy, but after a few days, we knew that we had a problem. He was black, and the other "brothers" in our company stayed away from him as much as possible. They warned the rest of us, "Never, never turn your back on him."

Bruce and I were on patrol one day when a call went out to all of us to keep a lookout for Jamal. He had been on MP duty at a gate and had failed to return from his lunch break. He wasn't responding to radio, either. The man who relieved him was working as a one-man post patrol, and now we were short. As we cruised the perimeter roads, we stopped to visit our buddies from Airborne. We had not been too concerned about a missing man and jeep, but all that changed when one of the guys asked why an MP jeep had just gone off on a side road heading for the bush with a young Vietnamese girl aboard. Bruce and I looked at each other, leaped off the sandbags, and jumped into our jeep. I slammed the tranny into first gear and Bruce grabbed the handset to request immediate backup as we headed for that side road. We soon reached the open gate, and the highway—tires squealing, red lights flashing, and siren wailing.

The road Jamal had taken was heavily overgrown and no longer in use. It wound around for several miles to the northeast of the airborne unit's helo-pad compound. Bruce and I both knew why he had gone this way and why he was ignoring the radio. From what the brothers in our outfit had told us, Jamal was capable of any type of abuse. Bruce and I wondered who the girl was and fervently hoped she would be all right.

I was doing nearly sixty miles an hour when we reached the cutoff. We could see the fresh tire tracks of a jeep. Once we exited the paved road I slowed to forty, shifted down one gear, and locked into four-wheel drive. We climbed a small grade that overlooked the rolling countryside. As I slowed, Bruce spotted the other jeep about half a mile ahead. It was parked in the brush several yards to the left of the dirt road. I floored the accelerator, but Bruce suggested that we slow way down and travel as quietly as possible, so our approach would be unnoticed. When we were about two hundred yards away, still on a slight downhill grade, I killed the engine and coasted, coming to a stop perhaps sixty feet from the other jeep. Bruce took up his shotgun and chambered a round. I took out my sidearm and checked to be sure that there was a round in the chamber, then concealed my pistol at my side as we walked toward the other jeep. There was no doubt it was the one Jamal had been driving.

Just past the jeep, I heard a young girl's voice crying and pleading in both Vietnamese and English, *"Please no do this. No hurt me."*

I spotted them first. Jamal, partly disrobed, was on top of the girl, fondling her. He was trying to remove her clothing with one hand while holding his .45 against her head with the other. She was resisting the best she could, but she was very tiny, and he about 6 feet tall and weighed about 200 pounds. He was so preoccupied he hadn't heard us arrive.

With both hands on my weapon, I placed the muzzle an inch away from his right ear and cocked the hammer back. At the sound, he shuddered and suddenly became very still.

"Before you move," I said quietly, "you should know I have my .45 an inch from your ear, and a Stevens pump is five feet away, pointing at your back."

Bruce added, "You know the training, you know the drill. Do it straight, and you'll live to face court-martial."

Jamal nodded and let go of his weapon. We had him lie on the ground, spread-eagled and silent. Bruce handed me the shotgun, then picked up Jamal's pistol from the grass, cleared it, and tucked it into his belt. He searched Jamal and handcuffed him.

I helped the girl up. She was crying and shaking, but we spoke softly to her, assuring her she was safe. In fairly good English, she told us that her name was Li. I was surprised that she knew us by name as well as by sight. We learned that she was the younger sister of Lin, our house girl—the same one we had tried to help several months earlier. Li was just eleven years old. When she told us that, I became so angry that I almost wished Jamal had resisted arrest; but looking at the little girl, I knew we had done our job right.

Jamal was court-martialed for kidnapping and attempted rape of a minor, and for being absent from his post in a combat zone. He was sentenced to thirty years in the military prison at Fort Leavenworth, Kansas.

It was rare when the five of us had a day off at the same time, let alone two consecutive days, but every once in a while it worked out that way. It was great just to relax. On one particular day off we spent some of the morning playing volleyball during a light rain. Later on we walked up to the canteen near the PX to get lunch. While we were there, one of our patrols stopped by. The two on duty bought hamburgers and had begun eating when their radio crackled, "X-ray 6: this is Handcuff. Over."

The call was repeated, but with their mouths stuffed full of food, they couldn't answer, so I answered for them. "Handcuff, X-ray 6. Go."

"Mills, why are you using the radio, and what's your 20 (location)? Over."

"Sorry, Sarge, but there is a hamburger-in-the-mouth problem here at the canteen. Over."

"Roger that! Stay put. You have a visitor on his way."

Our buddies on patrol took their food and drinks and drove on. We couldn't guess who the visitor might be. I had spoken casually a couple times with Colonel Wilson and BJ over the past few days, so I figured it wasn't either of them. Within a couple of minutes, a jeep pulled in. It was Wayne Cameron, our pilot friend who had helped us out at our trial. With a big smile he said, "If anyone of you misfits calls me 'Sir' or salutes me, I'll deck him." Then he laughed and shook hands with us.

"*Mister* Cameron, nice to see ya. What brings you here? How did you find us?" I asked.

"I had a recon mission near Di-An a couple days back. When I finished, I landed near the gate and found your old sergeant from the First Infantry. Anyway, he directed me here." Pausing for a moment, he continued, "I'm flying to

Vaung Tao in a week for a three-day R & R and wanted to know if you guys could go along. I have to ferry a Huey back to Bien Hoa on the return trip. Vaung Tao was a well-known in-country R&R area. Once it had been a resort town, on the ocean, and according to all reports, it was pretty nice. Our company clerk had told us long before that we only needed to put in our requests to get permission to go.

We put in a request for the five of us, and much to our surprise, four of us got passes. Kent had to stay and work, but he was good-natured about it as he joked, "Hell, with you four gone someone has to pick up the slack. That oughta be easy enough for one man."

On the appointed weekend, we met Wayne at the air base. There we boarded a twin-engine cargo plane, a C-130, I think. There was no cargo, only twenty or so GIs. Man, what a ride! This was a flight I would have paid to miss! To take off, this plane required all of the ground speed it could muster. Liftoff felt as if it was almost vertical; and strapped in, I felt like a 170-pound bag of spuds.

Some of these aircraft were equipped with small jet boosters, but not this plane. The two huge radial engines did all the work. The noise inside the cargo area was so loud we couldn't talk. Wayne had suggested we bring earplugs. We did, and they sure helped. As we readied for landing, a crewmember motioned for us to cinch up our straps, signaling that we would be landing in a couple of minutes. We were twelve thousand feet up, and we would be on the ground in two minutes? Hang on!

Descending was quick. The nose of the plane suddenly went down, and the tail went up. We were coming down at a near 45-degree angle. My visibility was good. I was sitting next to a large window on the starboard side, exactly even with the engine. I was amazed that I could actually see the change in the pitch of the propeller blades. It was as if the pilot had hit the brakes—hard! I had not realized that the pitch of the propellers could be reversed in midair.

We could see the center of the airfield below us. I'm not sure which was worse: flying with this wild bronco pilot or being scared shitless by the VC. We could hear the pilot laughing hysterically over the rumbling of the aircraft. They had told us that the pilots flew this way to give bored, homesick GIs a little fun and to avoid creating low flying targets for VC snipers—but until a flight like this actually happens to you, it is hard to imagine.

At fifteen hundred feet, we leveled off sharply, and we touched down just seconds later. The flight took less than twenty minutes. We were a bit wobbly as we made our way off the plane. Even Wayne, our gung-ho chopper pilot, was pleased the flight was over. Our pilot was in his mid-twenties, a captain as well as a comic, and was still laughing as he walked off the loading ramp with us.

"Sir, I would consider saluting," I started, "but I think my right arm is still inside the plane, plastered to the ceiling." He laughed all the more. Actually, he was a pretty decent guy, and he took the time to explain his maneuver to us. Wayne was well aware of such procedures.

We all crowded into a Lambretta taxi and headed for town. It was late morning when we were dropped off in front of our hotel. It wasn't exactly elegant, but it was a far cry from our hootches—it had two or three real beds to a room. We even had a bathroom with a shower, with hot and cold running water. Downstairs, we found a true restaurant, operated by the USO and the American Red Cross, a gift shop, and a movie theater.

I don't recall everything we did those three days. I know I slept a lot and enjoyed being clean. The food was plentiful, and it was good for a change. No one shot at us, and there was no bombing. It was absolutely quiet—as if the war was in another part of the world. We played and swam in the ocean and lay on the warm, sandy beaches—it was good fun! There were hundreds of Vietnamese shops and food stands. I have to tell you that Coca-Cola, Pepsi, and other U.S. drinks bottled in Vietnam were barely recognizable by taste. Mostly we chose canned drinks brought in from the States.

All too soon, Monday morning came and we were again sitting in the back of a plane. This was a much larger one, with four turboprop engines. About thirty of us were headed back to the base at Bien Hoa. The surge of power when the pilot throttled up those engines pressed us tightly against our harnesses. It felt as if we went straight up to three thousand feet before the pilot leveled off to a gentler rate of climb.

We arrived back at our company by 10:00 that morning, and by 3:30 p.m. we were back on duty and standing inspection in our guard mount. I can't say any of us was glad to be "home."

It had been really good to get to know Warrant Officer Wayne Cameron better. We saw him several times after that. He was shot down once but was unhurt and close enough to friendly troops to get help. The report said that he was on the ground for just a few minutes before he grabbed another bird and went back to work. He was a tough but very gentle, honest, and caring young man. Later, when he heard about our efforts with the kids and the young mothers, he flew in over two hundred pounds of food, all donated by the men in his outfit and their families. He also left a small refrigerator and a gas generator.

We asked him about the generator and the fridge. Apparently his maintenance sergeant had found the equipment in the parts dump. When he heard about the kids and about Wayne helping us, he rebuilt both units. He even installed a larger fuel tank on the generator. That little motor could hum quietly for a whole day. They were marvelous gifts. The five of us got permission to drive out to the air base one Sunday to attend church services. Afterwards, we met the old sarge and thanked him.

Three weeks after our trip to Vaung Tao we saw Wayne again. This time was similar to our first meeting. We were working convoy escort and security. Although we didn't realize it, he was flying the convoy commander, a colonel, who was directing our moves and watching for Charlie.

We had eight of our own MP vehicles, six of them mounted with M-60s, and there were three or four men per jeep. The convoy numbered almost thirty vehicles. It consisted mostly of larger trucks: flatbeds with tractors, deuce-and-a-halfs, water tankers and 3/4-ton trucks with quad-fifties or sixties. Several vehicles spaced at intervals within the convoy each carried upwards of thirty riflemen. This was serious stuff.

Lieutenant Richter was in command of ground security. For that reason, we were glad Sergeant Mitchell was coming with us. Our job was to escort the column and rendezvous with the next escort detachment. Lieutenant Richter was unusually quiet as we started off, a bit like a little kid still pouting. I don't think he was quite over the ass-chewing he had gotten from the G-2 major a couple of weeks earlier. Since then, he had been pretty sullen. We all felt that it would take very little to set him off, but as Mitchell pointed out, "We still have work to do." During a short meeting he added, "You guys do your jobs the way you've been taught, and I'll deal with the lieutenant."

At first we were able to maintain a fair speed. We traveled a good distance that morning, constantly scouting ahead and behind, watching for enemy movement. Unfortunately, we got bogged down with bomb craters and heavy refugee traffic—thousands of people on foot or on bicycles. We had to slow to a crawl with occasional stops. It took four hours to travel less than five miles. Suddenly the crowds just disappeared. We all talked about how strange it was.

The small chopper carrying the colonel had been busy, venturing out a mile or two each direction, and then returning to hover a couple thousand feet above the column. Then surprisingly we heard, "X-ray 2-3, X-ray 2-3. This Air Cover. Over." We were puzzled. That call number did not belong to anyone in our convoy. The transmission was repeated several times; then a light came on in my head.

"Hey, that's the number of our jeep that got destroyed at Di-An," I shouted. Quickly I picked up the handset and asked, "Air Cover—Wayne, is that you?"

A friendly voice responded, "Hey, I told the colonel here that I thought I recognized you guys. Glad to see ya!" Then he quickly added, "First, change your radio to your old Di-An frequency. We want to talk only to you guys right now."

We were mentally and physically scratching our heads trying to remember the radio setting. It had been four months; how the hell did Wayne remember it? Bruce did a quick twist on the knobs, just hoping. We hadn't even picked up the handset when we heard Wayne say, "Okay, I am guessing you're set now."

We could barely see his chopper; they were three miles south of us. The radio came alive again as Wayne began, "Five hundred meters south of your location there is a ravine that runs parallel to the road. It narrows and meets a bridge about three miles ahead." There was silence for a few moments, and then Wayne continued, "You have company coming; about five hundred of Uncle Ho's relatives are watching, and moving parallel with you."

We acknowledged the transmission. Since Sarge and the lieutenant were up ahead of us, we took the initiative. We moved all but two of the gun-mounted vehicles to the south side of the road and told everyone to be alert as the convoy continued slowly along. The lieutenant turned in his seat and saw our deployment. He stopped the jeep and growled, "Mitchell, what the hell do your men think they're doing back there? They must check in with me first."

Mitchell answered with, "Well, sir, I'm not sure, but I can guarantee you this—something's up and those guys are doing their job."

Since we had been traveling so slowly, it was not surprising that enemy ground troops could easily keep up. When we were stopped, it became even more dangerous. Wayne added the rest of the good news, "There is also a smaller group of black PJs moving toward the bridge. You copy?"

"This is ground cover. We copy," I responded.

I never thought I would hear a noncommissioned officer, especially a staff sergeant, buck an officer, even an officer like Lieutenant Richter—but Mitchell did. The lieutenant had gotten a reputation for giving some really off-the-wall orders. One the guys had overheard our radio messages and swung back to Mitchell and the lieutenant to relay what he had heard.

Richter was furious, "Why aren't these messages coming directly to me?"

Interrupting the lieutenant's tirade, Mitchell said, "Sir, if you want to survive, shut the hell up; pay attention, and listen!"

Kent and I parked our two vehicles next to the command vehicle Richter and Mitchell were in, now parked at the front of the column. We needed to explain what we were doing. We hadn't realized it, but apparently our mike or handset key had gotten stuck on broadcast. Bruce finally noticed it and released the button. Wayne was calling and said, "Put us on your speaker so your lieutenant and sergeant can hear."

Then a deep, gravely, southern-sounding voice came over our radio, "Lieutenant, this is Colonel Guthery. You're new in-country, and from what my pilot tells me, you've got some of the most experienced MPs and GIs you could hope for. Follow their lead and you'll not only survive, you'll get plenty of the glory."

Still fuming, the lieutenant took the handset from Bruce and acknowledged the message with a barbed, "Yes, sir!"

The column wasn't going anywhere very fast. We were still trying to maneuver around the holes in the road. Some of our troops, working ahead of the column, were throwing shovels of dirt and sand into the craters. As far as Wayne and the colonel could tell, the VC didn't think they had been spotted, so the Colonel gave us some rough ideas for a plan, leaving us free to improvise. Standing orders stated that U.S. military forces could not engage or fire upon the enemy unless fired on first. To the GIs in Nam, this seemed a little like stepping into the ring to fight, with your hands tied behind your back—not really very smart. Luckily, there were a few in charge who didn't buy into this theory of engagement. This *Bird-in-the-sky* (full bird colonel) was one of them.

We had our gun-jeeps in place, along with a lot of riflemen dug in alongside of the road, all guns trained on the ravine. We positioned others to cover the other side of the road. We hadn't seen any sign of movement, but we knew the enemy was there; they'd had to have seen the chopper. Wayne radioed that it looked like the VC would start an altercation in about thirty seconds. The good colonel let us know that he expected an appropriate response from us. This wasn't an exercise to get a VC body count, but he wanted them to understand that we knew where they were and that we were prepared to break a few rules to protect our own. I liked how that man thought.

Wayne brought the colonel's chopper down to about twelve hundred feet and hovered about half a mile from the road with the VC in between us. Now the VC knew they had been identified. Unlike Wayne's old bird, this chopper was equipped with two thirty-caliber machine guns. The colonel placed his sights at sixty to a one hundred yards from us and then squeezed off a hundred rounds. As the rounds tore into the ground many yards in front of us, we heard him yell to us on the radio, "Okay, men, you've been fired on. Open up."

We let go with the quad-sixties and fifties, and the riflemen's M-16s, along with our own M-60s and M-14s. Dirt was flying all across the berm above the ravine. After several seconds, Wayne called, "Cease firing, cease firing. The VC are on the run and heading back down the trail." After a few minutes Wayne added, "Okay guys, you've got that smaller group of Victor Charlies heading for the bridge. Knock on it and be careful."

Mitchell looked at us and said, "Who do you want to take with you?" We named three guys who had served with us in the field, and Sarge signaled them to come forward. That made the second jeep. Then I had a crazy thought. "How about it, Lieutenant, care to come along?"

Looking rather surprised and suddenly pale, Richter appropriated someone's M-14 and ammo, handed the guy his M-2 carbine, and said, "Hold this for me. I'll be right back." Then, to my surprise, he jumped—not into the front seat of my jeep (where his rank would have placed him), but into the rear seat—and our two vehicles sped off. The bridge was three miles away, and we were the only ones on the road.

Coming down a slight grade we saw the bridge. There was wide-open terrain on both sides of the road. We took the right side and the guys in the second jeep took the left, flying off the road at about sixty miles an hour (Those road races were paying off!). The roadway rose gently above us as we continued down the hillside into a large ravine. Both vehicles slowed to forty miles an hour. We landed simultaneously in the shallow sand of the gully, doing opposite 90-degree turns to face each other about sixty yards apart. Fifteen of the enemy stood between our two vehicles. We had caught them with their PJs down. They had explosives in hand they hadn't had time to plant. Best of all, we didn't fire a shot.

Lieutenant Richter called the bird to report to the colonel and about picking up the prisoners, "Sir, the bridge is secure, and we have fifteen N-V-A's."

It couldn't have been more than three minutes before two gunships were parking on the bridge. Prior to taking off with the captives, a Cahn Sat with chopper told us in fairly good English, "Three VC know you four," pointing to Bruce, Rob, Kent and me. "If you die, they get much piaster, much reward." He also said that one of these three was the Cahn Sat who had disappeared from First Infantry's forward outpost. That information didn't do a thing to help alleviate the prickly tingles going the full length of my body. It's nice to be wanted, but not that way!

After the choppers took off, we rechecked the bridge for explosives. The area was clean. We parked the two jeeps at the far end of the bridge, one on each side of the road, pointing in the direction where the convoy would appear. We contacted Mitchell and our bird again with the "all clear." Mitchell radioed back, "The column is on the go."

When Sarge drove up the lieutenant was as giddy as a high school kid after his first kiss. "Sonofabitch, what a ride." he blurted out with a big smile. "What a hell of a team you guys are," he said, looking back at the four of us. He went on to tell Mitchell that he had been wrong, and that all of us had been, well, closer to right.

Bruce walked over to him and said jokingly, "Lieutenant, sir, don't let the others see you like this." Pausing, he added, "Oh, and welcome to the Deuce Platoon."

Mitchell chuckled as Richter worked to regain his composure. Bruce stuck out his hand to the officer, and the young lieutenant responded by shaking hands with all of us.

Rob told him, "Never let anyone salute you in the field, sir. You'll probably be dead before your hand comes down."

Richter made a major 180-degree attitude adjustment for the better that day. Observing how we worked as a team impressed and changed the man. He had grown up.

After a few miles, we turned the convoy over to the next group. We refueled our jeeps and headed for home. Mitchell took a break from driving the lieutenant, handing that chore over to one of the other men. Seated in the right front of my jeep, he took out a cigarette and lit it. Then, after he had studied the four of us for a couple moments, he asked, "Okay, okay! Let's have it. What the hell did you do to that kid? You can tell me!" But we all just burst out laughing, Mitchell too.

"Mills, when you asked Richter to go along," Sarge began, "I thought you must have gotten sunstroke, but it turned out to be a great move." He concluded, "You probably saved his life today—and maybe for his whole tour of duty."

In retrospect, we just did our jobs, and the lieutenant had a ball being one of the guys for a change. Lieutenant Richter worked with us for another month or so; then he was transferred to a transportation company. We worked a couple more convoys with him. Once he even chewed out a young sergeant who was new in Nam for not listening to the "veterans." Lieutenant Leonard Richter took on a completely different demeanor; he was now part of a team—one of the guys. He learned to lead by questioning those with experience. He also gained our respect as an officer and a soldier as he learned to respect the men under him. Occasionally he asked why we did certain unorthodox things. We explained to him that our actions or reactions were usually from a "gut feeling," and that, day or night, we depended a lot on God for guidance and protection. None of us had ever been seriously hurt. I think he finally understood a little of what we were talking about.

Chapter 8
LESSONING TENSIONS

One of our duties as MPs was to provide twenty-four-hour security for the Tactical Operation Center on the II Field Force compound. This included security for the ranking officers, lieutenant colonels and above, billeted in and around the TOC facility. Pulling security for TOC put us in regular contact with our provost marshal. From the get go, he was one strange little man. He stood about 5 feet, 6 inches tall and must have weighed no more than one hundred and thirty pounds. He had a very unpleasant habit of staring at a guy's crotch when he spoke to him, seldom making eye contact. It was creepy being around the man, and we all tried to avoid him whenever possible.

The center (TOC) was really a compound within a compound. These officers did not have to endure the normal harsh living conditions the rest of us did, and for the most part, we peons didn't have a problem with that. Their quarters were single or doublewide mobile homes, forty to sixty feet long. They were equipped with hot and cold running water, full baths, air-conditioning, full-size beds, actual kitchens, and bottled water. Walking inside one of these babies was like stepping into another dimension—out of the war, with its grime, heat, and people trying to shoot you—into a real stateside home environment.

The mobile homes were flown in from Saigon by sky crane, a huge helicopter we called the praying mantis. As these units were brought in, some were temporarily stored on the vacant ground directly across from our company area. Later on they would be moved by truck or again by sky crane to the setup location. Every so often one of these mobiles would break loose from its cables and fall two thousand or three thousand feet, crashing on the ground. What a racket and mess!

Xom Demieux worked as a liaison, secretary, and interpreter for this group of officers. She also had security a clearance to go inside TOC. Some of our officers and noncoms didn't have that. Another of her duties was to oversee the civilian housekeepers. Meeting Xom (pronounced Som) was like a breath of fresh air in a country that was anything but fresh. She was strikingly attractive. She had been schooled in France and England, and spoke several languages fluently, including English, which she spoke without an accent.

I met Xom briefly just after returning from the First Infantry. Bruce, Rob, Kent, and I were working two motor patrols and relieving the security teams at TOC for lunch. We rotated through all eight positions, including the mobile homes site near where Xom usually worked. On the day we met, the tropical heat had built up to well over 110 degrees. Not a breeze stirred, especially near TOC. If there had been any air movement, it couldn't have gotten through the cluster of buildings and mobiles. It was so hot and humid that our bodies cried out for some cooler air. The majority of the civilian workers had retreated to whatever shade they could find. I stood in the blazing sun feeling as if I were roasting over a bed of coals.

"Why didn't I relieve one of the guys whose post is in the shade," I grumbled, "or perhaps at the TOC entrance where a cool breeze from the air-conditioning blows out every time the door opens?" No, without thinking I had marched right over to the hottest spot in the whole damn area—no shade, no breeze—no sense.

I had been standing near these mobile homes for about twenty minutes when I heard the door of the one nearest to my position open and close. The door was out of my line of sight, and figuring that anyone who came around the corner would probably outrank me, I prepared for a limp and sweaty snap-to-attention and salute. Much to my surprise, I heard the tinkle of ice cubes. Then a very attractive woman appeared, carrying a tray with five glasses along with a pitcher of something cool. Looking very Western, she could have passed for a young woman in the States. She wore white denim jeans and a light blue blouse. At nearly 5 feet, 5 inches tall, she was almost a foot taller than any of the Vietnamese women I had seen. Even in that heat, she was a vision of beauty and grace. We all agreed she made the best lemonade we had ever tasted.

Over a period of several weeks, Xom and I became very good friends. She had tried to help cut through some of the red tape and paperwork associated with my effort to adopt the two orphans. She lived in Saigon with her uncle and his family, but with the increased alerts and the danger of traveling alone at night, the U.S. Army had seen fit to give her the use of a much smaller trailer in the compound. She could stay there as needed, and often did so.

As we got to know each other better, I suggested a nickname for her. She was a fan of the American TV program on Armed Forces television called "Bewitched." Sam was a nickname for Samantha, the show's main character, and it was similar in sound to her real name. So I suggested "Sam" as her nickname. Xom had always liked the name Samantha. She liked my half-teasing suggestion so much that she had all new Army nametags made up with "Sam" printed in quotes between her first and last names.

Sam's father was French, and mother was half-Vietnamese and half-French. The Vietnamese had disliked the French occupation so much that, when she returned home from France, Sam took her maternal grandmother's family name and the more common dress of the country. As the hatred toward the French lessened, she switched back to her dad's name and to the Western attire. Sam was very western-minded and had frequently visited the U.S. with her father on his government trips. She had even studied for one year at a college near Boston. In looks and personality, she would have easily passed as an American girl. Sam was certainly one of the most beautiful women I had ever known.

After six months in-country, soldiers were eligible for an out-of-country leave, or R&R. Married GIs could go to Hawaii to meet their families, and single soldiers had their choice of a few different countries, including Thailand and Australia. A lot of the guys went to Bangkok, but Bruce and I decided on Sydney, and arrived there the end of March. Other than people driving on the wrong side of the road, we felt as if we had returned home to the States for a time. We were treated royally.

On our first night in the city, we walked about a mile to find a nice restaurant. Even in our civvies, our short hair and dark tans, gave us away; we were "Yanks." We had quite a meal of steaks, baked potatoes, vegetables, and other goodies. We could barely waddle out of there. We couldn't get enough fresh vegetables, fruit, and real milk.

As we finished our meal, four young ladies came over to our table and introduced themselves. For the rest of our stay, two of them were with us nearly all the time. No sex was offered or expected. It was almost as though they were the goodwill, GI-sitting ambassadors and protectors. These very attractive, young Aussie women accompanied us, mostly at night, and even visited us in our hotel room. They wouldn't let us buy them anything, and most restaurants, when we were in the company of these girls, usually wouldn't allow us to pay for our own meals.

I had looked forward to attending church services while in Sydney, as had Bruce. We couldn't find Bruce's church, so we went to mine. Several families there were quite eager to entertain us and they nearly fought over who would get to take us home. Finally a family named Stone took us under their wings for two days. They treated us to home-cooked meals and drove us on a tour of the city. That would be an easy place to visit again.

We had planned to see the world-famous Sydney Zoo. Situated on an island-like compound, the zoo was accessible only by passenger ferries. On the morning we set aside for our visit, we unintentionally overslept several hours, until nearly 11:00. We showered, dressed, and in thirty minutes we were in a cab. When we got to the ferry dock, we were surprised to see two of the Aussie girls. It almost seemed as though they had been waiting for us. There was a friendly exchange and they said something like, "What a surprise to see you boys here." Then they promptly excused themselves and left for town, and Bruce and I boarded the ferry. Arriving back at the dock about 5:00 in the evening, we joked that perhaps the girls would be waiting there for us, but they weren't.

Since we hadn't eaten breakfast and had only eaten a snack for lunch, we were starved. Fortunately, the better restaurants were within walking distance from the ferries. As we finished eating, who should show up at our table but the girls. We talked for a while and then Bruce and I decided to head back to our room to watch some TV. About an hour later, and well into an old movie, there was a soft knock on our door. Much to our surprise and amazement, there were our two "GI sitters" complete with popcorn and soft drinks.

Later as we talked and reminisced about this trip, Bruce and I came to the conclusion that the girls must have been professional hostesses employed by the two governments, possibly as a way to limit the spread of sexually transmitted disease.

Boarding the Boeing 707 back for Nam was difficult. It wouldn't have taken much convincing for us to stay in Australia. As we were headed for our seats on the plane, Bruce suddenly stopped and looked around. Feigning surprise, he said, "Damn. I don't see the girls anywhere."

Back in Nam we returned to the hot and sweaty job of MPing at the 552nd.

During our time away, our infamous colonel, the provost marshal, had written some new rules of conduct for anyone visiting the post. One part had to do with appearance. "Hair will be military with no beards. Uniforms will be clean and in good condition," or words to that effect. We were to issue citations to those men coming on post who didn't meet these criteria. Most of us agreed it was bullshit.

GIs from all branches of the service came on post for several reasons, but most came to visit the PX. A lot of these guys, soldiers and Marines, were just coming in from combat and a long stay in the bush. Their uniforms and appearance were pretty rough. We didn't feel we could automatically write a guy up for such an infraction, so we devised a series of warnings and verbal explanations of the rules, giving the men enough time to conform or to leave the post. If they were coming to visit the PX, we gave them an hour to clean up. This gave most GIs more than enough time to buy what they needed, get a cold drink, and leave the post.

Our "poor attitude," as the colonel called it, really sent him into a rage. However, if we didn't receive any lip from a soldier, we just gave warnings. Unfortunately, if they returned later still looking disheveled, we had no choice—we had to cite them. That didn't happen very often. There were only a few instances when our efforts to be fair were not appreciated.

Rob and Kent were on post patrol one day, while Bruce and I were on roving foot patrol around the TOC area. This included the officers' mobile-home park and the adjacent PX. We got a call from Sergeant Smith to watch for an overloaded jeep of GIs from a nearby bivouacked cav unit. The jeep had blown through Gate Five, nearly running down our man on duty. Then the occupants had saluted with an obscene gesture. Rob and Kent had been patrolling near the gate and were in pursuit. The errant jeep seemed to be heading toward the PX. Bruce and I each carried a sidearm and a shotgun. Bruce ran to our jeep, whipping it onto the north perimeter road to block one side, and I flagged down a kid driving a five-ton crane and had him park it across both sides of the road.

Within two minutes of receiving the call, we were in place. We stood in front of the vehicles with our shotguns ready. We heard the siren of the pursuing MP vehicle long before we could see either vehicle.

The cav jeep came in sight a quarter mile north of us as they raced around the curve near the 199th Airborne. Looking through our field glasses, we watched as they nearly rolled the jeep. We could hear the tires bawling, begging for mercy from the overload. It looked like there were ten guys in or hanging onto the vehicle. The GIs were yelling, laughing, and singing. The MP jeep was right behind them, red light flashing and siren blaring. The cavalry came to a screeching halt not more than ten feet from us. They seemed almost hysterical; three of them were laughing so hard that they fell off the jeep and rolled around on the ground. It was hard to be angry with them.

Unfortunately, Kent and Rob were not in a forgiving mood. Besides giving the uncomplimentary salute at the gate and having made the MP there dive out of the way, the cav driver had forced Kent and Rob off into a ditch.

Without warning, Rob grabbed my shotgun, pumped a round into the chamber, flipped off the safety, and fired one round into the air. The Stevens was the loudest personal weapon I had ever heard. Tossing it back to me, he ordered the other soldiers to dismount from their jeep and to form a line along the side of the road, and produce their IDs. The fired round had caught everyone a bit off guard, and everyone's attention was riveted on Rob.

In the nearly seven months I had known Rob, I had found him to be a hard-working, fun-loving, young man. I had seen him scared in combat, but I had never seen him flinch. He always did his job well, and seldom used foul language. Now he was practicing several new dialects, and I realized that until that moment I hadn't seen him really angry. Right then he was five notches hotter than furious, and close to blowing. Before he could get himself into deep trouble, Bruce and I thought we'd better help him out. Kent took Rob by the arm and walked off to the canteen trailer for a cold drink while Bruce and I sorted things out.

A young lieutenant and a corporal were in charge of the cav group. Both were just nineteen. Earlier that morning they had escaped an ambush unscathed after several days of heated combat. From what they described, it sounded like a miracle that no one had gotten so much as a scratch. They had pulled out of their fire area about 0200, arriving in Long Binh Province not more than an hour before our meeting. They were bivouacked a mile west of the tower and Gate Five. As it turned out, they weren't even sure where they were because they had lost their maps.

The young lieutenant and the rest of his command explained that they were "so damn happy to be alive and to see an American military post," they had just plain lost it.

We found several cans of 3.5 beer (the Army brew) and a few empties in their jeep, but the soldiers weren't drunk—not on GI beer—they were just happy.

Sergeant Mitchell was not on duty that morning, but he had been in the PX. Hearing the round from the Stevens, he hurried out to see what was going on and hurried over. Bruce and I decided to write up both the lieutenant and the corporal for failing to make a gate stop, having an overloaded vehicle, speeding, and not being in control of their men. We chose not to report about the beer, the recklessness, or the finger saluting. They were surprised we went so easy on them.

While we were writing their citations, one in the group commented about how cushy we had it at a headquarters company, and how we probably never had to face a real firefight.

Mitchell was not in uniform, but he had his sarge's growl working when he introduced himself to the rest of the group. Then he explained, "The man on the gate and these four men served with the First Infantry in a forward observation outpost on the Cambodian border."

They seemed impressed. Mitchell also told them about how we had hit a mine and about the firefight that followed. We couldn't hear all that was being said since we had moved a few yards off to finish up with the corporal and the lieutenant, but the man who made the comment about our work being cushy came over and told his lieutenant what Mitchell had said.

Looking at Bruce and me, the young officer asked, "Is that true?"

We nodded and said, "Yes, sir."

The corporal stuffed his ticket in his pocket and moved the jeep off the road into the PX parking area. Then he did something unexpected and totally on his own. He marched (and I mean marched) his men over to where Rob and Kent were sitting. Then to a man, they all apologized, including their lieutenant. Then the corporal told his men, "No one will go into the PX until we do the same with the MP on the gate." And they did.

Another situation involved some visiting leathernecks from up north. They were not a happy group of Marines. We had very little contact with Marines since few were stationed in or around the II Field Force area. We had a great deal of respect and admiration for the hellish combat most of them had been through, but when they were off duty and visiting other posts, there always seemed to be fights.

On this particular day, Bruce, Rob, and I were on a three-man motor patrol and had just finished relieving the tower guard for noon chow. Even though it was the start of the Vietnamese autumn, it was sweltering. On our way back to our main gate, we observed a Marine Corps deuce-and-a-half right in front of us. We noticed the left rear tire was flat. We stopped them intending only to alert them about the tire, as it was almost impossible to hear or feel a rear-flat from inside one of these vehicles until the casing started to come apart. There were about twenty or so Marines in the back. Everyone was pretty sullen.

There was none of the usual talking or joking around about MPs—not even the expected middle finger or name-calling.

The truck had no doors, and a canvas top over the cab. Bruce approached the driver's side and, stepping up on the foot peg and grabbing the cab-handle, he noticed an officer sitting on the right. Bruce didn't have a hand free to salute, but he did offer the greeting, "Good afternoon, sir; Sergeant." There was no response from either.

Addressing the driver Bruce explained, "We won't hold you up, but we wanted to make you aware of the flat tire, left side rear."

The three were not pleased we stopped them—an attitude that quickly spread to everyone riding in the back. Everyone was dirty with uniforms that were badly tattered. Because of the group's surly attitude, Rob and Bruce wanted to check the vehicle's authorization papers and conduct a safety inspection.

I took them off to the side and said, "Hey, guys. We don't know what they've been through or what they're coming from. And even with their bad manners they still haven't done anything wrong." Then I added," And besides, it's hotter than hell out here. Do you really want to sit here and do the paper-work?"

They shook their heads slowly as they considered what I had said. I walked around the truck to the passenger side, saluted the captain, and said, "Good afternoon, sir. Thank you for stopping. You're free to proceed," and waited for what seemed like an eternity for the officer to return the salute. Then I went back to my place behind the wheel of the jeep and drove away, leaving them sitting along the side of the road.

Entering our gate, we stopped momentarily at our company office and checked in with the desk sergeant. Then we went to our hootch where we picked up some cold pop along with our mail and headed to the canteen for a our lunch before we returned to work.

While eating, I heard the familiar flapping sound of a flat tire. At first I didn't make the connection. But who should drive up but the Marines. "I sure never expected to see these guys again," I muttered.

Their captain, who was probably in his mid-twenties, acted like a Marine, but he took it too far. He was rude to all Army personnel regardless of rank and only showed a bare tolerance to officers who had more on the collar than his railroad tracks.

Carrying their M-16s, the Marines climbed off the truck and headed for the front door of the PX. Seeing this, we quickly left our food and drinks and ran headlong to cut them off. As we ran, we asked them repeatedly to stop, but they ignored us. We got to the main entrance just a couple of steps ahead of them.

We saluted the captain, saying, "Good afternoon again, sir," and waited for him to return our salute. He just stared at us with a slight smirk on his face. After nearly a minute of this game, I said to him, "Sir, it's too damn hot for this. We are willing to render all military courtesy to you, and we expect no less from a Marine Corps officer." Slowly and grudgingly he brought up his hand and saluted us.

Bruce must have been overcooked by the sun, and said, "I've had enough of this strutting peacock." He and Rob were about ready to off-load their entire citation books on this man, and his troops. Again I was able to restrain them.

"Sir," I began, "I must inform you that weapons are not allowed in the PX." I then pointed to the notice on the door signed by the provost. I suggested that they place all their weapons in their vehicle, leaving one man to stand guard for a few minutes. Saying nothing, the captain tried to push his way through. I grabbed his arm and, because he was slightly off balance, I was able to move him a few yards away from his men. He did not take kindly to this maneuver.

Up till then, he had refused to speak to us. Only the driver and sergeant had spoken to us out on the highway. The captain now made it plain he intended to alter my sex and the rest of my anatomy, and he told me to get my hands off of him, which I had already done. At this point I was getting pissed too.

Looking him in the eye, I said, "Sir, we really don't wish to slow you up. But first you need to know that my MOS (Military Occupation Service) of 95 Bravo-20 (Military Police) is in no way voluntary. My being here is not voluntary." He was plainly angry, but I continued, "But understand this, sir. I do take my work very seriously, just as you do yours. If you don't comply with this order, I will write you and your men up for failure to follow general orders and the basic rules of conduct on this post. That will also include unkempt uniforms, lack of haircuts, and unauthorized beards."

He still stood there glaring at me.

I continued, "Sir, that's all bullshit. You know it, and we know it. It's unfair to treat anyone coming out of combat that way."

He started to relax a little, as I continued, "I can give you an hour and a half to clear the post." He stiffened slightly again, but I put my hand on his arm (which was a no-no). "That will still give you and your men more than enough time to shop the PX, get a burger, or go to one of the clubs for a sandwich and a beer and to have that flat tire changed at our post motor pool."

Right then his sergeant walked over, holding a copy of the post's new standing orders about clean fatigues, haircuts, etc. In a near whisper, he addressed his captain, "Jerry, sir. These guys really are bending the rules for us. Hell, sir, they could get busted for this." The captain took a look at the rules, and the sergeant added, "I was just talking to a sergeant from one of the Army infantry companies. He said the MPs on this post really go out of their way—even getting into trouble themselves—just to be fair to all GIs."

The captain turned around, looked at his men, and said to the sergeant, "Have the weapons placed in the truck and put Simpson on watch. Relieve him in fifteen minutes."

The sergeant hollered, "All right, you mud-balls. You heard the CO and these coppers. Let's get it done." And they did, in double time! A man stayed with the truck, and we pointed out where he could get the tire repaired. The captain was still wearing his sidearm; as he reached down to take it off, Rob told him, "Sir, officers and NCOs are allowed their sidearms." The captain left it on, saying nothing.

We recovered what was left of our lunches and went back on patrol. A little over two hours later, the Marines exited through our gate. The tire job took a while longer than expected, but everyone seemed to be in a much better mood and some of them waved and joked, even calling us a few uncomplimentary names. It felt good to see them acting normally, and we saved ourselves one hell of a lot of paperwork. Returning our salute, the captain hollered, "Good luck, Army!" You could have knocked us over with a slow breeze.

A few days later we did have to write up a Marine lieutenant for being drunk and for striking an Army sergeant. He was locked up overnight. The sergeant chose not to press charges, so the next morning we delivered the lieutenant back to his company and commanding officer. His CO was the captain we had met a few days earlier. As we left there bivouacked, I think the lieutenant was wishing he'd gone into the Navy.

Late one night we were in the company club watching a movie when we heard a series of short bursts of automatic weapon fire. Reportedly, these rounds, although not aimed at our compound, originated near the ice plant and Widow's Village across the highway. A few moments later, Mitchell came running into the club and spotted Bruce and me. He said, "Find your three friends. I need the five of you to get over to the village and see what's going on." Looking around, he finished with, "Take my jeep. It's parked near the orderly room."

Bruce went after the jeep, and I headed for our hootch where Paul and

Kent had been sleeping. Hearing the shooting, they were slightly awake. I hollered, "Hit the floor, we're going calling."

Bruce slid the jeep to a halt at our front door and came in to change into pants and boots, as I was doing. Cut-offs and sandals are not ideal attire for this kind of work. In four minutes, we were dressed and in the jeep along with an M-60 and our other weapons. I took the wheel and, locking into four-wheel drive, started for the gate. Rob met us at the gate, and as he jumped into the back said, "Mitchell said to tell ya, he'd have some backup for us soon." Looking at our gear and his own weapons we'd loaded, Rob asked, "Would someone please tell me where we're going?" As soon as Bruce finished tying his boots, he gave Rob a quick rundown.

Making a hard right onto the highway, we headed for the dirt access road into the village, perhaps a hundred yards west of the gate.

As we approached the village, I felt a chill go through my body; I think we all did. Once inside the village I turned off the headlights, using the blackout lights instead. Leaning over toward Bruce, I asked quietly, "Did anyone say where we were to meet the backup?"

He said quietly, "No," then snickered, "it's top secret."

I shifted into first gear, and we crawled forward, the engine turning just above idle. Our blackout lamps were useless, except perhaps as targets, so I switched them off as well. I was quietly humming a favorite hymn, and someone else was softly saying a prayer. We didn't go on any assignments alone.

It was so dark we couldn't even see our hands in front of our noses. Bruce whispered for me to stop, and as I did, I could hear the safeties being switched off on all the weapons.

Rob placed my rifle next to the gearshift and said softly, "Locked, loaded, off safe, at your right knee."

Bruce was on the radio asking the desk where we were to meet the rest of the group. It was hard to make out what was being said, but what we did hear did not give any of us that warm, fuzzy feeling.

"No help's coming," Bruce whispered.

"Why not?" came a chorus of four, in not quite a whisper.

"They got lost," was the answer.

"What the hell does that mean?" someone asked. We weren't sure if the rest of the squad was lost on post, in the village, or in the latrine. A few minutes later I heard a voice humming another old familiar hymn.

Our eyes, still straining to see anything, were now adjusting to the dark, but with no moonlight and just stars, we still couldn't see a thing.

Bruce had me make a turn to the right, thinking there was a road there, but we ended up bouncing through an open field. Still in first gear we crept along. Suddenly there was a big bump and an even more sudden stop. The jeep's front wheels dropped into what must have been a small drainage ditch, nearly catapulting the three in the rear seat out of the vehicle.

"Is everyone all right?" I asked in a whisper.

The jeep was stuck fast; and three voices from the rear seat all said, "Hey, nice going, Mills."

"Well, at least I didn't shoot it this time," I replied. Mumbling now to myself, I added softly "Gee, I haven't shot a jeep in over four months."

Bruce leaned over and said, "They're out of season, anyway."

All this bantering helped to ease the fear and tension that had increased when we learned that no backup was coming. No backup was pretty serious stuff.

Bruce notified the desk that we were stuck. He was told to either hold on until morning or start walking back right then. We had a pretty good idea of where we were, as we could see the compound lights not more than two hundred yards to the north. But because it was pitch-black, we decided to stay put. All five of us got out of the jeep and sat on the ground. We concluded that if any trouble were to come, it would be from the opposite direction from the compound lights. We formed a semicircle with our shoulders together and the left rear tire our resting point. Facing out from half circle and our rifles across our laps, we radioed the desk that we were staying put.

There was no doubt about it: we were brave; we were heroes; we were stupid and scared shitless! Our bodies shook slightly from the adrenaline. Fear has a tendency to alert all your senses, but my heart was already beating so loudly I couldn't hear a thing for about twenty minutes. My eyes were opened so wide they hurt.

We spoke in whispers as we talked and told jokes (it's really hard to laugh in a whisper). We took turns sleeping, two at a time. I guessed it was about 3:00 in the morning when my turn came. I put my head down on my knees and was instantly asleep. We had to keep the radio on, but quit using it because the handset squawked every time we keyed it. We even covered the lighted dial so as not give our position away.

I was asleep all right—it took three good jabs in my ribs to wake me up. "What's up?" I mumbled.

Rob whispered, "Just listen." For a few seconds, I didn't hear anything. Then, for a short moment, I thought I could hear muffled voices.

"Did you hear that?" someone else asked.

I answered in the affirmative, but I couldn't be sure. Then, a few seconds later, came another sound—much closer. These were definitely voices; Vietnamese voices.

Kent suggested we do a quick "free fire" or "mad minute." This meant laying down a somewhat controlled area of weapon fire. No target, just shooting.

That little voice inside me said to wait, and I said, "You know, we're not sure who the hell is out there. We have less than an hour until dawn and fifteen minutes past that before we can see. I sure don't want to kill some old mamasan or kid going pee."

It was really hard to say all that in a whisper, but we agreed to hold our fire. Most combat units in this situation would have opened fire, not knowing who or what was out there. That was the longest hour and fifteen minutes I have ever spent in prayer. My senses were strained, just trying to hear, see, or smell, to be able to detect anything. The sky began to turn purple as the horizon beyond the compound offered a hint of the coming day.

"All right, let's get up slowly," I said in a loud whisper. "Do a couple of deep-knee bends to loosen up."

We took a few deep breaths then started walking in a low crouch, moving in the direction of the voices. After about eighty yards we came upon a group of about fifteen refugees—a half dozen young kids, parents, and grandparents. At first we thought we had found the source of the voices, but an old mama-san held up her hand as a quiet sign and pointed on ahead.

In another fifty yards, we came upon a second group. These were not refugees; these were Victor Charlies, nine of them, and they were sound asleep. We quietly made a circle around them, and then I fired two short bursts into the morning sky from my M-14. (I had wanted to do that all night.) Startled, they bolted upright. Without saying a word, they slowly placed their hands on top of their heads as Paul and Kent collected their weapons. Then we searched each one, collecting pistols, knives, and a few grenades. As we marched the VC back to our jeep I saw that it was parked directly in line with both groups. If we had fired during the night, we would surely have hit the family and perhaps missed the VC all together.

We could hear the radio crackle from several yards off as the base tried calling us. "X-ray 6, this is Hand Cuff. Over."

"Phone's ringing, honey," cracked Kent.

As the others kept a close watch on our unfriendlies, I started the jeep and, with a whole lot of throttle, backed it out of the trench. Rob picked up the handset and called in.

"Handcuff, Handcuff. This is X-ray 6. Over."

They answered quickly, and we explained our situation and told them we were bringing in nine VC. As we approached the highway, three jeeps (one of ours and two from G-2) met us. A master sergeant, two captains, and a major got out of their jeeps to check out our find. They couldn't believe it! Ten minutes later another jeep arrived. Xom Demieux had been brought in to assist with preliminary interrogation. Even at 5:00 a.m., she was beautiful. At 5:15 we left the captive VCs with the G-2 contingency and our long-lost backup and returned to the company area. We were beat.

Back in the hootch Sergeant Mitchell stopped in as we got ready for bed. "Sorry about the backup. The best we could muster was placing some units along the highway."

Jokingly, I asked, "Can we put in for overtime?" and we all managed a short chuckle.

We had been scheduled to go on duty in an hour, but we hit the lights-out button in our brains. We'd already been replaced on the duty roster. As he turned to leave Sarge said, "A helluva job, guys . . . good work!"

A few nights later, Bruce and I were both on patrol working with green replacements, giving them a little on-the-job training. I liked working with the new men because I didn't have to do so much of the paperwork and driving, but Bruce hated it and wouldn't let the new guys drive or do much except sit.

About midnight, the patrols stopped at the bunker near our main gate to harass Rob and Paul a little, since they both had new people. Then we walked over to get some coffee from the mess hall (the only safe thing there we could ingest). As we were standing around drinking our coffee and talking, a jeep from the 720th MP stopped outside the gate. The gate guard hollered, "Hey, Mills, these guys wanna talk to you and Bruce." With the exception of ours, all the gates were closed and locked at dusk. This was the only after-dark access to the compound.

A sergeant from the 720th had stopped outside our gate and asked, "Are you Mills?" I answered in the affirmative. "Our patrols spotted jeeps of yours going down into Little Hanoi village a half hour ago. It's off-limits, ya know."

The village in question was a suspected Viet Cong meeting place, filtering men, weapons, and food in and out of the area. It was partially visible from the tower.

The sergeant continued, "BJ reported that one of your men is up there now trying to break into a house of a young Vietnamese woman." the sergeant added. "BJ's already up there waiting with the other patrol. We thought you guys might want to handle this one yourselves. Should I report it to your desk sergeant or DO?"

If at all possible, each unit tried to keep their dirty laundry contained within their own company. I thanked the sergeant then ran to the "jail" to discuss this with Sergeant Smith, our Desk Sergeant. Mitchell was supervising patrols in Bien Hoa and would be unavailable for over an hour.

Smith gave me the go-ahead, explaining, "Mills, I'm shorthanded. Take Rob and Paul off bunker duty and leave the new men in their places. Go! Knock on it." Then he yelled as I left the building, "Use your friends from the 720th as backup."

"Roger," I hollered back.

Until then there had been no report of any of our jeeps missing, and it was embarrassing to have another MP unit telling us about it. We didn't have any idea who would be dumb enough to pull such a stunt. These were serious infractions: being in a known off-limits area, the misuse of a government vehicle and trying to break into a house. All these offenses were court-martial offences—if the soldier lived through the night.

Not wanting to chance the radio, I asked our radioman to contact the men in the tower via field phone. We asked them to look at Little Hanoi through the nightscope to see if they could detect any movement and to signal us by a light as we drove by. As we passed by the tower, one of the guys made a series of circular motions with a flashlight, indicating "all clear." A few minutes later we arrived. BJ and his two patrols were waiting for us.

We had eight men; the four of us from the 552nd and four from the 720th as backup. All four vehicles were equipped with M-60s. We four carried our M-14s and sidearms. Just as BJ and one of his men pointed out our stolen jeep, we heard some banging and a loud voice telling a girl to come out. After listening for a few seconds, we made out faint Vietnamese voices saying "GI, go 'way, go 'way."

We looked at each other and said in unison, "Sergeant Green."

Bruce asked BJ and his group to tune one of their radios to our frequency so we could talk to them directly. If things went wrong, they could call our company for help. This was unorthodox, but what the hell.

"Lock and load, safeties off," I said softly, and a series of mechanical clicks followed. We drove down the small trail-like road. After a few yards of trying to see with the blackout convoy lights, I said, "Screw this, I'm no friggin' owl!" and I switched on the headlights just in time to be surprised by a water buffalo crossing right in front of us.

Paul was on the machine gun in Bruce's jeep, and Rob was on the one in mine. Slowly passing the parked jeep, we could see a rifle on the front seat. We were only fifty yards from the highway, but it felt like miles. Fear dragged us down like emotional quicksand.

As we got closer, we could almost make out Sarge's slurred language. Paul and Rob stayed ready on the M-60s while Bruce and I left our vehicles and proceeded on foot. Approaching the village, we could see a row of small, one-room, stucco buildings with uneven, tar paper roofs. They were connected in a long line fronting the main street. Doors in back opened into an alley. The main street was only ten feet wide; it went at a slight left angle for several yards, making it difficult to see beyond the headlights of the jeeps. We turned on our flashlights, shoulder-strapped our rifles, and pulled out our sidearms. Then Bruce heard a faint little voice from the darkness calling us by name.

Bruce touched my arm and whispered, "Hold on, Vic. Someone's calling us." I couldn't hear anything but my breathing. My heart sounded like a snare drum.

Bruce swung his light to the right, and there stood Li and her older sister Lin in the doorway motioning for us to come in. Even though we knew these girls, we approached with extreme caution. Behind them stood a man whom the girls introduced as their uncle. Moving closer, we recognized him as well. He was one of the locals who had helped rebuild the temple for the kids. In Vietnam we were never sure, especially at night, whose side anyone was on. The man told us that the GI was at their back door and that the more the man drank, the more confused he was about what house he wanted.

We flashed our lights around the room and carefully but quickly crossed to the door on the opposite wall. With the help of the small, outside, overhead light strung between the buildings, I could make out Master Sergeant Green through the window sash. Lin said softly, but firmly, "VC come. Go fast." Nothing like a little incentive. As I threw open the door, Sarge fell in, flat on his face. While he raged on, Bruce grabbed one sweaty armpit and I grabbed the other, and as fast as we could, we half-dragged, half-carried his six-foot, two-inch frame to the jeeps. Sarge yelled and cussed at us all the way. Placing his hands behind him we handcuffed him and loaded him on the floor in the back of Bruce's vehicle. We had left the engines running, so Bruce turned his jeep around. I had left mine facing the opposite direction. As we started back toward the highway, Bruce drove forward and I was in reverse. That way we could maintain good visibility with our headlights pointing toward the town and the road. We stopped where Green had parked the other jeep. After gagging Green, Bruce and I got out while the others stayed on the machine guns. Flashlights in hand, we quickly checked over the vehicle for possible booby traps—a grenade tied to the inside of the gas tank or under the pedals. We found nothing. I turned on the ignition and kicked the starter. With a whir, it was running.

Turning to Bruce, I said, "Let's get the hell out of here."

Rob answered "Amen" as he jumped from the machine gun into the driver's seat of his jeep. We slammed all three jeeps into four-wheel drive and got out of there as fast as those seventy-five ponies could move them. At the highway, I asked one of the other MPs to sit in the rear seat of Bruce's jeep to keep Sergeant Green stable. We made a new speed record and arrived at the gate and the jail in less than eight minutes. The whole task took only half an hour, but man, what pressure.

Bruce commented dryly, "I'd rather go back to the First Infantry outpost than go through this again." We were all in agreement.

For some time Green had been telling everyone how "short" he was. He would be heading for home and retirement in a couple of months after nearly thirty years of service. He had been acting strangely, actually friendly, with everyone. He even said he was sorry about sending us out to Di-An.

Both Mitchell and the CO returned about the time we finished our reports. Captain Gordon walked through on his way to his quarters and asked why Green was locked up. After Smith explained the situation, the CO asked if it could be written up in a manner to avoid a court-martial. Smith answered that this would be up to the arresting MPs, but since there would be a preliminary report of the infractions on file with the 720th, things would be a little more complicated.

Master Sergeant Green did have a court-martial: he lost some rank, paid a fairly big fine, and caused a lot of embarrassment for himself and his family. At one time, Sergeant Green may have been a good soldier (he had started in the Marine Corps prior to WWII). But, like the first sergeant, he was an extremely mean individual: mean to the men in his command as well as to the nationals. If you didn't play by his rules, you were somehow given an exit to other duties—usually something like door gunner on a chopper. This attitude was prevalent throughout our immediate chain of command, right up to the provost marshal.

During my fifteen months in Nam, I knew of several good young men who would have done practically anything to transfer out of the unit. Some did and were killed or permanently injured as a result of being sent into a different combat role unprepared. They had been sent to combat as cannon fodder!

Chapter 9
Bar Fights and Water Buffalo

Some time after the Tet offensive, personnel at TOC in Bien Hoa went through channels and requested the five of us by name. Once again, we were assigned to bolster their security. The Air Force security personnel needed to free up some manpower for their perimeter. All of us who had been on the original detail were pleased and surprised that TOC management had specifically asked for us. A few of the guys who had served at TOC with us before had rotated home, but most of us were still available. Three more men to the detail and we went to work from 6 o'clock in the evening to 6 in the morning.

Much of the time it was just plain boring. The only excitement was traveling to and from TOC. However, something did come from our serving again at Bien Hoa. The powers that be liked our work so much they recommended three of us for a special assignment. We were led to believe it would be more mentally stimulating than simple guard duty or patrol. We were sent to Saigon to play detective.

Involvement in the black market by U.S. military personnel, as well as by U.S. civilian workers, had increased many-fold since Tet. The three of us were to get a much closer look at how the black market operated—from the inside. Our assignment involved investigating, gathering evidence, assisting with arrests, and providing security.

Through our provost marshal's office at II Field Force and the Saigon office, Bruce, Dave, and I were temporarily assigned to the Criminal Investigation Division (CID) in Saigon.

Dave was the new guy in our little group. We didn't find him; he found us. He had worked on patrols and guard duty with several of the 552nd regulars. He soon found that these partners were undependable. Dave had also noticed that we were singled out for many of the "dirty-end-of-the-stick" details that Top came up with. He realized that even though some of our assignments were dangerous we always returned. He had also seen that if neither Mitchell nor Smith was around, we usually had to go without backup. After working with our TDY group from the Deuce Platoon, he decided that it was safer to be with any of us than with anyone else in the company.

The drive to Saigon went smoothly. Prior to the Tet offensive, this had been a beautiful city. After the offensive, its latent charm seemed somehow bruised. It was a port city, a kind of diamond in the rough.

The jeep we used carried bogus markings on its bumpers. We were told to report to someone who would be waiting for us at the USO club. Until this point, we had been told only enough to confuse the hell out of us; our assignment was "to act as security" for a nonexistent supply company.

When we arrived in Saigon, we stopped at the USO club as instructed. Taking our gear and weapons inside, we stretched out in some recliners to wait for our contact. Half-reclining in my chair, I caught a glimpse of one of the girls working there. She looked very familiar, and I guess she thought she knew us too, because she kept shooting glances our way from the far side of the room while she worked. The club was housed in what was probably a former warehouse. It was very large. There were several other GIs in the building that day, and all of the hostesses were busy visiting and serving them cold pop and food.

I nudged one of Bruce's boots with mine. When one of his eyelids finally opened, I motioned toward the girl and said, "Don't we know her?" He agreed that she did look familiar, but he couldn't place where we had met her.

In a few minutes, the girl walked over to us, and it hit Bruce and me at the same time. "The USO club out near Di-An," we both said. She was one of the seven girls we had met on our way out and again on our return trip nearly three months later. Her name was Gail. She was a beautiful, black woman, tall and slender. She looked to me like a young Lena Horne. It had been almost four months since our last visit, and we were surprised that she recognized us.

"Let me get you something to eat. Then we can sit and talk a while," she suggested. "Hamburgers all around?"

We all agreed, and in a short time she brought us a tray full of hamburgers, fries, and cold drinks. We asked how she was able to remember us from all the GIs.

As she served us, she said, "When you are as scared as we were, you don't easily forget those who were able to take some of that terror away and make you feel really safe, even just for a few hours." Swiping a few fries she added, "And without trying to take advantage of us either, which you guys probably could have done." She leaned over and gave Bruce and me a big kiss and said, "That's for all the girls, but since they're not here, it's mostly from me."

Dave had been asleep, but he woke up when he smelled the burgers. He got to meet Gail, but he didn't get a kiss.

As we ate, Gail pulled up a chair and told us, "Most of us from Di-An were sent to Saigon just before Christmas, but after the VC attacked, many of the girls in our group requested to go home. I stayed, and so did two others."

She helped herself to more fries and said, "I can't blame the others for wanting to go home. I wanted to leave pretty badly too."

"With all the fighting, why didn't you?" I asked.

"I have a brother here," she began. "And we can visit every few days. He's in the Navy, stationed at the port, driving a truck."

After we finished eating, Gail cleared the table and disappeared into the kitchen for a few minutes. Returning quickly, she had a perturbed look on her face like a mother might have when speaking to her young irascible children. "What mischief have you two been up to?" she demanded with a twinkle in her eye. "There are two men at the front door asking for you."

We thanked her for the burgers and told her how good it had been to see her again. She gave the three of us a goodbye hug saying, "Be careful, and God bless you!"

The two men were from the CID. We followed them to a building downtown where we were interviewed and briefed. From the briefing we learned that we were expected to handle some preliminary investigations, which was great. Here was an opportunity to put into practice more of our MP training. Unfortunately, our work in the city turned out to be about as exciting as watching rust form. We did get to follow a few suspects and make a few arrests, but for the most part we did a lot of waiting and report writing.

Most of the time we wore civvies. These clothes were issued to us since we hadn't brought any with us. One of our last jobs was to tail a container truck from the docks. We staked out the gate, spotted the truck, and began to follow it heading south out of Saigon. Bruce and I were driving a civilian copy of a Jeep Wagoneer, while Dave and two other men used the smaller M-151 jeep.

This assignment was really comical. If the term "dumb as dirt" were listed in a dictionary, the two enlisted men we were tailing would have been pictured as the definition. They had chosen a gem of a vehicle: a bright orange tractor truck pulling a flatbed trailer with a red container on board. They also had a Vietnamese national sitting with them.

They turned onto what appeared to be a seldom-used dirt road. This led to a large ocean inlet and an old abandoned wharf of empty warehouses.

When the truck stopped, we parked off the road in some high grass about a hundred yards away. Dave stayed behind with the vehicles to monitor the radio. This put him in a good position to drive up quickly as backup, or to help with any prisoners we might take. The rest of us took our weapons and a walkie-talkie and pushed our way through the trees and underbrush. This was good cover. Five minutes after we were in place, a military car approached. Dave alerted us by radio.

When the car stopped, three Army officers got out. Right then two more officers appeared from an old building on the wharf. All five converged at the rear of the truck where the driver and his two cohorts waited. The highest-ranking officer was a major. Using bolt cutters on the lock, he swung open the doors of the container. Then all but the Vietnamese man climbed into the box to look over their booty. The Vietnamese government man quickly reached inside his loose shirt and pulled out his .38 revolver, giving us the high sign. We emerged from the foliage on the double, surprising our quarry. We placed all of the men in custody, and called for more back up.

The ride back to town was interesting. Even though it was only a short distance, I had a ball driving the tractor-trailer rig back to headquarters. Bruce drove the staff car, and Dave drove two of the prisoners and our agent in the Wagoneer. The others rode in the little jeep. Later, Bruce said that it was rather funny because the major, whom we had handcuffed, was nearly in tears. He kept insisting he was just trying to help, but no one bought his story, including those at his court-martial.

From time to time, we also helped inspect duffel bags and packages that GIs were sending home, usually just before they rotated back to the States. The rules stated clearly what you could and could not send home. Firearms and drugs were on the list of no-nos. Some GIs even tried to mail home rocket launchers. It was amazing what we found, and what ingenious tricks were used for hiding the contraband. In spite of our vigilance, some illegal equipment and drugs did make it back to the States.

Our assignment in Saigon was cut short, and we were quite happy about it. Before we left, one of the men in charge called us into his office and told us, "You have done a great job during your short time here. We'd like to have you stay on. I can get promotions for you as well as a nicer place to live." This guy was so cloak-and-dagger, we never knew whether to salute or kneel to him. His rank was "top secret."

"We've talked it over and well, sir, it's not the challenge we had hoped it would be," I explained.

Command there gave us "a job well done" just the same. My two friends shared my attitude and sentiments: "Just give us a convoy, a checkpoint, a bar fight, or a vehicle accident to investigate any time!"

On the morning we departed Saigon, we dropped in at the USO club where we had been invited for breakfast. Afterwards we said goodbye to Gail and the other girls. They did a great job in a rough place—true ladies, every one of them. We also had the pleasure of meeting Gail's brother, Lucas, before we left. He seemed like a great guy.

Outside of Saigon we came upon a traffic accident involving some GIs and Vietnamese nationals. We assisted with traffic control and administered first aid, then reported the accident by radio to one of the MP companies in Saigon.

By noon, we were back at the 552nd. We checked in at the orderly room to catch up on any changed or newly posted orders that might have come through during our absence and to pick up our mail. Our new assignment was waiting—convoy duty. After reading our mail and opening our care packages, we met with Smitty and the others who would be working the convoy. We were going back to visit Di-An for a day. Army Intelligence had reported some increased VC activity in that region since Tet. This assignment was going to be a joint one with the First Infantry MPs, some old friends from the Deuce Platoon. It would be great to see them again.

The rendezvous point was about ten miles southeast of our compound. Once there, we would take over the MP duties. The plan was for us to take the convoy to the junction at Di-An and meet up with the First Infantry MPs.

We turned in early since we would be heading out the gate by 4:30 a.m. Fortunately, our mess sergeant was on R&R, and there was a real mess sergeant filling in. It was actually safe to eat in the mess hall—a great change, even for a few short days. Sarge was a cooking and cleaning fool. He threatened to get rid of all the Asian help if they didn't do the job to his satisfaction. That arrangement would have been fine with most of us. The locals were given one day to get things right. He let four of them go for not washing their hands before they handled food or utensils.

At 3:15 a.m. the mess sergeant woke up only those men who had convoy duty. As he walked past our bunks, he said simply, "I have *real* eggs, *real* ham and fried potatoes, along with *real* coffee made with *real* water that I stole from another mess. I also have some fresh cereal and *real* milk." And as he walked out the back door, he finished with, "Chow in fifteen minutes." Squinting at my watch, I could barely distinguish the big hand from the little hand, but they seemed to be indicating that it was just past 3:18. That's early in anyone's Army. We fudged for ten more minutes, but the allure of real food was just too good to pass up.

Breakfast was as promised; there was even some fresh bacon, probably pilfered from one of the other mess halls on the compound. The mess sergeant must have been related to Norman, our supply sergeant, for he did whatever it took to do the job right.

We exited the compound on time. There were twelve men, five gun jeeps, and one regular jeep. Sergeant Smith was taking his turn as supervisor. With the exception of Smith and his driver, all of us were veterans of other road-work. Only a few had the long stay with First Infantry Division MPs.

With gas tanks and "jerry" cans full, we were under way. Even though I was driving one of the jeeps, I found it hard to shake the sleepies, especially after a big breakfast. Bruce had to talk to me to keep me awake, but he was having the same problem. It was still dark out with just a hint of color on the eastern horizon.

To help our maneuverability, Smith told us to keep our speed at thirty miles an hour. At that rate we would reach the rendezvous point within a few minutes and still be early. Arriving fifteen minutes ahead of schedule, we found the convoy waiting for us.

As one of the jeeps from Saigon MPs was driving off, the driver hollered, "Hey, Smitty, watch your ass. You've got a 'gung-ho' lieutenant in charge of that convoy!"

Smith waved and quickly found the lieutenant. Besides being an arrogant SOB, the young officer was determined to make a name for himself by getting the convoy to our destination in the least time possible, standard regs be damned. In order for the other units along the way to offer security and supplies, routing and scheduling were critical.

Smith reminded the lieutenant, "You know, sir, it's important to maintain the correct speed and to follow the schedule, and not to be too early at check-points. That could be dangerous." His warning fell on deaf ears and a conti-nent-sized ego. Smith turned and talked to us about the best way to proceed so that we could stay on schedule.

"Hey, Smitty, don't you have the Deuce frequency?" I asked.
Smitty nodded.

Bruce suggested, "Call 'em. You'll probably be able to get a message to their lieutenant or sergeant about this hotshot. Let them know that he is either going to have us arriving early at every CP (checkpoint) or broken down along the way."

We had slipped a couple of thermos bottles of hot coffee into the jeep. As Smith sipped his coffee, he wrote out a short message. Handing it to his driver, he said, "Send this message to the First Infantry. Here's their call sign." Then, walking over to my vehicle, Smith picked up the mike to our radio and called back to the 552nd. Mitchell was on the desk, and Smith reported this new twist.

As it turned out, notifying command of the changes in our timetables saved the day. Sergeant Mitchell worked through channels to reorganize times of checkpoint arrivals. This strategy worked just fine, since neither Smith nor a sergeant from the transportation company could make the lieutenant understand the importance of a schedule.

The lieutenant was hell-bent on breaking speed records and pressed everyone to drive faster. The demolition team working with us slowed things down some when they checked bridges, culverts, and suspicious patches of roadway. Our designated speed was supposed to be twenty miles per hour, but whenever possible the lieutenant urged the big rigs to go much, much faster. Smith kept working to keep the lieutenant contained and constantly reminded him of the standing orders, which really pissed off the young officer.

One of our jeeps broke down and had to be towed behind a truck, leaving Bruce, Rob, Paul, and me to work out of one jeep. Our group sometimes needed to run a few miles ahead of the column to secure a bridge and to check for mines. At one point, we followed our local "bomb-squad" up the highway about three miles so they could check out a small bridge. Half a mile before the bridge, we spotted a line of trees that might give cover to the VC. We turned off the road, leaving the demolition guys to do their job, and went to set up some security for them—but we really goofed.

We needed to find a place that was off the main road but that had easy access back. The road we took went across a huge paddy field and looped back to the highway near the bridge. Several other little roads or paths crisscrossed the whole area, but none of them offered a feeder back to the highway. The one we chose was a little wider than most and rose nearly ten feet above the rice fields. It gave us excellent visibility of the surrounding country on our side of the highway; but when we reached the end eight minutes later, and perched ourselves on the service road berm, we realized our predicament. Two deep ditches separated us from the main road. We were sitting ducks should we be attacked from any direction. We had no way out, except to return the way we had come. The road was only eight feet wide, and somehow we needed to make a U-turn if we wanted to get back to the highway.

The "explosive" boys were combing the other side of the road and under the bridge looking for explosives. Rob and Paul found the squad's sergeant and explained our situation. They asked to have the explosives group stand by when they were finished to provide some cover for us while we got out of our sticky jam. The sergeant agreed, and our two MPs told him that we would stay put until the "bomb squad" had completed their work. Then we would pull back. We were giving these guys some real entertainment. This whole thing had become quite embarrassing.

We positioned ourselves, watched, and waited. About fifteen minutes into our wait, I spotted a water buffalo coming up out of the paddy seventy-five yards to the rear of us. "Hey, where the hell did he come from?" I hollered. The others turned, equally surprised; none of us had spotted him earlier.

The beast began to walk slowly toward us, acting rather confused. As the warm breeze blew from his direction, it became obvious that he had been wallowing in a freshly fertilized rice paddy. Apparently he was also sexually primed, probably searching for a mate. He kept moving toward us, occasionally letting out a loud bawl.

At first his strange behavior fascinated us. Then we realized that we were definitely sitting where he wanted to go. Bruce joked, "Where do you let a water buffalo walk?"

When the animal was about thirty yards from us, Bruce and I became concerned. Although probably used to people, he was a wild bull. We hollered at Rob and Paul to approach slowly. These animals weigh upwards of two thousand pounds and can have exceedingly touchy dispositions. Anything or nothing can set one of these brutes off—a ton of Asian bovine playfulness!

"What is that dumb shit doing?" Rob yelled back at us.

The animal stopped fifteen yards from the jeep, looking left, then right, then to his rear (he couldn't see over that), and back at us. Suggestions were flying. From that distance, did the jeep look like the object of his affections? (He must have been sniffing that methane much too long!) We could not understand how our jeep in *any way* resembled a cow. But I liked Bruce's comment the best when he said, *"We're parked in his place and he's madder than hell!"*

With no warning the animal lowered his huge, horned head and charged the jeep. I hugged the machine gun turret as tightly as I could to keep from getting thrown off, and Bruce jumped to the ground. The bull rammed the jeep and the impact made the vehicle lurch forward. The rear end of the jeep looked like a 10-ton truck had hit us. Bruce yelled, "Hey Vic, get the hell down from there. He's getting ready for another charge."

My rifle had become wedged in the sandbags at my feet. Off balance, I managed to reach over to the sixty and switch off the safety with one hand. Squeezing off a short burst into the air, I looked back to see the water buffalo pirouette and make a strategic retreat. I didn't want to kill the animal, just scare it back into the water long enough for us get out of there.

At first it looked as if the M-60's bark had discouraged the animal from any further attraction to our jeep, whatever it might have been. The buffalo was indeed heading for the water. Bruce got in the front seat saying, "If he hits us once more, we'll go over the edge into the ditch."

Suddenly we heard the thundering hooves of the bull. He rammed us once more, crumpling the whole backside of our poor vehicle. This was not a good place for GIs to travel on foot, and I had finally reached the point of being willing to kill the animal. The M-60 could no longer be pointed low enough to shoot in front of him because the floor of the jeep had buckled slightly and tilted the turret forward. Finally I drew my .45 and cocked it. As the bull came at us once more I fired, and the round hit the dirt inches under his nose. The dirt that kicked up must have stung his snout, because he stopped abruptly, shook his head back and forth, and emitted loud groaning sounds.

During all of this there was a farmer standing off on one of the other path laughing at the whole spectacle. Bruce had called to him in Vietnamese for some help, but he was laughing too hard to respond.

Ferdinand came in for another charge, shaking his head, heavy foam flying from his mouth and nostrils. We were very close to wearing his hoof prints on our backsides. In the midst of the charge, my .45 rang out a second time, striking the beast right between the horns. I could actually see the bullet bounce off the thick bone, removing a little of that tough hide. The force of the bullet drove the bull's head down, plowing his nose into the hard soil. His knees buckled and he nearly did a somersault. Dazed and wobbling, he managed to get up. For a few moments he just stood there a few feet away, glassy-eyed. The farmer was no longer laughing, but yelling at us to leave his animal alone. His English was pretty good.

Paul and Rob had been standing on the berm at the front of the jeep, but neither could see the bull well enough to get a clear shot at him. They could see the partially caved in tailgate of the jeep though, and knew all too well we needed to get out of there fast. The shooting could attract the VC.

Keeping an eye on the buffalo, I finally extracted my M-14. The animal was stunned and slowly began to move away. I knew if we didn't get out of there fast, the battle would soon be over and would probably end in the buffalo's favor. He appeared to be taking a breather as he tried to clear the foggy mist out of that small brain of his.

Bruce had managed to turn the jeep around. It seemed like a good time for us to vacate the premises. Both Rob and Paul were yelling, "Be careful!" (As if that thought had never crossed my mind.)

Then, with the meanest set of eyes I had ever seen, the water buffalo turned toward us again. He lowered his head, let out a bellow, and thundered toward the front of the jeep. Bruce used all the power the engine had, swerving to miss the last charge. As we sped by, one of the animal's huge horns hooked just inside the left rear wheel-well, tearing the sheet metal and nearly flipping us into the adjoining paddy. The jeep's momentum saved us. It spun the beast 180 degrees, rolling him down the embankment and on into the water.

Bruce slowed the jeep so our two buddies could jump in. We could hear the farmer yelling as we sped off. Rob looked at me and said, "Smitty isn't going to believe this." He keyed the mike and called Smith.

"We were just damn fortunate that there were no VC around," I said. "During this encounter, who would we have fought first?"

The convoy column was five minutes from our location. It took us almost that long to find our way back to the highway where our friends in the bomb-squad had been enjoying the show from their ringside seats. They were weak from laughter. Their sergeant said, "That was a great match, men. How about a return engagement?"

"Someone's really gonna be pissed about the jeep," Bruce said.

"Shit, I'm just glad to be alive to talk about it," I responded.

Sergeant Smith was laughing when he drove up, and he laughed even harder when he saw the jeep. When he finally composed himself, he said, "Hell, there wasn't much else you could have done, guys. Don't worry about it." Corroboration from the demolition personnel ended the report.

When the rest of the column showed up a few minutes later, the farmer was still furious, claiming we had killed his water buffalo; but as we looked off the side of the road, we saw the animal alive and well, still looking for his cow. As far as Smith was concerned, this delay was a godsend—the convoy had been moving much too fast, overshooting checkpoints.

We walked over to our mangled jeep and prepared to move out. The Cahn Sat assigned to the convoy called to us to wait. We had ponied up some local currency for the farmer, but the Cahn Sat said, "Animal was wild, not belong to farmer. He lied to GIs, but not to me."

The old farmer was still standing alongside the highway a few yards from us, looking bewildered and dejected. As we walked past him heading for our jeep, we stuffed the piasters into his shirt pocket, anyway. He had put on a good show too!

Pushing the speed of the column finally cost the lieutenant time. We had been back on the road for just a few minutes, traveling over fifty miles per hour, when one of the heavy trucks blew a radiator. This truck was carrying howitzer ammunition. After finding the problem, the mechanics informed the lieutenant that they couldn't do a road fix; the vehicle would have to be towed. While the truck was hooked up to for towing, the maintenance sergeant did a quick inspection of all the other vehicles, checking their radiators, hoses, and oil levels. A few were in need of some quick attention. Some trailer chains and hitches were loose. Two hitches were broken.

The breakdown delayed us twenty minutes. When we began moving again, the lieutenant slowed us down to thirty miles per hour. With all of our earlier bursts of speed, we arrived at Di-An just twelve minutes late. The good lieutenant was congratulated for doing "such an outstanding job!"

We stayed one night with the First Infantry MPs and slept in our old tent-hootch. It was great seeing the lieutenant, the sergeant, and some of the guys again. A few of them had gone home, and a couple had been killed during the Tet offensive. Chief was still there but was getting very "short," and happily told us so.

While there, Smitty had a talk with the sergeant and lieutenant about the 552nd MP Company, and our performance while we had been with the First

Infantry. Both the lieutenant and the sergeant praised our work and effectiveness. Then Smith was given a tour of the motor pool so he could see what was left of the 552's jeep, X-23. No one had done anything to it since we left. Smith was amazed.

The lieutenant and the sergeant hinted that it was hard to understand how some of the officers and noncoms in our company at II Field Force could ever have been placed in command, but they couldn't come right out and say so. They told Smith that the commanding officer of the First Infantry had wanted to give awards to all of us in the Deuce Platoon for a "job well done" but that our CO had refused. Until now, Smith had only heard bits and pieces about our stay with the First Infantry. Now he really understood that all of us had done our job.

The lieutenant again refused to let us salute him, insisting on a handshake instead. He and his sergeant wished us all good luck.

We gassed-up our jeeps, and were ready to roll. Just as we were fixin' to leave, someone from the radio shack ran out and handed a slip of paper to the lieutenant.

Looking at Smith and at us, he said, "A small group of our infantry and MPs are doing a search-and-seal operation just past the first village on your return route. Would you be able to assist as backup for a few minutes? We're still shorthanded, and they've asked for more help."

Smith looked at us and we nodded. "That's fine, sir, we'll be glad to help," he said.

The lieutenant introduced Smith to a Vietnamese sergeant whom we already knew. He climbed into our jeep and laughed when we told him how it had become damaged. This man was a member of the South Vietnamese Army—a friend. He showed us a quicker way to the village, a real "head 'em off at the pass" maneuver.

Paul, who doubled as one of our mechanics, could fix anything and had repaired the disabled jeep we had been towing. Now all of our vehicles were operational. Other than being badly bent, our mangled jeep still ran okay, and Paul was able to adjust the machine-gun mount to function properly. That was very comforting.

We moved along one of the red clay roads, so numerous in the area. The foliage came right to the edge of the road. It wasn't really dense yet, but it was getting thicker by the mile. It was still early morning, and the day had not yet reached its hottest point. I was feeling a little uneasy about all of the brush and trees crowding in so close. The area seemed to be part of an old rubber-tree plantation.

Because we were on a temporary assignment, we had left all but one radio tuned to the First MP channel. About ten minutes out, a call came from the group we were to assist. Bruce looked up at me and said, "It sounds like the sergeant from the outpost."

I was standing in the back and holding on to the M-60 for balance. I said, "Too much wind noise. Can't hear him clearly."

Smith's jeep was right ahead of us, and he motioned for us to get on the radio. I picked up the handset and listened for a moment. Then I pressed the button and said, "Hey, Sarge, Mills here along with Bruce and the rest of us."

"Hi, guys, thanks for helping," the young noncom replied. He wanted to know where we were, so I read off a couple of landmarks. They were accurate, and he told us about a turn coming up in a mile.

"Smith, do you monitor?" I asked, and he waved.

The foliage was like a thick forest now. We turned off the main road and onto a something that was really just a wide cow path. After another two hundred yards, we spotted a couple of 3/4-ton trucks and some GIs. We pulled in and parked.

We were in a village that consisted of ten huts of earth and grass. Occasionally a piece of corrugated steel siding could be seen. A path separated the huts, three on one side and seven on the other.

All the civilians were tense. Apparently we had missed something. Then we saw it! In the middle of the path between the huts lay an infant girl. She was lying face up and had been crying so hard and long that her voice was nearly gone. A group of the villagers were just standing around, not able to do anything. A young woman in the midst of the group was nearly hysterical—obviously the child's mother. The others were trying unsuccessfully to console her.

Smith's driver was standing with Bruce and me, wondering why no one was trying to help the infant. Suddenly he bolted away from us and headed for the baby. Bruce hollered to Rob, and as the well-intentioned kid passed, Rob put his right foot up and grabbed the young man's arm, rotating him gently to the ground.

Rob knelt down and whispered, "She's a booby trap." The kid turned white as a sheet.

Bruce and I went back to our jeep and got our bayonets. Walking slowly back toward the child, we were met by Rob, who took my blade and said to me, "My turn . . . but guide for us." Along with two men from the First, we all went down on our knees. A little boy walked up and handed me a small piece of sugar cane. I poured a few drops of water on it from my canteen and carefully placed the tip of it on the baby's lips. She stopped crying instantly. She squirmed a little as she sucked on the cane, and then dropped off to sleep from exhaustion.

We studied the area around the child before touching anything. Someone from the First MPs suggested, "There aren't any bomb experts close by. Maybe it would be more humane to just shoot her."

I had heard of GIs doing just that, but it was not an acceptable solution to us—not today, not here! We were no experts, but we had to try. My thoughts went in prayer to a Higher Power. Although the baby had been crying, she really wasn't hurt yet. The Cahn Sat and two others from the First kept everyone away as we studied the situation.

The day was warming up, and Bruce said softly, "She's dressed too warmly." She was wearing a heavy shirt, and a blanket was tucked partly around and under her little body. We carefully unfolded the top part of the blanket, which was more like a tea towel. Checking for wires or strings, we opened the front of her cotton shirt.

Bruce whispered, "There it is; the string."

Following the string carefully across her chest, we cut away part of the blanket. As she slept, we used our bayonets to carefully and slowly dig a six-inch trench around her, similar to a small box. This whole process was new to us, but we knew if we didn't do it correctly, we might all be blown to hell. We continued to work and silently pray.

We had heard that sometimes the VC would bury a second piece of twine or wire; one end would be tied to the charge and the other to a hut pole or tree. We found none.

Rob stretched out flat on the ground. With his head near her left side, he said with a smile, "She needs changin'."

On her other side Bruce whispered, "I can see the pin. It's a grenade—looks like one of ours."

Kneeling above the baby, I asked if he could see where the string was attached.

He said "No." Then he quickly added, "Hold it, Vic. Take another look, Rob. Can you see the grenade?"

I carefully removed some loosened dirt in front of Rob. There was the pin, and Rob answered, "Yeah, but it's turned the wrong way."

I took out my pocketknife to cut the string, saying, "You know if we're wrong we'll have less than five seconds."

"So let's not be wrong," whispered Bruce.

He watched as Rob slowly placed his left hand just above the baby's bottom and arched her back slightly; Bruce slid the grenade out.

Tossing it to me he said, "A dud!"

Letting out the breath we'd all been holding, we stood up and stretched. The VC had been practicing some of their psychological fireworks. I picked up the baby and handed her to the anxious young mother. Through tears of joy, she thanked us over and over again.

Before we could leave, the interpreter told Smith something very upsetting he had heard from several of the villagers. Just a few yards away from where we stood, two priests of some sect were *cleansing* the village and the Vietnamese blood by killing infants and toddlers who were of mixed race.

Bruce, Rob, and I followed the Vietnamese sergeant along a trail through the trees. We could hear faint, muffled cries as we came upon a small clearing and a shrine. The body of a young mother, perhaps sixteen years old, lay a few feet away. A man and woman wept uncontrollably over her. Our interpreter explained, "She, their daughter. The priest kill daughter and her son, because of mix blood."

What brutality! The infant was only a few months old.

A few yards further, we found a large flat rock that appeared to serve as a sacrificial altar. It had been used very recently. This was the most gruesome scene I had ever witnessed during my tour of duty. Continuing on, we reached another clearing where we came face-to-face with two men in monk-style robes. A baby was lying on a block in front of them. One of the priests had raised a machete up, above his head, but he froze as we entered the circle.

We gasped in disbelief.

Bringing up my .45, I cocked it and pointed it at the priest. "Put down the knife," I ordered.

Smith, who had followed us, asked if I was sure of my actions. In response, Rob and Bruce unlaced their sidearms, saying, "We're in total agreement!"

Smith said, "That's good enough for me," and he took out his .45.

The priest just looked at me. I asked our guide if the priest understood English. He said that he was sure they both knew exactly what I was saying. To be certain, I instructed the ARVN sergeant to tell the priest in Vietnamese once more, "Carefully put down the knife," and to let the priest know that if he tried to carry out his execution, I would fire. The message was sent and understood, but the knife headed for the child anyway. I fired, and the round struck the blade. The impact broke the man's wrist, and the machete went flying from his grasp. Bruce holstered his weapon, walked over and picked up the child, and we quickly retreated to the jeep.

Smith just shook his head and said, "We're done. Let's get the hell out of here and back on the road."

No family in that village would take the baby. The mother was the young woman who had been killed earlier. We asked Smith if we could bring the baby back with us. Of course he said "no," but he did so with a wink. In short, we all could have gotten busted for taking the infant with us.

The woman whose baby had been booby-trapped was forced to leave the village. Her baby was also of mixed blood, and it was just a matter of time before she would have to face a similar tribunal and fate. Bruce and Rob told the ARVN to have the mother get her belongings. We would take her to live in Long Binh at the "Temple Hotel," as we jokingly called it.

Smith said, "You guys be sure that when we get back you take these three directly to the other families, and don't let anyone see them in your jeep."

Taking a deep breath he added, "Because if you get caught, I don't know you." We agreed. Civilians weren't supposed to ride in military vehicles, although the CO, Top, and the master sergeant had frequently had prostitutes picked up in our jeeps and brought to the compound. Apparently the difference was "privilege of rank."

Other than a short break for lunch, we made no further stops on our trek from Di-An to II Field Force. Our ARVN interpreter had returned with the First Infantry, so communicating with the young mother was difficult, but she knew she was safe. Although she was not much older than fourteen, she did an excellent job of taking care of both babies. It was late afternoon when we drove past our gate and turned onto the Widow's Village access road. The girl and the babies were warmly welcomed at the temple. We stayed only a few minutes and then headed back to base.

Our involvement with the nationals and our renovation of the old temple resulted in weekly ass-chewings by the CO and Top. Each time we were told to stop, and each time we saluted and said "Yes, sir!" But we continued helping the families.

A day or so after our return to base, Rob and me were on our way to visit the kids when a house girl ran up to the jeep with a note from Sam. She had some packages for the displaced families. Rob made a fast U-turn and headed for our favorite trailer park.

Sam was glad to see us, and while we talked, she loaded five heavy packages into the jeep. "Vic," Sam began, "I explained to the officers and staff about all you guys working with the kids in the temple." Pointing to packages she added, "The officers' wives have sent some things to help."

I was very surprised and pleased at their generosity. One of the officers returning from TOC saw us loading up and stopped to meet us. This was my second face-to-face encounter with a general. We snapped to and saluted, but before we could offer our military greeting, he gave us a "general" wave and said, "Stand at ease." This guy was really down-to-earth. (He played a great game of chess too.) The general had heard from Sam about our CO and Top chewing us out over the temple project. He asked us a few questions and invited us to stop by to see him anytime.

A week later, while Sam was in our hootch visiting us, our clerk dropped off two very large boxes addressed to the five of us.

"This ought to keep you out of hot water for awhile," the clerk said with a laugh. "Top and the CO are fuming."

Inside were thank-you notes to us for our work in the Widow's Village along with some really nice *new* things for the kids and moms at the temple. Sam read the return address, and with tears streaming down her cheeks she said, "Look at this, Vic. General and Mrs. Johnston on this package, and Colonel and Mrs. John Downey on the other." The general, whose wife had sent the package, was the same officer whom we had met returning from TOC. We were never called on the carpet again for our efforts with the orphanage—not by our CO, Top, or the provost's office.

For a week following the arrival of the packages, the alerts were crazy, preventing us from visiting the temple. Red alert meant imminent danger; yellow was for caution, blackout status; and green was all clear. The alerts were changing frequently, sometimes as often as two or three times day and night: from red to yellow, back to red; from red to green, and back to red again.

For that week the five of us lived at the tower, a common detail during heightened alerts. There were no breaks. We ate C-rations morning, noon, and night. When we weren't on red alert we could heat the cans of food. This we did by burning C-4, plastic explosives we called play dough. We cut hunks off the block of C-4 and rolled them into long thin snakes. We would place a loose coil of the claylike explosive under a 5-pound coffee tin and light it. That stuff burned slow and white-hot. There was no danger. You could hit C-4 with a hammer, drop it, or throw it and it would not explode. It required a special blasting cap to detonate it.

The tower was a miserable place to stay for any length of time. The floor of the first level, our entrance, was dirt. There were no showers, and the only latrine was a hole GIs dug outside. Since it was so dangerous to go out at night, the first-level dirt floor was our latrine. Even after shoveling and raking, the dirt floor smelled foul with urine and defecation. The wall of the tower was brick and concrete, a foot thick. The second level, or main floor, of the structure was thirty feet above the dirt area. It was large, very open, and built even tougher than the guard bunkers. Surrounded by three times the sandbags, it was like having a bunker atop a thirty-foot cylinder.

Generally, we had two M-60s, a grenade launcher, and our rifles in the tower. Some of the bunks were down below, but because of the stench we took turns sleeping topside. The four floodlights brightened the night. Periodically, two or three of us would go down the ladder to make a security check around the perimeter. The railroad ran along the southeast side of the tower, giving excellent cover for an enemy trying to infiltrate our position.

Early one morning at the end of the week, the "all clear" finally sounded. Within a few minutes our relief showed up. Although we were very tired, we all wanted to stop for a short visit with the kids at the temple.

It was nearly 8 o'clock, and we thought it strange that no kids were outside playing. As we were getting out of the jeep, one of the older women held up four fingers and motioned toward the rear of the building. Picking up our weapons, we looked where she had been pointing and saw two men running away to join up with four others. They were headed toward the railroad tracks. Bruce, Rob, and I ran out the back door, and Kent got on the radio. Then he joined Paul to look around the building. I was running a few yards ahead of Bruce and Rob. Suddenly I dropped to the ground. I lay quietly, and my two friends joined me.

"What's up, Mills?"

Scanning the area in the early morning sun, I said, "They could have blown us to hell two seconds after we turned onto the village road. So why didn't they?"

"Maybe we caught 'em off balance," Rob said quietly.

Bruce added, "Well, they probably knew we wouldn't fire on them with the kids so close."

Pausing for a moment, I concluded, "They want us to follow. Did we surprise them or is this a trap?"

We moved more carefully and slowly, and as we approached the tracks, the brush and shrubs got thicker. Dropping to one knee, and looking for anything out of place, I noticed a bush off to our left a few yards, partially uprooted. Then the three of us saw some string not quite covered by dirt. I brought up my M-14 and fired a short burst into the bush. It exploded, setting off a second blast that took out a small tree twenty yards to our right. Rob let out a howl as if he had been hurt, and two heads popped up forty yards out. Rob and Bruce each fired one round, and the two heads dropped. Moving carefully forward, we found the two wounded Vietnamese. After searching them, we half-dragged, half-carried them back to the jeep. We didn't see the others anywhere.

Kent and Paul were in position near the jeep when they heard the shooting and the explosion, and they quickly got in radio contact with our unit. As we made our way back to the jeep, we waved to the mama-san who had warned us. She smiled and made the sign of the cross.

An hour later airborne troops captured the remaining four Vietnamese. They claimed not to be VC, but seemed to be anti-everything—America, South Vietnamese government, and even Ho Chi Minh.

Days and weeks of boredom were periodically punctuated by the occasional ten to fifteen minutes of stark fear and terror when we were suddenly thrust back into the reality of Nam. This was the case for nearly all personnel—officers and enlisted men alike. In what might be called "safe areas," MPs had more activity and perhaps less boredom by the nature of their work. Besides taking care of the occasional bar fight and post security details, we also had the responsibilities of dealing with traffic problems on and off post, and of investigating GIs involved in vehicle accidents. We were kept busy most of the time.

Even though the Tet Offensive was two months past, it left everyone on edge. For that reason, when troops from the field stopped by our compound for a little relaxation, we tried to be tolerant, giving out warnings more often than citations. None of us liked landing hard on GIs who were just off combat and only wanted to blow off a little steam. Sometimes their actions ran them smack-dab into trouble, and we had to take care of the problems. This duty was the hardest and the most disliked part of our work.

MPs were not very popular, and some of these kids were huge and had attitudes—they seemed constantly pissed off. Trading punches with them was not a smart thing to do.

Bruce and I were on one late-night post patrol, and Rob and Kent were working the other. About midnight we got a call to go to the main post club to check out a reported fight. That could mean anything from a verbal argument to throwing chairs. Since Bruce was driving, I entered the building first. Everyone was sitting quietly—a very abnormal picture. I noticed that a pool table had been overturned and that other tables and chairs were strewn all over the room. Suddenly someone grabbed me and I was flying through the air. I remembered a cute little platitude, "It's not the fall that hurts; it's the sudden stop at the end." I bounced off an upended pool table and slammed into the far wall.

My flying lesson had lasted less than a second and had covered a distance of roughly twenty-five feet, when all of my bouncing was done. I was too surprised to be scared and too numb to care. Mentally, I was still standing at the door. I looked up and saw a familiar face sailing toward me. It was Bruce, also coming in for a hard landing. In a few seconds, when my head cleared, I saw our "flight instructor"—a specialist fourth class, in cut-off jeans and an olive drab, Army T-shirt standing near the door laughing at us. He was waiting for the next person to enter. Knowing that Kent and Rob would be right behind us, I yelled one of our radio codes, "Ten-ten," which, loosely translated; means "Duck." This confused our very large and very drunk friend. He took a few steps away from the door toward us. Rob had paused just long enough to get set. He came up behind the GI, placed his nightstick between the man's legs, and brought it up sharply into his groin. Even when a man is drunk, that maneuver is very difficult to ignore. Then Rob brought the nightstick to a horizontal position across the GI's legs and he fell, beautifully! (MP school hadn't been a total waste after all!)

Getting to my feet, I bent down to retrieve my helmet and nightstick. Rob had turned his back on his opponent when Bruce yelled to him, "Hit the deck!"

A second, smaller man with a large bottle was headed for Rob. Moving in a semi-crouch, I side-armed my nightstick across the man's nose and forehead, knocking him out cold.

What a mess! Both men were part of a cav unit that had just finished a month of fierce fieldwork and combat. I felt sorry for them, but they had hurt a lot of people in the club and had assaulted the three of us. We handcuffed them and loaded them into our jeeps. Sergeant Mitchell drove up just as we finished interviewing witnesses and getting first aid.

"What the hell happened to you three?" Sarge asked.

Right behind him came a captain, the CO of the two fun-loving "kids," to check on the ruckus. Then he recognized his men.

"What the fuck is going on here?" he demanded. "What have your MPs done to my guys? Can't my men have a little fun without getting busted every time?"

We saluted the captain, and Mitchell asked if we could make an oral report so that everyone could hear. We agreed and we all went back into the club. A medic had been in the bar and was helping to patch up the injured. Luckily, no one was seriously hurt. No broken bones, except for the man I had hit with my nightstick. His nose had assumed a slightly different angle. Bruce and I, now bandaged, had been bleeding from deep scratches on our heads and forearms.

Looking at the damages, their CO pleaded their case, saying, "Many of my guys were either killed or seriously wounded." With a change in attitude, he asked if he could personally discipline his men. The officer reminded the four of us of the lieutenant in Di-An. It was obvious this officer cared about his men, and that he was hurting too.

Mitchell gave us the option, reminding us what we could and could not do. He left the charges up to us. As we huddled with Sarge discussing our options, I said, "Let's charge them with being drunk and disorderly, and issue them just a simple citation."

Bruce recommended that the captain assume the responsibility for these two men, having them pay all damages out of their own pockets. Sarge liked the idea and presented it to the captain. Since the officer really didn't have much of a choice, he gladly accepted and followed us down to the jail.

We kept the two men overnight and released them to their first sergeant the next morning. A few days later, I was surprised that both of these men stopped by looking for us. It was one of the rare days our group had time off together, and we were getting ready to head over to the temple with some newly arrived packages. Bruce and I recognized the men instantly, but they had been so drunk, they had no idea who we were. We flagged them down, and they pulled their jeep over, close to our hootch. The guy I conked had his nose in a splint, and he read from a slip of paper the names of the four MPs they were looking for.

I held up two fingers, "Well, you have two of us, and if you'd like to see the other two, you could give us a ride over to the village and see them as well."

We loaded the boxes and ourselves into their vehicle and drove to the temple. On the way, the bigger man said, "Our CO said you guys reduced the charges against us. We just wanted to thank you personally." Both men had been fined and reduced in rank. "The citations were nothing compared to a possible court-martial," the big one told us.

We felt they were sincere. This was the first time anyone had ever thanked us for writing them up. It's true that they would have been looking at serious charges if we had gone by the book, but I knew they didn't want to be in Nam any more than I did. These guys had been involved in a lot more combat than we had, and they had seen many friends wounded or killed. Who can say how any of us would have reacted had we been in their position?

As we approached the temple, we spotted Rob and Kent outside playing with some of the kids. The big guy asked us, "What is this place? What are you doing here?"

"We collect families and young mothers needing help," I told him, and I introduced them to "my two kids," the girl and her younger brother I was still hoping to adopt.

The two men spent nearly an hour there playing with the kids. They even helped feed a couple of the toddlers. During that hour, they found what we had learned a few months earlier—that there was more to being in Vietnam than the war and the killing. As a result, we had some new recruits. Two weeks later, they showed up with a wonderful surprise—a crate full of supplies. There were clothes for the mothers as well as for the kids, jars of baby food, and boxes of baby cereal. Best of all, they brought a 13-year-old girl who had been, as one of them put it, "GI mistreated," with her mother and her 10-year-old brother.

"Is there room for them here?" one of the men quietly asked.

We said there was, and we added them to our growing family.

The two men continued to bring gifts and care packages until they rotated home. About a month after the big man's tour ended, we received a large package he had mailed from home. It weighed almost ten pounds, and he had addressed it simply, "Temple Hotel, c/o 552 MP Company." Love and care are contagious!

After being in Nam for a while, I developed a severe rash on the insides of my legs, around my crotch, and under my arms. It itched constantly and at times was very painful. I found that I was not alone; many of the guys in my outfit suffered from the same ailment. When we perspired it was like throwing salt on the problem.

Sleeping was difficult; I scratched until I bled, and ended up with open sores. No matter how often I showered, or what bar soap, creams, salves, and powders I used, there was little or no relief.

The main reason for the rash became evident one evening. It was nearly dark when Bruce and I were relieved from tower duty. Most of the afternoon had been clear and hot, but looking toward the southeast we could see clouds forming from the vapors rising from the earth. This weather pattern kept moving toward us, bringing torrents of water. I had never seen anything like it before.

After we briefed the men relieving us, we gathered up our gear and headed for the jeep to finish our shift with three hours of motor patrol. By the time we reached the jeep, we found ourselves in a torrential downpour. The jeep was open and had a mounted M-60. Since the weather had been clear all day, none of the canvas tops had been installed, and our rain gear was still in our lockers. I took the machine gun off the mount and wrapped it in our two flack jackets as best I could. Then I put it under the rear seat where it was partially protected from the rain and inevitable rust. Unfortunately, our rifles had to stay in the open.

The raindrops were as large as silver dollars and came down so heavily that it was difficult to see the road. A few minutes later we parked in front of the orderly room. One look and everyone began laughing hysterically at us. We hadn't a clue why, until we looked at each other and burst out laughing too. From the waist up we were covered with foamy bubbles.

Mitchell was desk sergeant, and when he heard the commotion, he came out to see what was going on. He laughed as well, and instructed, "Check out a covered jeep, loose the sixty, and get changed before going back on patrol. I'll give ya ten minutes."

Our housemaids worked very hard for the five bucks per month we paid them. They cleaned our living quarters and hand-washed the laundry. Even though our company was rather small compared to other outfits, the girls did the laundry almost daily. I was buying a large box of detergent every week.

That's one hell of a lot of suds. Until this experience I had not had much interest in how the laundry was done, but I began to watch more closely.

The detergent box called for only a cup of soap for a washer using perhaps ten to fifteen gallons of water. I watched as Lin and two other girls who worked in our hootch dumped a quarter of a box of detergent (eight or more cups) into the laundry tub of clothes and added only two or three gallons of non-potable water. Then they went to work scrubbing. Their hands had gotten quite sore and sometimes even bled. There was no rinse cycle. The girls simply hung the laundry on a line and gave it a cursory spray of water from a hose.

I mentioned this incident and the problem of the rash in a letter to my older sister. She promptly wrote back saying that the sores sounded very similar to diaper rash. My friends and I thought this was quite humorous; it made no sense to us. According to the letter, though, there was a solution to this and it was on its way. My sister sent a box of laundry soap from a new company. The stuff was biodegradable and had no irritants. (I didn't have any idea what that meant at the time.) My sister had also included several bars of an antibacterial bath soap, so we worked on making some changes.

We showed Lin how to use the new laundry powder, explaining that the directions on the box were for a washing machine. The amount of soap for a normal load was just a quarter of a cup. There was a lot of resistance from the girls as I introduced them to the idea of *rinsing* the laundry.

We set up a barrel to heat the water to a notch above lukewarm. It was unbelievable how just these subtle changes—warm water, thorough rinsing, and the new soap—could make such a huge difference.

A few days after all of this, Bruce, Dave, and I were ordered to appear at a court-martial in Saigon to testify against an officer we had arrested. Bruce and I conned Mitchell into letting Rob go along as well. Originally we were to spend the night, but upon arriving we were met by a major who said that the trial was over. The defendants had changed their pleas to guilty the night before and would only be going in for sentencing. He thanked us for showing up.

After five minutes of paperwork with the major, we headed to the USO club for a doughnut and something that resembled real coffee. As we walked in, we spotted Gail sitting at a table with her brother. She waved us over to join them. We ate doughnuts and drank coffee while we visited. The man and wife who managed the club came over to say "Hi," and to thank us for taking such good care of their girls.

One girl was new in-country; she'd arrived just a week earlier and was still learning about balancing the heavy tray of dirty dishes. I was in a direct line with her as the tray began to tilt, so I jumped up, steadied the load, and carried it out to the kitchen for her.

It was the first time I had seen this area of the club. Stepping out the back door to take a look around, I noticed an old wringer washing machine sitting just off the steps. The girl who had been doing the balancing act followed me outside a minute later, bringing me a fresh cup of coffee and a cinnamon roll. Thanking her, I asked, "What is this machine used for?" It was not connected to water or power. She said she didn't know but that she would ask the manager, and she disappeared back inside.

In a few minutes, the whole group came out back. The husband said, "At first we weren't sure what Debbie was talking about, but now it's clear. We used this machine at the old location for washing dishtowels and some personal laundry. It's too small for us here; we have a much larger one now."

"Can we buy it?" I asked.

Looking puzzled for a moment, the man then said "No, but you boys can have it. It works fine, and we do have to dispose of it."

With one mind, the four of us reached into our pockets, pulled out some of our military "funny money," and donated it to the club.

Bruce looked at me and asked, "You can't put this thing in the back of a jeep, so how do you plan on getting it back to the post?"

"I don't know," I answered, "but there's got to be a way."

Gail's brother, who had overheard the conversation, walked out to the back step and said, "Hey, no problem. I have a load of medical supplies going to the Long Binh post in two days. You're four miles west? Hell, I'll bring it out to you then."

"Sold!" we agreed. "We'll buy you lunch too," I added.

Two days later our washing machine was delivered. We had constructed a level platform with some lumber scraps. Paul made a power hook-up that worked like a charm. Lin, her sister, and the other girls were excited. Two of the mothers from the temple who also worked for us brought some of the kids' laundry to wash in the machine.

The effect was amazing. Several of us consistently used the new bath soap for our showers and the new laundry soap for washing clothes, and the girls gave our laundry a thorough rinsing. Within a couple of weeks, the rash problem had all but disappeared. The local medics took note of our good results and gave out special instructions: "Where possible, thoroughly rinse all laundry."

Our new laundry process brought another welcome benefit—the girls' hands healed up. Several of the other men in the outfit wanted to buy the new soap for their own use, so my sister sent more boxes as gifts for them. Sisters do come in handy!

About this time, most of us from the old Di-An group went on convoy duty out of the area for several days. When we returned, we were surprised to find a new first sergeant and to learn that a new commanding officer was on the way. What an improvement! Top was a soldier's soldier. Those men who had gotten along well in the old "club" days didn't care much for him. The 552nd already had spit and polish. What we had not had was leadership; and these new men brought that and more to the unit.

Although nothing was said openly to us, it was quite evident our new head cadre didn't care much for our provost marshal. According to our clerk, their comments were not very flattering.

We never learned the fates of our previous first sergeant and CO, but we heard plenty about Master Sergeant Green. He was the NCO who had tried to rape a number of our house girls, and also who had been the main one responsible for so many men having been sent to field duty. He pleaded guilty to charges of an attempted break-in at Little Hanoi and of being in a restricted area. Green lost a stripe and was fined, but I wished that he'd been brought up on abuse charges and sent to Leavenworth. He retired back to the States to suffer his embarrassment with family and friends.

One night before a movie, Top asked if he could join us at our table. As we chatted and waited for the film to start, he said, "I notice that generally the same group of men are assigned the rough details, and that the five of you are generally in the mix. What gives?"

"Well, Top," Rob began, "the twelve to fifteen of us all served with the First MPs at Di-An as punishment."

"What do you mean, punishment?" Top demanded.

"Mills here was sent to the field because he helped to keep a young house girl from being raped," Bruce explained. "He confided in his former AIT CO about the situation, and the guy turned him in."

"Most of the others of us were sent to the field for similar kinds of things," Paul said. "It was obvious the First Infantry needed extra manpower, and the first sergeant and CO here used it to their advantage."

"We heard that some guys just plain transferred out," Top said. "Is that true too?"

Bruce held up his index finger, slightly raising his left hand, and said "Ray Torres was a friend of mine. He wouldn't bend from what he knew was right. After several weeks here, before the need with the Big Red One came up, he went to 199th as a chopper gunner. He was killed two weeks later, but the last time I saw him he looked happy. He told me that he was at peace, and that the 552nd was not the normal Army." Bruce slowly wiped his eyes with a sleeve, and lit a cigarette.

Top listened, and seemed to respect the combined experience we had gained from the First Infantry duty. Apparently he was also aware of our performance during Tet, and he wanted to know why we usually volunteered for things that seemed to be dangerous. Why were we being singled out for so many of these jobs? "The five of you—why you five so often?" he asked.

We were all quiet for a few moments, thinking. Then I said, "We found it much safer working a hot spot than waiting back here on the compound. We trust each other. We know what each other will do, and usually know when they'll do it." Pausing for a moment I added, "Some of the older guys now seek us out because we do the job, and we do come back."

Rob added, "It was safer for us to do a job at Di-An, knowing the dangers we faced, than it was to sit here in this compound not knowing what was going on. We were outcasts here because of our commitment to duty and survival. We just didn't fit into Top's club."

"When a new man with a clean training record showed up," Bruce began, "he instantly became a good candidate for the First Infantry MP." Sitting quietly for a moment, he slowly added, "They held this big stick called 'field' or 'combat duty' over everyone's head. It was punishment to be sent out there from this cushy headquarters work. It was actually more to protect the first sergeant's and the CO's butts; no offense."

Top nodded, "None taken."

As the conversation continued as others added comments as well, explaining that a guy could be accepted at II Field Force if he drank, used drugs, abused the house girls, and didn't rock the boat.

As Top glanced around the table, he noticed that none of us was drinking alcohol. He seemed genuinely surprised and asked if we didn't drink anything stronger than soft drinks. "Oh, yeah, the coffee in the mess hall," I cracked. That brought a chuckle or two. "I don't drink at all, but sometimes these guys might have a beer or two—seldom anything hard. This was partly the reason for our 'popularity' with the unit."

"Or lack of it," Paul chimed in.

Top began to get the picture, and he asked if Captain Gordon had been in command during the whole time. We all nodded. While we were talking, more MPs who had served in the field joined us and added their views on "Life with the 552nd."

The lights then went out, and we settled back to watch the movie. About ten minutes past the credits, I turned to Top, only to find his chair empty. Leaning over to Bruce and Rob, I said softly, "Do you think we said anything we shouldn't have?" They just sat there blankly, probably wondering the same thing.

A week or so after our conversation with the new first sergeant, our old friend Wayne Cameron had a chance to fly to Vaung Tao for another three-day weekend. He sent a note asking several of us to join him. When we asked Top if we could take a run to the coast for an in-country R&R, a strange thing happened. All of the soldiers who had served with the First MPs and who had not yet rotated stateside, and who wanted to go, received a pass.

We returned from R&R a half day late due to bad flying weather and met our new CO, Captain Roland Fairchild. We were impressed. For the first time during my tour of duty, the 552nd was alive; and finally well.

Shortly after returning from the Vaung Tao trip, we were told during a company formation that the Army was giving us the opportunity to trade our outdated M-14s for M-16s. The catch was (there's always a catch in the military), all of us had to agree to it. The newer men who had never had to use their weapons complained about the weight of the 14s. They thought it would be great to have the lighter 16s. It was true that the M-16 was a lot *lighter* weapon. Those of us who had been around had heard from the field that the M-16s were not totally *dependable*. That was probably why every "grunt" GI in the field wanted to trade their weapons for ours.

The CO told us that on the following Saturday, we could test-fire both weapons to see which we preferred. From what I had been told, that may have been the first time the military gave troops their choice of weapons. I was eager to see a new M-16 up close, to fire some rounds through it, and to find out if it was as formidable a weapon as the old M-14. I also wondered if this was going to be an honest test, or if we were going to be spoon-fed some military BS.

It had rained most of Friday night and into early Saturday morning, but the day quickly warmed up. Those men who were off duty drove to an area northeast of the 90th Replacement Company, a couple of miles past our fuel and ammo depot. Top and the CO met us there, along with an Army major, a lieutenant, and three noncoms (two from the Army and one from the Marines). They brought ten M-16s with them. We tried them out and fired as many rounds as we wanted. We also learned how to clean, and reassemble them. This was a simpler weapon. After an hour or so, we were asked what we thought of them and if we would care to switch.

As I had often done during my training in the States, I held up my hand to ask a question. Several of us from the First Infantry assignment had been talking seriously about the M-16s. I indicated that we had some reservations. The major turned to me and said, "Soldier, this isn't basic. Your ass is on the line just as much as anyone else's. Speak up."

"Sir," I started, "many of us here were TDY with the First Infantry MPs for several weeks. There wasn't a day that went by when some GI, Marine or Army, didn't try to trade his 16 for one of our 14s."

Then another one of the former TDY guys said, "Whenever our M-14s were used heavily, not one ever failed in the field. It's more accurate, hits harder, has better range, and it can take rough treatment."

After a few more comments were made, I said, "I would rather take my M-14—as heavy as it is—into combat, with fewer cans of rations, and know that my weapon will see me through, than gamble on this," and I pointed to the M-16 someone was holding up. Holding my M-14 by the sling I moved beside the Marine sergeant and dropped my weapon into the muddy water. To the major, I said, "Sir, if you can drop the M-16 into this trench of mud and water, bring it up and match my fire, I'll trade."

Gunny glared at me, and growled, "You don't treat your weapon like that, soldier, at least not in the Corps."

"I know, Sarge," I answered, "but nearly all of us have been doing it every day by diving into smelly, stinking rice paddies or muddy trenches. The weapons get plenty dirty, but muddy or not, they still have to fire. If they don't, a lot of people back home will cry."

The lieutenant and the major agreed, and under a lot of protest the Marine slowly lowered his weapon toward the water. That test went against every grain of his military training. I understood and respected his position. We all tried to avoid treating our weapons like that, but in the heat of warfare, we weren't always given the choice of battlefield conditions.

Gunny was still moving reluctantly, so the lieutenant took the M-16 from him and threw it into the muddy water. "I think this is what these men had in mind, Sergeant."

"Yes, sir!" he groaned, protest still evident in his voice.

We truly felt sorry for the Marine veteran. Several of us were standing a few feet from the trench. Unexpectedly, the major dropped two more M-16s into the water.

"One at a time, Gunny," said one of the officers, "pick up a weapon and fire it on full auto, short and long bursts."

He picked up the first one, let the water drain out of the barrel, pulled the bolt mechanism back to inject a cartridge into the chamber, and pointed it toward the open range. He squeezed the trigger. "Pop! Pop!" then nothing. A cartridge jammed in the chamber and it was stuck open. Gunny slid the bolt back and freed the bent cartridge. Again he pointed the barrel out toward the field and squeezed the trigger. One "Pop!" and it jammed again.

Handing this weapon to one of the Army sergeants, he grabbed another M-16 out of the water and fired just five rounds before it jammed. Clearing the rifle, he tried again. It fired once more before it quit. The third effort was even worse. This time the lieutenant picked up one of the remaining M-16s and fired only three rounds before the barrel split nearly six inches, blowing the breech apart and slightly injuring his right hand. A medic quickly cleaned and bandaged the wound.

Bruce, Rob, Paul, and some others had placed their M-14s into the muddy water along with mine. Top came over and asked us quietly, "Will they fire all right, boys?" We just smiled, picked up our own rifles from the muck, and aimed them at the cardboard targets a hundred yards out. We each fired twenty-one rounds, in short and long bursts, without a hitch. When we examined the targets, we found fifty-eight new holes.

In their effort to sell us on the M-16, the demonstrators had come with some arrogance. They left a bit more humble. They didn't say much as they drove away. The Marine did tell Bruce and Rob that he much preferred the M-14 the Marines used when he first came to Nam. Sometimes in their zeal to improve something, people don't stop to consider how well the original product has proved itself.

Top jokingly said, "Okay, you monkeys, weapons inspection in ten minutes." It took us an hour to get our rifles clean. Top and the captain came down to the hootch and asked why we had been so sure our weapons wouldn't fail. We opened the breach bolts on our 14s and Bruce explained, "While we were with the Big Red, we found that the best cleaner and oil available was the Army's aerosol bug spray. We combined the spray with a new lubricant from the PX, called WD-40. Now the weapons won't rust, they keep clean, and they never fail to fire properly."

After the first sergeant and the CO had carefully checked our weapons, Paul said, "We gave the same treatment to a couple of the M-60s that we've been keeping here in our hootch. Since we're usually the ones sent on patrol, we wanted to be sure our weapons would operate okay."

Handing our rifles back to us, the CO said, "Since the first sergeant and I are new to the company, we've been looking over your files. We like how well all of you have worked together."

Top added, "Keep it up, guys. We wouldn't mind being in your bunker during a firefight."

As they were leaving, Paul said, "You can join our group anytime, Top, Captain."

Yep, the 552nd finally had someone who could spell "leadership" and who knew its meaning. It was mighty nice for change. Mitchell and Smith seemed to approve as well. I think we all slept a little better.

Chapter 10
A Glimmer of Light

By the end of March 1968, I felt as if I could finally see a glimmer of light at the end of the tunnel. Even though there were nearly seven months left on my tour, I still had the feeling that my time was short. Bruce and Paul were scheduled to return to their homes in Utah sometime in August. Rob was from the East Coast and would be going home about the same time.

A lot of the guys we had served TDY with in the field had rotated home already. Moods improved as the time to leave moved closer; but the guys were also less enthusiastic about working certain details, such as convoys or patrols through the Widow's Village. The five of us voiced no such reluctance because we enjoyed staying busy.

Although we experienced only limited combat while we were in Long Binh Province, a few guys also faced some personal challenges. Paul was one of them. Bruce and I were on post patrol one afternoon and stopped by our hootch for some cold pop. Bruce waited in the jeep while I went inside to retrieve the drinks. Paul was sitting on his footlocker at the far end of the building. Because I had just come in from bright sunlight, I couldn't see clearly; the darkened room played havoc with my vision for several seconds.

"Hi, Paul. What's up?" I said. There was no response, and I continued into our club.

As I started back out a few seconds later, my eyes were already adjusting to the darker room. As I slowly walked over to Paul, I noticed several empty cans of Army and Vietnamese beer, and a few still unopened. Tears ran down Paul's face and onto the pages of a letter he held in his right hand. What really alarmed me though was the pistol in his other hand. I put my cans of pop down on another footlocker and sat down next to him.

Paul had always been a clearheaded, quiet, young man. He was also the only one of the five of us who was married. He often spoke of his wife. I had no idea what was going on, but with a prayer in my heart, I put my arm around him and asked, "What's wrong? Can I help?"

It was obvious he was in pain over a problem at home, and I knew he felt helpless. All kinds of possibilities ran through my mind. He wanted me to read the letter. I said I would if he'd give up his pistol. At first, he refused, and mumbled something about killing himself. I knew he had a church background and that he and Bruce were of the same faith. For several minutes we talked about some familiar passages from the Bible.

Finally, after repeated requests from me, Paul handed me his pistol and the letter. I could neutralize the weapon, but not the letter. His wife had written that she didn't plan on staying home while all of her girlfriends were having fun going out. She wrote about some guys she had already partied with. She described a time when she and three young men took a couple of six-packs of beer "up to the lake" and "had a *very* good time." She even included a blow-by-blow recounting of her infidelities. Paul had received several disturbing letters from his wife for many weeks, usually begging him to come home, but this was the worst "Dear John" letter a GI could receive. It was painful even for me to read.

It finally dawned on me what was really going on in the letter. I said,

"Paul, this is only a goat! She's just trying to get to you, and she's doing a damn good job of it. She's not doing any of this stuff." Paul looked at me as I added, "She's just lonely and hurting too."

It wasn't long before Bruce walked in the main door looking for me. "Hey, Mills," he called out as he walked down the aisle. "What gives? Let's go! Smitty's is about to blow his top."

Paul was sobbing with his head on my shoulder.

I pointed out a particularly graphic paragraph in the letter for Bruce to read. He gasped in disbelief as he read it and said under his breath, "*Son . . . of . . . a . . . bitch.*"

Paul had wanted to put in a request for an emergency leave, but he wasn't sure of what our new first sergeant and CO would say.

"On your feet, Paul," I ordered. "We're going to the chaplain's office right now. Either he or the Red Cross should be able to get you home for thirty days."

He looked at Bruce and me blankly.

Bruce added, "Look, Vic, we've gotta get that damn jeep from in front of this hootch or Smith is gonna have all our hides. *Let's move it, guys!*"

Paul slipped on his boots while I locked up his pistol. Then three of us ran out the door, dove into the jeep, and sped away. We couldn't hear whether Smith called out to us, but when I glanced in the rearview mirror, I saw him heading for our hootch. After that, we didn't look back.

We dropped Paul off at the chaplain's office with letter in hand. Most of us knew Captain Tulley, the chaplain, and felt he was a great guy. I knew he could help.

As Bruce pulled back onto the north perimeter road I told him, "We've gotta go back and square this with Smitty."

Bruce agreed, but added, "Let's make one circuit first and then we'll call in. Besides, you forgot our drinks!"

As it turned out, we didn't have to make that call. We were being radioed. "X-ray 6, X-ray 6, this is Handcuff. What's your 20 (location), over?"

We were passing the PX parking lot, and as I picked up the handset we could see five guys there, tangled up in a fight.

"Handcuff, this is X-ray 6, we are at Papa X-ray. Five Golf India's fighting. Request backup. Over."

"Ten-two-four, backup en route. Handcuff clear."

We were temporarily off the hook when we heard the call for assistance go out to the other unit. Turning into the parking lot, Bruce hit the lights and siren, and the fight immediately stopped.

"Okay," I began. "Everybody line up and get your ID out."

Bruce then asked, "Would someone like to tell us what this is all about?"

Before anyone could answer a staff sergeant ran over from the PX. "Sorry for the ruckus guys. You turn these knot-heads over to me and they will be firmly dealt with. You have my word!" the sergeant assured us.

"That's probably all right, Sergeant," Bruce said. "But we'll have to wait for our sergeant and clear it through him. He'll be here in just a minute or so."

When Smith and his driver showed up, the staff sergeant tried to get to Smith first to throw his two rockers around: his E-7 versus Smith's E-5. I stepped in front of the E-7, "At ease, Sergeant. Please stay with your men."

Smitty looked at me, then at Bruce, and asked, "Where have you guys been?"

Before we could answer, Smith quickly added, "Cuff the sergeant and put him in your jeep. Write up the others for fighting and send them on their way. Both Mitchell and I have had dealings with this sergeant and his men before."

The other sergeant could hear us. He didn't much care for Smith's orders and started toward us, but I rotated him around until he was up against our jeep.

"You're going with us, Sergeant." I cuffed him before he knew what had happened and sat him down on the back of our jeep. Smith came over to talk with him for a minute. All but one of the men received a citation.

"You guys are getting off easy," Smith told them. "Now get the hell back to your unit, and have your first sergeant contact our desk sergeant in the morning."

Smith explained later that the sergeant and his men had been involved in many other incidents. Twice Smith had let them go with a promise from their sergeant that proper and firm punishment would be given. The sergeant had done nothing. Apparently Mitchell had experienced a similar incident or two. Now this sergeant's account was past due and payable.

With Smitty in tow, we transported the sergeant to the desk. Bruce and I took care of our part of the paperwork, and Smith told us, "Go find Top. He wants to have a word with you two." Almost two hours had elapsed since we had dropped Paul off at the chaplain's office.

We found Top in the mess hall drinking coffee with the CO. We walked over to their table and came to attention.

"Excuse us, sir," I began. "We were told to report to the first sergeant."

The CO looked up at us and smiling slightly, said, "Put the bullshit aside for a minute and sit down."

"Yes, sir," we responded, wondering which of us would feel the boot of authority first.

"Look," began the captain, "neither one of us is real big on pomp. It takes too much time and energy, and it's usually too damn hot anyway."

We tried to explain why we were late getting back on patrol, but lighting a cigarette, Top said, "Your friend is, as we speak, on his way to Bien Hoa Air Base. They're holding a plane for him." Looking at his watch, he smiled. "No, he's probably airborne by now, heading for a thirty-day emergency leave, thanks to you guys."

The CO added, "Had we known about the severity of Specialist Walker's personal problem we would have approved it in company long ago." Pausing for a moment, he added, "But with all that we've heard about this company, I wouldn't have trusted us either."

As we got up to leave, we both saluted saying, "Thank you, sir; First Sergeant."

Once outside, we both gave a sigh of relief. Looking skyward, we saw a DC-8 flying overhead, and Bruce said, "He'll be landing in Oakland in about twelve hours."

Shortly after the new leaders took over, we began having more intense inspections during guard mount. There were an increased number of inspections of our quarters too. Many of the men who had been in company longer than I didn't take kindly to this. They thought that those of us from the field, the old Deuce Platoon, had something to do with the changes.

During one of the guard-mount inspections, Fairchild gave a two-minute speech about morale and ended with, "There will be no more hard drinking, and no tolerance for anyone using drugs. I'll give you a choice: give up the drunkenness and drugs or go to Leavenworth. If you need help kicking either habit, we'll do everything we can to assist you, and we'll keep it in-company if you're sincere. First Sergeant and I know who you are. It's now up to you. We will give you twenty-four hours to come forward."

It was amazing! The drugs vanished. The drinking didn't stop entirely, but there was a big decline. Only one man was badly hooked on drugs, and he got the help he needed. He was back to work in two weeks, clean and ready to go. This individual rotated home five months later as a proud vet who had done his job.

After a few months in-country I found my uniforms seemed to have shrunk—even the new ones. In truth, I had gained some weight. The house girls began calling me "Mop-dit," which was a kind Vietnamese term for "too fat." I had been eating PX canned food and the goodies sent from home, but the real culprit was far too many Cokes, Pepsis, and Dr. Peppers. I couldn't stand to drink our so-called potable water. By the end of March, I had ballooned from under 160 pounds to nearly 200 pounds.

Sam came to my rescue. The mobile-home officers were having clean, mountain spring water delivered from the States to their mobiles. I don't know where it actually came from, but it was very good water. I had asked Sam if our hootch club could be included in the order. At first Sam wasn't sure how her boss would react to this new business arrangement, but he finally told her, "As long as they pay for it, it's fine with me." He didn't much care for the potable water either.

Two weeks later, we had fresh spring water in our hootch's club and in the orderly room. The captain and first sergeant chipped in as well, expanding the order. Although the water wasn't ice cold (actually it was lukewarm), it was wonderful.

During the first month of nearly no sodas or PX food, I dropped twenty pounds. I felt better, slept more soundly, and perspired less. My heart went out to all the guys in the jungle who had to dip their canteens in a local stream and to make it drinkable, using purification tablets.

Bad water, extreme weather, and the Viet Cong were not the only hazards in Vietnam. Sexually transmitted diseases presented a silent but pervasive threat. During my tour in Nam, I stayed away from sexual relations with any of the Vietnamese women. This wasn't due so much to lack of interest as it was to my desire to survive. I had heard of too many GIs who had "social diseases," some of which were considered incurable. Although every PX carried condoms, there was no guarantee they hadn't been tampered with.

While working foot patrol with Rob around the PX, we witnessed a frightening sight. Four young Vietnamese women were sitting in the storeroom using something similar to hatpins to poke holes in the boxes of prophylactics.

Many Vietnamese girls erroneously believed that getting pregnant by a GI would mean an automatic marriage and a ticket to the States—a gift from Uncle Sam. Others coerced by or sympathetic to the VC, thought to put GIs out of commission with venereal disease.

When we saw what the girls were doing, I said to Rob, "See if you can find Sam, and tell her that we need her for official business involving Vietnamese nationals." Then I stationed myself where I could watch both the door to the stockroom and the main floor of the PX. A lot of GIs were in the PX that day. I was glad to see Roger, our company clerk, among them. Although he was not an MP, I could have him call for backup. Roger was standing twenty feet away from where I was hiding. Not wanting to yell, I threw a box of toothpaste at him. As he turned around, he saw me motioning him over. He came very reluctantly. The man wasn't very friendly, and no one seemed to like him.

I told him, "Go out to the jeep and call for backup." He acted as if I had just given him a 5-pound box of Tootsie Rolls, and he dashed out of the building. "I hope they don't use their sirens when they drive up," I muttered.

The PX manager came over to see what was going on. I suggested he not sell any condoms for a time, and requested that he let me know should any of the Vietnamese help suddenly leave the building. He agreed.

Within a few minutes, Rob and Sam arrived, entering through the rear loading- door. I told them Roger was using our radio to call for help. I explained to Sam in more detail what was going on. She stayed on the PX side of the curtain, Rob went back down to secure the rear service entrance he and Sam had just used, and I took up my position across from the storeroom where the ladies were still busy with their hatpins. Sam stuck her head through the curtain and said softly, "Roger said to tell you that they're on the way."

I turned to Rob him the "okay" sign.

Sergeant Mitchell and his driver, a new kid in-country named Tom, showed up first. Rob joined me and indicated that another unit was in place at the rear of the building. Then he left Tom to stand by the curtain and I asked Sarge to peek into the storeroom to check things out.

After a few seconds, Mitchell growled, "Shit, I've seen enough. You two handcuff the women."

The women were frightened, and they cried. Sam questioned them for a few minutes and then made a search, but found nothing. She said, "The VC operating in this area put these workers up to this sabotage. To keep their families safe, they were forced to comply."

We heard a slight scuffle on the other side of the curtain. Roger had tackled a Vietnamese PX employee who was trying to escape, and with Tom's help had handcuffed the man. When Tom and Roger pushed the man through the door of the storeroom, all four girls started chattering at once. We didn't need an interpreter to understand. The man was a VC contact. Wisely, Tom had searched him and found a loaded Chinese-made, semiautomatic pistol. We called G-2 in to claim their prizes. I was concerned about the women and hoped they would be treated fairly. Sam said she would follow up and help if she could.

As Roger and Tom walked out ahead of us, I told Sarge, "You know, if you really want to make Roger's stay in Nam mean something, put him on a few patrols. I think you will see a big change in the man."

Rob agreed, and Mitchell nodded thoughtfully and asked us, "Would you two want to work with him?" We both answered in the affirmative.

A few days later, Roger rode with Bruce and me. We let him drive a little and he got to use the red light and siren whenever we had to stop someone.

"Ya know," he said slowly, as he sat at the canteen for a break, "I've been in the Army for five years. This is my first assignment as clerk to an MP company." Pausing, he added, "I've gotta tell ya. I like playing cops and robbers. This patrol was the most fun I've ever had."

We found him to be a good man, a good clerk, and a pretty good MP too.

Many of the clubs hired Vietnamese girls to "manage" their clubs, and ours was no exception. These *ladies*, simply put, were prostitutes, easily given to the call of the "almighty piaster." As far as I could tell, the only thing they seemed to manage well was their allotted time in the sack with a GI. Some of us were not in favor of these girls being on post all night because of security problems. Our weapons were out nearly all the time, and the girls had access to any of them, whether in a hootch where GIs were sleeping or in our clubs.

Our squad club was built between two hootches. The guys hired Ti Ling to keep the club area clean and serve the drinks (we had only pop and coffee). In each hootch there were one or two separate rooms at the front door for the squad leaders. Ours had two, but one was empty and it became Ti's room, for . . . well, you get the picture.

I paid her little or no attention. She was not particularly attractive and wore very heavy makeup. From what guys said, she was good at what she did. Nearly everyone in our company, as well as half of the GIs on the compound, had been with her. I suppose I presented her with a challenge. Captain Fairchild, the first sergeant, Mitchell, Smith, and I were holdouts. So, every time I went into our little club, she'd smile at me through her crooked brown teeth and say, "Why you no like Ti Ling? You go with Ti Ling now to room, I make you boo coo happy!"

"Ti, I like you just fine, but I'm not interested," I would say nearly every day. But I have to give her credit; she was persistent. Several times I found her sitting next to my bunk waiting for me to wake up. I had given her several reasons why we would not get together. None of them cut much ice. So, I was still a challenge to her. Even Bruce and Rob had given in.

Much of the time I was successful in ignoring and discouraging Ti; however, over time she became even more aggressive, and it got more and more difficult to sidestep her. There was one morning when I could not avoid her. I was the only one in our club when she showed up at 10:00 in the morning, late for work. I was enjoying a cup of coffee, waiting for my partner Bruce, who was in the latrine. When Ti walked in, I suddenly knew how a mouse felt when a hawk circled overhead. "Heaven help me," I muttered. The "hawk" began to look more like a vulture with every pass. Even though I was on duty, I knew, as did she, that someone would cover for me if I wanted to take the plunge.

She poured herself a cup of coffee, sat down across from me, and said, "Hey, Bic, we go now into little room, make love; and I make you feel very good."

As we sat at the table drinking coffee, an idea flashed through my head. I answered, "Ti Ling, I feel very good, now; but maybe you're right." Her eyes got real big. Sipping from my cup I added casually, "You know, Ti, back home I am a transit operator." She didn't have a clue it meant bus driver, and I left it that way.

She listened very intently and showed great interest in what I was saying. In the past, my comments to her were generally curt, so it probably appeared to her that I could be weakening, and perhaps be planning to have something more than just coffee.

"Tlansit opo-ata?" she asked.

"Close enough," I responded. "I drove a special bus." She nodded that she understood. "Back home I am paid to pick up girls every day." Pausing for effect, I watched her eyes as I sipped some coffee. "At times I pick up several women late in the evening and drop them off at their homes very early the next morning. Sometimes I start early in the morning and go on until late at night." Ti was pouting now as I explained further, "For my work, which I was really good at and enjoyed, I was paid more than fifty dollars each day."

About half way through this, Bruce entered the club. Smirking slightly, he got some coffee and joined us at the table. He nodded in agreement whenever she looked at him.

Ti said something in Vietnamese that, roughly translated, meant she wasn't quite buying my story. I was supposed to have turned in my city employment card when I left Seattle, but instead had kept it. Taking the tattered document out of my wallet I showed it to her. There was also a picture of me with my ex-girl friend, the one I had helped move to Spokane. The photo had been taken at a county fair there; my friend was dressed up in a saloon costume and I, as a gambler. That helped my story immensely.

I gave Bruce a wink, and we were all quiet for several moments. Then I turned to Ti Ling and said, "Because I like you, I will only charge you . . ." I paused as if I was working on a calculation in my mind. I was hoping she wouldn't see through this fabrication, and take me up on my silly offer. I continued, "…yes, for Ti Ling only twenty-five American dollars. You do have American dollars, don't you?"

She looked at me in disbelief and then at Bruce and asked, "You tink Bic say true?"

With a straight face, he nodded slowly in agreement. She got up from her chair, retrieved the coffeepot, and without saying a word, warmed up our coffee. She never bothered me again.

It was strange how news traveled. A day after my conversation with Ti, Sam knew all about it, and we had a good laugh. I was off until the next afternoon, and as we joked and talked, she invited me to have dinner with her in her trailer. I jumped at the chance to have a meal that was not from the mess hall or a C-rations box.

Sam knew her way around a kitchen, and I enjoyed the meal. Afterwards she pulled out a beautiful and expensive guitar. She played and sang several French folk songs as well as some American ones. I never expected to find so much beauty, grace, and wonderful music in the midst of a country in such turmoil.

I taught her a few songs, and we took turns playing her guitar. The evening was going perfectly up till 1:00 a.m., when the siren suddenly sounded a red alert. I went outside to use the MP field phone, which was close by. "Hi, Smitty, I'm up in trailer park with Xom," I explained. "Could I be picked up?" Walking along the perimeter road in the middle of the night during a red alert was not a really smart thing to do—not with so many nervous trigger fingers out there. Smith said he'd have someone meet me with my gear in a few minutes.

Sam had come with me. As I hung up, she said she had told her family she was changing her name to Samantha. I nodded approvingly, and we walked back to her trailer. We hurriedly closed the curtains and turned off the lights. As I made my way to the door listening for the sound of a jeep, I felt her warm arms wrap around me from behind. I turned to meet our first kiss, warm and full of wonder. We made our final goodbyes as a tap on the door told me I was late getting outside. When I opened the door, I was surprised to see Sergeant Mitchell.

"Hi Sarge, I had expected one of the regular patrols."

"Come on, Mills," he grumbled, "I'm tired of driving."

"Right, Sarge." As I hustled out the door I said, "Smitty said—ah—Sergeant *Smith* asked me to check the trailers for any lights."

Mitchell chuckled slightly. Looking back at Sam's he said, "I think you did a good job in checking her lights. Come on, we'll check the others on the long way back to the jeep." He handed me my pistol belt and a flashlight. "The rest of your gear is in the jeep."

As we walked through the trailers toward TOC, we observed only one mobile with its lights on. We knocked several times, but there was no answer.

Sam suddenly came up from behind and said, "I have the key, Sergeant. General Burke is in Saigon." Opening the door, she entered and turned out the lights.

"Thanks, Sam," I responded.

Mitchell and I checked on the two MP guards posted at the entrance to TOC. They were scared, green kids. After we talked and joked with them for a few minutes, they settled down some.

"We've got to get to the tower. They've reported some movement," Sarge told me as we made our way to the jeep. You know," he added, "if you get caught with that girl, you could get busted!" In a second breath, he added, "Might be worth it!"

I agreed. Hell, if I got busted for everything I was doing—seeing Sam, working with the orphans, and so on—I'd be the only GI out of half a million with negative rank. I'd have to pay the Army just to be in Nam. Now that was a dark thought.

There was a half moon out that night, and as I climbed into the jeep, a gun jeep, I said, "This bright moonlight will certainly help us in using the nightscope."

Mitchell agreed, but added, "The down side is, it's easier for Charlie to see us too."

As soon as I snapped my MP armband on the sleeve of my Army-green T-shirt, we headed for Gate Five, the best and fastest way to the tower from the mobiles.

"We're taking a slightly different approach," Sarge began. "Patrol one is manning Gate One; Gate Five has two new men from the post com-center. Patrol two is a rover, checking both north and south perimeters, and all the bunkers on post. Everyone will have to stay awake tonight. They're mostly green kids in our bunkers and in the tower. The corporal is in charge there though, and all the patrols are experienced men."

Out of left field, he asked me, "It's none of my business, but I'm curious. What the hell did you say or do that got Ti Ling so pissed off?"

Thinking for a moment, I simply said, "Basically, Sarge, I just gave her a big, long explanation of what 'no' means. Why do you ask?"

"Well, she just up and quit today. Went back to the construction boys."

As we approached Gate Five, I could make out two guards pointing their weapons at us, so I flicked on the red light for a second as we came to a stop.

"Hi, guys, how ya doin'?" I asked.

"Fine. Who are you?"

"We're from the MPs."

Mitchell chatted with them for a minute or two to help calm them down. Then he casually explained, "You know, boys, since most of the danger will probably be on the other side of the fence and highway, it might be a good idea to keep your weapons pointed more in that direction."

They were shaking so hard, it was a good thing for us that their fingers hadn't gotten any closer to the triggers. As Mitchell continued to work to quiet them I checked their weapons and I found that each had a round in the chamber and the safety off. If there had been a little more moon light, everyone could have seen me turn forty-nine shades of pale. Even Mitchell shivered and winced a little when I told him the good news.

Removing the rounds from each weapon, I clicked on the safeties and made sure each selector switch was on semiautomatic. Then I handed their weapons back and explained what I had done.

Leaving Mitchell for a moment, I walked over to the nearby bunker, which was being manned by some of the 199th, and called softly, "Frank. Hey, Frank, are you in there?"

"That's Sergeant Francis E. Mulkahy, if you please, you dumb-ass cop!" came a familiar gravely voice. A tall, lanky frame came out from the rear of the squat structure and began to saunter over to me.

"Hey, Frank, ah, I mean Sarge, congratulations," I said as he approached holding three fingers on his sleeve to indicate three chevrons.

"How many men do you have in the bunker?"

"Just three of us—me and two new men, and they're scared out of their skulls."

By this time, Mitchell had joined us and I explained, "All the gate guards are new in-country, Frank. The two on this gate damn near fired on us. Don't sneeze."

Even though the gates were locked at night, most of us felt that they were the weakest links in our perimeter.

"If you can, Frank, kinda watch out for these guys too. They're more likely to shoot one of us or themselves, than the enemy," I said.

"The tower has been reporting some activity all evening," Mitchell shared with the new sergeant. "We don't know what that means yet. We've gotta get up there to take a look-see." He turned back toward the gate where the two new men were standing, and added, "We may have to come back through here in a hurry, and I sure the hell don't want them shooting at us."

Frank nodded in agreement. Mitchell said he would tell the guards what was going on. Frank said, "No, Mitch, let me do it. I'll talk to them right now. You guys get on your way. We'll cover your ass on your return trip."

Mitchell liked the idea and, as we started toward the gate, Frank asked if we had some extra M-60 ammo.

"They brought us the wrong can of loose rounds," he told us. As I handed him an ammo can, he added, "Oh, by the way, Mills, I like your uniform. Cutoffs and a T-shirt; is that the new MP look?"

Anyone who has ever been in combat or who has been truly scared knows that humor is a real aid in settling nerves. It can also help to make one more alert. I was grateful for Frank's light touch just then. He was good with his men, but he was willing and able to work with anyone.

As we climbed into the jeep, Frank went over and introduced himself to our two gate guards. He helped them open the gate, and we sped off.

Nothing was said for a few moments as I drove up the road, but then I turned to Mitchell and said, "*That* must be the reason for this VC movement and alert."

"What in blazes are you talking about?" he demanded.

Starting to chuckle, I said, "This must be Ti Ling's revenge."

I had caught the good sergeant a little off guard, and he burst out laughing.

The gun jeep we rode in was probably the first vehicle with a full tank of gas that Mitchell had found in the motor pool. As we got nearer to the tower driveway, I asked if the M-60 was loaded. He said it was, and I asked him to lock and load my M-14, since that would have been really hard for me to do while driving.

Placing my rifle on the windshield frame, he said, "On safe."

As he checked his carbine, I radioed in that we were about to turn off the highway into the tower driveway entrance. "Please advise the tower: ETA one minute."

I couldn't always explain why I did certain things, but if I got an intuition to do or not to do something, I responded to it. At times things would happen so quickly there wasn't much time to explain an idea, but this was how most of us from the field had learned to work; especially the five men in our tight group. This was how we worked and survived. Perhaps it was instinct.

As soon as I started my turn into the driveway, I suddenly felt impelled to check the railroad and the area around it. By the time I hit the dirt shoulder where the asphalt highway met the driveway, I had slammed the jeep into four-wheel drive, removed the safety on the M-60, and taken the pin out of the turret. As I drove the jeep on the southeast side of the tower, I wondered why the floodlights were not on. Perhaps that was what spurred my actions. Turning on the headlights, I drove hard for several yards to the downward edge of the berm stopping at a 20- to 30-degree angle. Sitting twenty-five feet above the rails we came nearly face to face with a half dozen armed and very surprised VC walking up the side of the berm toward the tower.

Mitchell couldn't believe what he was seeing and voiced his reaction eloquently: "*Sonofabitch!*"

Still in the driver's seat, I reached high over my head to the sixty and squeezed off a few short bursts, mostly over their heads. I wasn't trying so much to hit any of them; I just wanted to say, "Gotcha! We see you!"

Sarge fired ten rounds from his carbine, and I let go with a few, better aimed, rounds from my rifle. With the projectiles kicking up sparks and dirt from off the rails and rail bed, our visitors suddenly wanted to be elsewhere, and they took off running down the berm, disappearing around the curve of the tracks. They never fired a shot. As they ran, I sprayed the underbrush on both sides of them, emptying my rifle.

As we backed up from the edge of the berm, Mitchell looked at the tower and said, "Where the hell are those guys? Why aren't those damn floodlights on?" Then he turned to me and asked, "How did you know?"

"I didn't know, Sarge. It was just a feeling, maybe because the floods were off. I'm not sure."

Two of our guys met us at the arched doorway to the tower. They laughed and said, "Hi, Sarge! You guys cleaning your guns?"

I was pissed and grabbed one of them and forced him up into the jeep to man the sixty while telling the other to lock and load his rifle. "You sorry bastards have no idea what just went on here, do you?" Even in the dim moonlight, I could see the color fade from their faces. Sometimes a little fear ain't bad.

Looking back at the man on the machine gun, I added, "If you see, or even hear, something move, you open fire. If you hear a twig snap, you open fire. It's unlikely you'll ever get another break like the one you guys got just now! Try to stay alive until morning and remember—there isn't a safe place in Nam."

Sarge was steaming, and he growled his approval. We found out that these guys had been in the bottom level of the tower trying to heat up some cans of rations. I hadn't seen Mitchell that angry since the incident with our former first sergeant a couple of months earlier.

"You sorry bastards should get down on your knees and thank whatever deity you believe in that you're still breathing," Sarge told them.

Then we went topside to the observation floor of the tower. I had forgotten that the corporal was in the tower. Immediately Sarge asked him, "Why aren't the floodlights turned on?"

The floods were as important to the tower defense as the floods at the bridge bunker were—perhaps more so. It was post S.O.P. (standard operating procedure) to have them on.

The corporal answered, "I thought we'd be less conspicuous." It was the wrong thing to say.

Mitchell reached out with both hands and tore off the corporal's stripes. He turned to the other guys and told them just how close to dying they had come. "You all better understand this, and fast—this is no fuckin' joke! This ain't basic; you're not back at Gordon. This is for real. Another half minute, and you'd all been wasted!"

While Sarge did his dressing-down, I switched on the floods and moved one of the two M-60s to the eastern side overlooking the rail bed. Giving a "shoot sign" to Mitchell, I sent another forty to fifty rounds out to the tracks and into the bushes. Since I had an expanded field of fire, I sent a few more rounds into the area around the curve and at the edge of the berm. I'm not sure if this action was "by the book," but we had learned at the Big Red One that it was important to do a follow-up action with some noise so the VC wouldn't think we were unprepared and come in for another, closer look. I think we confused the hell out of Charlie that night, because we didn't hear anymore from them.

The alert lasted six hours. Dropping Mitchell off at his hootch, I took the jeep back to the motor pool. Dawn was now long past and I needed a few hours in my bunk. Walking back toward my hootch, I suddenly saw a huge ball of fire rise into the sky. I yelled, "Hit the dirt!" and dove for the ground myself. A second or two later, we heard the blast and felt the concussion as it swept through the company area. The enemy had hit our fuel depot again. This explosion was not as severe as the one we had suffered a few weeks earlier, but it still got everyone's attention. Army Intelligence was really on the ball that morning, because three minutes *after* the fuel dump went up the siren sounded the alert again—only fifteen minutes past the *all clear*.

I ran back to the motor pool and got the jeep again, intending to pick up Mitchell. But Smitty stepped out into the street and stopped me.

"Hi, Smitty, what's up now?" I asked.

"You go get showered and hit the hay. The alert is only yellow, not red," he explained. " Keep your gear ready, and I'll take the jeep back to the motor pool."

After I cleaned my weapons, I headed for the mess hall for some milk and doughnuts. Then I did what Smith had recommended, except in reverse. I went to bed first. When I woke up, at about 2:00 in the afternoon, I was pleasantly surprised to see Paul's smiling face. He was in a good mood.

"Hey, you best get your butt out of the sack. We're partners today, and you've only got thirty minutes till guard mount."

"Welcome home, Buddy," I said as we shook hands. "What's our alert status?"

"Oh, all that ended about 10:00, just about the time I got back. Charlie's afraid of me, ya know," he cracked.

"Hey, you're a little early, aren't you?" I asked. "You weren't due back for another two weeks."

He was all ready for work, and he followed me to the shower area so we could talk. As I got ready, he filled me in on his trip. Everything was fine at home. He and his wife had had a long talk and had gotten some counseling from their church. As it turned out, she had not been dating. She was just mad at the Army. Anyway, he and his wife decided that he should return to Nam earlier than scheduled, so that he could get home sooner.

By the time I was ready, we still had fifteen minutes. I picked up my weapons and gear, and we headed for the jeep that Paul had checked out. We drove to the mess hall for some coffee and cold cereal. Bruce and Rob were just finishing when we joined them. It was great to have Paul back on the team. Some of the guys ribbed me about my late hour with Sam in her trailer, but I just smiled as we headed for guard-mount inspection.

Everything settled into a general routine once more, which gave me more time for the kids. Evidently the temple was gaining a reputation. A group of guys from a construction battalion brought in a 12-year-old girl with a 3-month-old baby. It still bothers me to think what we did to some of those innocent people.

I was still trying to adopt the little girl and her brother. The paperwork and process resembled a yo-yo. It was up, then down. During one of the upswings, Top had given me permission to go into Saigon. There were even more applications. Sam knew I needed to get into the city and that a ride was needed. She told our favorite one-star general about what I was trying to do. Sam served as the general's interpreter, and she had already been a real help to me as a translator during some of the adoption interviews. The general arranged for me to be his driver for a day, since his regular driver was on a week's R&R in Hawaii. I suggested it might be a safe idea to take Rob along as an extra man. The general agreed.

Captain Fairchild and our first sergeant gave us the written orders to drive the general and his interpreter (Sam) to Saigon. Casually the CO asked how I was so familiar with Eagles and Stars (colonels and generals). I just shrugged. Having two GIs along made the general feel easier about traveling. There had been a few reports about stepped-up VC activity in our vicinity. I don't know why the general didn't use a chopper to fly into town.

Most GIs rarely get to know officers as people. This man was very much like Colonel Wilson, a down-to-earth, no-nonsense kind of officer with a good sense of humor.

When we arrived in Saigon, we dropped the general off at the main operations building not far from the presidential palace. He gave us his personal pass to use the vehicle, and instructions on when and where to pick him up. Since Rob and I were in our official MP garb, I really didn't think anyone would stop us.

At the Vietnamese Consulate Building I filled out several more forms. Sam was indispensable when we talked to the people at the Consulate. Their forms were written in Vietnamese, and in very poor English. By the middle of the afternoon, I finally began to realize what I had feared: neither of the two governments seemed interested in having me—or any GI—adopt a child. Although no one would come right out and say so, it was obvious. I was serious about adopting, though, and so I went through the drills just the same.

We picked up the general at the appointed time and headed for Long Binh. Rob drove while we all discussed the number of exceptions for each adoption rule. Even the general found most of the rules ridiculous. Over the next few months I made more trips to Saigon. Representatives of the Republic of South Vietnam even came to see me a few times, always with the same results: just one more form to fill out.

From April to September of 1968, everything settled into an uneasy but peaceful pattern of existence. There were very few enemy contacts or incursions into Long Binh Province. Every so often the VC would air mail us a few rockets resulting in little or no damage. Their favorite target was the air base in Bien Hoa.

Each day became a repeat of the one before—always hot and humid, with all of us wanting to go home. That was the real battle—the battle of being so close to rotating home you could smell Mom's hot apple pie, and still having to wait. Only time was the solution for this problem.

It was the end of July when Bruce, Paul, and Rob packed up for their flight back to the States. I was sad, but happy for them. For over a month, they had been packing and sending home large boxes of personal belongings and mementos.

The morning of their departure, Top found us in the mess hall and asked, "Hey, Mills, would you rather take these bums to the air base yourself, or shall I send them on the bus?"

"Of course, Top. I'll drive 'em," I said as I jumped to my feet.

"Here's the motor pool slip. Go get a jeep and find another man to ride with you."

"Hell, I'll go, Top," Kent yelled from across the room. "I'll ride shotgun."

Top nodded approvingly, and he strolled back to the orderly room. It would be the last trip for the five of us. I knew my friends were eager to get home and resume their lives with their families. I was glad for them, but this was still a bittersweet occasion. We had spent a lot of time covering each other's butts. I would be hard-pressed to trust anyone else. The five of us had so much in common.

We left the compound early so we could stop for a few minutes at the orphanage. I was glad to see all the kids, but I wondered what would become of them after the others and I went home. The women and some of the older kids cried. The Vietnamese people held no inhibitions when it came to showing their feelings. They were always so honest. We, on the other hand, have so many hang-ups; so much baggage. There is a lot in life we miss.

As we sped along the highway and through several little villages, we came upon a wide, open plain. Out about 150 yards stood a row of thin, concrete telephone poles. I slid the jeep to a stop and Bruce asked, "What's up, Vic?"

"We're early, guys," I said. Looking at the poles, then at my three departing team members, I pointed to the M-60 and held up my M-14. "Betcha a buck you can't hit one with the first round." Bruce took my rifle, Rob grabbed the sixty, and Paul hauled up Kent's rifle. "Careful you don't hit the jeep guys," I said laughing.

"That's your kind of game, Mills!" responded Rob, as he fired a couple of short bursts.

Nearly all of the rounds found their target. Pieces of concrete flew off as tracers and non-tracers hit the poles! I paid my dollar—Army script, of course, and we reminisced about the many hours of patrol and guard duty we had pulled together. We talked about our stay at Di-An, and the guys there. Sharing some shade we stretched out on the ground under a tree while we talked. "That was good duty," I said softly, "it probably saved our lives." The five of us were in complete agreement.

When we got to the airbase staging area, we ran into three guys from the Deuce Platoon who were flying home too. We had a cold drink and more good talk. Kent and I tried to look more important than we were. Finally a very young lieutenant came over to us, and in a high-pitched voice made it clear that personnel not boarding a flight were "dismissed!" He made us wish we had been in our MP armbands and helmets on. We did what groups of GIs always do—we promised to write and to visit.

Kent and I stepped away from the staging area and watched them board. Then we headed back to the jeep. Driving out of the town of Bien Hoa, we stopped along the side of the road to watch the DC-8 climb into a partly cloudy sky.

I chose the right front as I got back into the jeep. Perched on top of the seat back, I held on to the M-60 turret, and then settled back down into the seat. My mind flashed back to my first hour in Nam and the bus ride down this same road through the same town and villages. It seemed as if it had been just the day before. Until that moment, I hadn't thought much about that day. Now the memories flooded back—the street vendors, the milling people. We had gotten to know a few of the locals since then, and they called out our names and waved as we passed by.

I sat quietly as Kent drove slowly along the narrow road through the hamlet. Approaching the open field again I climbed up behind the M-60 and fired a long burst at one of the middle poles, hitting it over and over again. Kent commented on how skillful the other three and I were. As I took my seat once more, I wondered out loud, "What career can a guy get into with this kind of a skill? Sharpshooter or marksmen, maybe? I can shoot jeeps, snakes, and oh, that ever-friendly pet, the water buffalo!"

Chapter 11
SAM AND THE KIDS

It became increasingly clear that there were some serious personal problems I needed to deal with, but Vietnam was not the place to do it. I still had to survive several more weeks of duty. My ex-wife had written several times, even sending pictures of my son Micheal. She suggested that we might get back together. For my son's sake I did consider this, but only briefly; it wouldn't work. Then there was Sam. We were no longer just bending a few rules; we were mangling them.

Shortly after seeing my three friends off, Roger came into the company club looking for me. "Hey, Mills, there you are! Been lookin' all over for you. Top wants to see you ASAP."

"Okay, I'm on my way."

Stepping into our orderly room, I stopped at Top's desk. "You sent for me, Top?"

"Oh, yes. Hi, Mills," he said, looking up from a stack of papers. "I have some news for you, but I'm not sure if it's good or bad." Shuffling through some papers, he picked up one that looked very official from command in Saigon. "Here it is. This may help you get those two kids." Scanning the directive, he continued, "Okay. If you extend your tour of duty by two months, actually nine weeks, you can receive a six-month early out from active duty."

I kept listening for the catch, but Top assured me, "These regs are bonafide, and if you have an 'early out' it would be a cinch to adopt those two kids. The paperwork should fly through channels."

Thanking Top, I collected the forms and headed for my bunk. I had gotten serious about Sam and had asked her to come to the States with the kids and me. We could be married as soon as I was separated from the Army. We talked about this possibility, and although she seemed excited about the prospect, we came to no definite decision. I had already made arrangements in advance to fly the kids and Sam to San Francisco, where they could stay with my older sister: just in case Sam said yes, and the adoption was approved

So I extended my tour the nine weeks, but I wanted to leave the spit-and-polish of soldiering behind. Top told me that I would not be assigned to pull any more hazardous duty. I told him that if my experience could be useful to new men coming in, I would just as soon work. It would help to pass the time more quickly.

A few days after signing my extension papers, the Vietnamese government turned down my latest request for adoption. They maintained that I would be in-country eight days past the official date of my application's expiration. There would be no extensions. The main reason the officials gave for not approving my previous applications was, that under my earlier military requirements, I would still have to serve an additional six months stateside. In getting rid of one problem I ended up with another—eight days. It was clearly a no-win situation no matter what I did. Sam's uncle, who was in the Vietnamese legislature, tried to intervene, but he was abruptly turned down as well. Even Top, the CO, and Colonel Wilson tried to intercede on my behalf, but to no avail.

Sam and I continued seeing each other, and there seemed to be a genuine bond between us. Although she hadn't actually said yes about returning with me to the States, she certainly hadn't said no. She had collected a lot of information on Washington State and the Pacific Northwest. At times, she even seemed giddy about the prospect of going to America. Even her family seemed pleased.

A couple of weeks after the final adoption refusal, I found a note from Sam on my bunk. This was not unusual; we regularly communicated this way—she'd leave notes on my bunk, and I'd leave notes on the door of her trailer.

Her message was only two lines. It read, "Vic, our being together probably wasn't meant to be. Stay safe and have a wonderful life back at your beautiful Washington." She signed it, "Love, Samantha." For many days I tried to locate her. Even her general was surprised. He had been told she had returned to France. At any rate, I never heard from her again.

For the next couple of weeks, I was filled with anger and hurt. I felt lonely and betrayed—by my own nation and by the South Vietnamese government I was trying to help. I felt like the world's most gullible SOB! The CO and Top were concerned about my sudden change in attitude. Both knew the series of disappointments that had quickly challenged my life. I still did my job, but some of the guys, including Kent, thought of me as a 175-pound bomb waiting to explode.

During this time of trial, I had many long talks with my chaplain friend and also with Colonel Wilson before he rotated home. With part of my free time, I assisted the chaplain with the services and however else I could help. I found it difficult to go to the orphanage, and made only short visits. In my heart and deep within my soul I felt I had failed the little girl and boy. I had really looked upon them as a daughter and a son. One day Jim, the chaplain, understanding my state of mind, made me drive him out to the orphanage for a long visit. It truly helped.

Having friends and work also helped, and I gradually came back to being myself.

"Mills wake up." Roger was shaking my bunk. "Come on, Damn it. Vic, wake up. We got trouble man! Vic! Get up!" the clerk finally yelled into my ears.

That did it; I was up. "Okay, okay; I'm up already."

"The CO and Top want to see you ASAP."

I struggled to sit up on the edge of my bunk, only to see Roger disappear through the door of the hootch. It was mid-morning. I had worked bunker guard duty the night before and had been asleep for only a few hours. I slipped on my shower thongs, cut-offs, and a T-shirt. Then, half awake, I staggered and tripped my way to the orderly room. When I stepped inside I made a sleepy effort to come to attention, but no one even acknowledged me. Roger handed me a cup of coffee, a tip-off that I wasn't going back to bed for awhile.

The first sergeant, the captain, and Kent were studying a map.

"Mills, get over here and tell us if you're familiar with this road and the surrounding area," Top growled anxiously.

Something was not right, that was plain to see. My superiors seemed highly concerned and angry. With a quick look at the map I said, "Yes, sir. We did two convoys down this stretch of highway four or five months back. The second one cost us a jeep, and the country nearly lost a water buffalo." Then I asked, "Why? What's up, Top?"

"We loaned out two new men to help on a convoy," began Top. "Their jeep broke down near here," he explained, pointing to an inked circle.

The captain now grimly took over the discussion, saying, "And the major in charge just left *my two men* there to fend for themselves." Then he added, "Everyone else in the zone is tied up with TOC security. The generals are meeting here around noon."

The CO and Top looked at me and then at Kent.

Top asked, "Can you guys find those two boys and get them back here?"

"Sure," I answered. The radio operator had just come in through the back door, and I turned to him and asked, "Tom, have they seen any VC?"

"Maybe," he answered, holding a piece of paper in his hand. "Captain, they just called in reporting a group of men moving across the paddies and grass about half a mile out from them."

The captain spelled out what he wanted. "Whatever it takes, bring those boys back. *Now!* I expect to see you back here as well." He added, "I can't guarantee you backup, but we're trying."

"The backup would be nice, sir," I responded, "but we understand the situation."

Kent and I looked at Roger, and Kent finally said, "Well, are you coming or not?"

Roger looked questioningly at Top, who nodded, growling, "Get out of here."

Roger let out a huge, "*All right!*"

Then I told him the specific jeep we wanted. "Get it off patrol if you have to, but get it."

The radio operator piped up, "That jeep is on patrol. I'll call it in right now."

"Lights and siren," I added. I gave Kent and Roger a short verbal list of the tools we needed—an extra M-60 with five cans of ammo, a full box of bandoleers for our M-14s, plus two M-79 grenade launchers and forty rounds. Then I ran to my hootch to get dressed and get my gear. In less than ten minutes, we were driving through our gate with Kent at the wheel. Roger had grabbed a bunch of doughnuts and a thermos of coffee from the mess sergeant.

I was glad to see that the jeep had nearly a full tank of gas. I told Kent, "Keep it on the floor, with lights and siren."

This vehicle was the fastest jeep in the pool and handled the best on the road. It was a Kaiser-Jeep and would outrun anything in the area. As we blasted down the highway, I was still working on getting dressed. It was only a few miles to the highway junction cutoff where we had assisted several convoys; the latest, some months back—the last real job our team of five had worked.

Roaring along, we noticed that the 720th and 716th MPs were lining the highway, and BJ and his partner were moving traffic off the road ahead of us. Apparently they knew we were coming. We were doing nearly seventy-five miles per hour. When we reached the intersection, I hollered at Kent to take the turn in third gear at forty-five miles per hour.

Kent responded with, "You're crazy, man! We'll flip."

I assured him, " I know this vehicle. Just do it."

We were doing over fifty as we rounded the curve. Cutting into the right dirt shoulder, the tires bawled their complaint. We were soon back up to seventy-five miles per hour.

Kent leaned toward me with a big grin and yelled, "I want to take this sonofabitch home with me. Think it'll fit in my duffel bag?"

I laughed as we continued to race against time.

We had eaten the doughnuts and spilled most of the coffee. We did manage to sip some of what was left as we passed the mess-kit cup around. Because of the general's motorcade and meeting at II Field Force, I knew there wouldn't be a backup from any unit close to II Field Force.

I began to calculate our ETA and rendezvous.

Roger tapped me on the shoulder and said, "Vic, X-ray 3 is calling us," and handed me the handset.

"X-ray 3, this is X-ray two-niner. What's your situation? Over."

"Mills, this is Lucas. We have what looks like thirty-plus Victor Charlies about five clicks out. Fifteen minutes ago we counted over fifty, and we can't figure out where the others went. Over."

"Lucas, check your flanks and your rear areas—*now*. Fire at anything you see. Repeat. *Fire at anything you see*. Hold on. Our ETA is about five minutes."

I guess my instructions were clear because I heard their M-60 barking into action as he answered.

Looking at our speedometer, I hollered at Kent, "Anything left?"

"No! This vehicle is not supposed to go eighty. We're nudging that now," he hollered back.

"We're less than five miles away from them," I yelled again. "Click off another three miles, then slow it down to fifty."

He nodded.

Turning to Roger, I yelled, "Get on the sixty. Lock and load it and your rifle." All three M-14s were ready too. As Kent slowed down, I placed our rifles above the dashboard and hood. Reaching back, I pulled up the second machine-gun, opened the front leg stands and set it up on the hood as well.

Grabbing the handset, I called, "X-ray 3, this is X-ray two-niner. We are less than two miles from your 20 (location)."

The radio crackled and Lucas exclaimed excitedly, "Hey, Mills, how'd you know they were behind us already? We caught 'em and they've moved back, but they're still on three sides. Over."

As we rounded a long sweeping curve, we could make out a half dozen VC lookouts about five hundred yards off the road. They were looking so intently in the opposite direction they hadn't heard us coming. Roger and I opened up on them with the two 60s. They were so completely surprised that four of them dropped their weapons and took off running.

As we left the curve, we saw a more ominous situation ahead. About twenty-five VC were on the blind side of the roadway from the stalled jeep, moving along a gully toward our friends. The rest of the enemy force had moved on, leaving this group behind to take care of two GIs in a broken-down jeep. Our speed was down to forty now, and I pointed out a spot off the right shoulder where we could come in behind them. We couldn't have planned this better— the VC in this group still hadn't seen or heard us, even with our earlier burst of gunfire.

Kent shifted into four-wheel drive as we came off the blacktop and onto the shoulder overlooking the dry-wash gully. We bounced down the side and into the shallow part of the wash where we came to a stop, and began firing our two M-60s and an M-14. Roger had even gotten off a couple of rounds from the grenade launcher. I guess it sounded like half a battalion as the explosions and .30 caliber rounds ricocheted all around the enemy kicking up clouds of dirt. The VC never fired a shot. They just threw down their weapons, squatted on the ground and placed their hands on their heads.

After a few moments, Kent moved the jeep back to the shoulder of the roadway. He positioned himself so that he could see the surrounding country. Taking the sixty off its turret and setting it on the hood, he used the jeep as cover. Lucas came running up to assist Roger and me with the prisoners. One of the first things I told the VC to do was to strip down. I wasn't about to pat down twenty-five enemy troops. We were sure someone understood English well enough, but they played dumb and refused my orders.

I told Kent, "I think that now they know that there are just five of us, they might be thinking of un-surrendering."

" Vic, they've never heard of *the five* before," he said with a smile.

With Kent and Roger manning the two machine guns and Lucas holding his rifle, all trained on the enemy, I stepped over to the jeep's radio. Keeping the prisoners in sight, I picked up the mike to call in and flipped on the external speaker, "Handcuff, Handcuff this is X-ray two-niner. Over."

"X-ray two-niner, X-ray two-niner, this is Handcuff. Report. Is that you, Mills? Over."

"Handcuff, this is X-ray two-niner. That's affirmative. We have rendez-voused with X-ray 3. Both Mike Papas okay. We have captured twenty-five VC; I say again; twenty-five Victor Charlies, who refuse to cooperate. Can-I-shoot-them? Over."

I looked up at Kent and Roger. Both looked surprised until I winked at them. Then they understood what I was doing. Twenty-five prisoners against five of us could make for a tricky situation. I didn't want to shoot them, but I didn't want them to know that. And I didn't want to be shot either. I was trying to pull off one hell of a bluff.

"X-ray two-niner, X-ray two-niner. This is Handcuff. Over."

Taking up the mike again, I answered, "X-ray two-niner, go."

"Mills, this is the captain. If they won't cooperate, shoot the bastards! Over."

"X-ray two-niner. Roger. I will shoot the prisoners. Over," I responded, hoping that the CO was playing the same game I was.

Things began to look better. The captured VC certainly didn't know our CO, but the ones who understood enough English believed the order to shoot and quickly jabbered something to the others. By the time I'd hung up the mike and turned around, our Asian friends were buck-naked. It was that fast. They understood us quite well. We picked up their weapons, leaving their clothing on the ground.

"X-ray two-niner, be advised. Backup is on its way, compliments of the U.S. 9th Cav and an ARVN company of infantry. Do you copy? Over."

"This is X-ray two-niner. Good copy. Thank you, sir."

A few seconds later Kent hollered, "The 9th Cav just called in wanting to know if we were the MPs requesting taxi service."

Looking where Kent was pointing, I saw diesel smoke and dust. What a beautiful sight! As they passed by the disabled MP jeep, their motor pool sergeant and another man dropped off to look it over. The column stopped at our checkpoint. Two officers, one an ARVN lieutenant and the other a U.S. cav captain, along with two staff sergeants jumped off the two lead APCs. Pointing to one of the prisoners, I said, "This man is either an officer or sergeant because the others kept looking at him."

The cav and ARVN units took over the prisoners. They checked the captives' clothing and allowed them to dress before loading them on two trucks. We walked to the other side of the road where Lucas had been talking with another sergeant showing him where he and his partner had first seen the VC. The sergeant deployed two other APCs and thirty riflemen. Two hundred yards apart, they began to sweep the open grassy areas on both sides of the rice field.

About twenty minutes later, our other jeep pulled up with the sergeant and mechanic inside. Our other MP driving said, "The fuel pump went out, so these guys put a new one on."

As the E-5 sergeant climbed out of the jeep, Kent said with a smile, "Just send the bill to Haig."

We thanked the captain and the sergeants for stopping by. They had been on their way to bolster security for the general's meeting, but this was a good stop as well. While the rest of the command went ahead to set up their command post, a third of them had been sent to assist us. Now they'd have to catch up.

As we drove off, we saw some of the cav troops bringing in additional prisoners. It had been quite a morning..

"Let's get back. I'm tired," I told Kent as he accelerated up to speed, with the other jeep close behind.

Kent informed the company that we were on our way back. It was just past 1:00 p.m. We had been gone nearly two hours. On the way out, we had driven hard and fast to get to the stranded men. I considered the difference it had made to save that five or ten minutes. Without our efforts, those green kids probably would not have fired on the enemy; they didn't have enough experience. It's likely they would have been killed.

Driving back to the 552nd compound, we noticed a lot of gunships overhead. We had almost forgotten the general's staff meeting. There was a lot of local traffic at the intersection, but being a cop, I simply drove around and through it.

As we entered our compound Top was coming out of the orderly room to meet us. We dropped off our two machine guns to be cleaned. Captain Fairchild came from the other direction. With our gear in hand, we stopped at attention.

Fairchild said, "Good job, boys."

We learned later that the CO and Top planned to file charges against the officer of the convoy for needless endangerment of his men. I never heard what happened. From what we knew of the captain and first sergeant, we guessed that somebody, somewhere, was probably holding his head in his lap.

That was my last taste of combat. I have always been grateful that I saw so little fighting in Vietnam, and I salute and honor those GIs during whose tours the hell never let up. My next few weeks included a short stay at TOC at the Bien Hoa Air Base and at our compound. I would have been sent back to the 90th Replacement, but they had been hit with rockets earlier that week, so I stayed put. I pulled bunker duty and rode on patrol a couple more times, but the last two weeks in Nam I was completely off the duty roster.

The time just dragged. It was hard staying busy, but I was allowed to drive Kent to his plane. He left a few weeks ahead of me.

With mixed thoughts about things at home and about Sam, I visited the orphanage and the two kids more often.

I was scheduled to leave for the States on November 26, 1968; however, one Sunday shortly after I returned from services, Top gave me different news. He came into the hootch saying that I had been rescheduled and was to leave eight days sooner—on the 18th—the eight days I would have needed to complete the kids' adoption. Had I only known this sooner, I could have taken the kids home.

November in Southeast Asia is summer, and the median temperature reaches the 110-degree mark. The oppressive heat reminded me of when I first arrived in Nam, nearly fifteen months earlier.

A week before I was to leave, I was summoned to the chaplain's office to meet some friends of his. They were civilians, two unmarried sisters who had lived in Southeast Asia since the Second World War. Although not missionaries from a church, they were sincere and dedicated ladies. They asked to visit the orphanage, so the chaplain drove us out in his jeep. The sisters fell in love with all of the kids and their mothers, and the feelings were mutual. They asked if they could take over running the orphanage after I left Nam. I was pleased, and knew the other guys would be also. These two women, who so loved the Vietnamese people, would continue what we had started.

As I got ready to go home, I had a new problem—all of my old uniforms were too small. Although I had gone from 200 pounds back to a more comfortable 175, I was still fifteen pounds heavier than when I arrived in-country. I sat in the mess hall having coffee with Top and a couple of others and said, laughing, "It's funny, but I need new uniforms that I'll wear for less than a week. Seems like a lot of expense for such a short period of time." They all nodded in agreement. With all that I needed I wasn't sure it could be pulled off within just four days.

Two days before I was to leave, my new duds arrived. Immediately I took them to the two women who ran the sewing and alterations concessions for the company. The barber who shared the small building gave me a quick trim. All of them were very kind, and the women made sure that my "unies" were finished by the end of the day. When I picked them up, the seamstresses cried and said, "We very sad for us and very glad for our good friend, go home."

At first they wouldn't let me pay for their work; however, as I left, I took out all of the Vietnamese currency I had (about three times the bill) and put it in the hands of the older mama-san, saying, "This money won't buy anything back home. You are my friends. You take it." With more tears and hugs, they accepted.

For some time our three little house girls, Lin, her sister Li, and their friend had wanted makeup kits. They had seen ads in the many magazines and newspapers that would filter through our living area, and Sam had shared a little makeup with them. I took the last of my military funny money and bought a kit for each of the girls. Billie, one of the girls from the Red Cross Center, went with me to the PX to help pick out something appropriate for 13-year-olds. I made sure Billie would be with the girls when they were given their gifts so she could show the young ladies how to use them. All the gifts were a success.

Most of my personal items had already been sent home—souvenirs and such. I now packed whatever I could manage to stuff inside my duffel bag. The girls came to say goodbye and to show me how they looked in their makeup and in the jeans and halter-tops that Billie had given them. They cried, and jokingly Li and her sister Lin tried to climb into my duffel bag, saying, "We go home too, with Meo." (Meo was as close as any of them could get to pronouncing "Mills.")

Chapter 12
MY TICKET HOME

"Where are the CO and Top?" I asked Roger as I shouldered my duffel and overnight bags and headed out the door of my hootch for the last time.

"They're in the orderly room waiting for you," he answered.

As we walked toward the orderly room I had bittersweet feelings about leaving. When I arrived in Nam, it seemed this day was so far away; perhaps even unreachable, but now it was here. For a long time, I could not understand why anyone would wish to do more than one tour. Now I knew. It was the people: sometimes a true love interest, sometimes just friends with whom one has worked so successfully. I had experienced all of the above. I had three love interests: the Vietnamese people, all the families we had helped, and Xom.

Memories of the past fourteen months flooded my thoughts like old movies: all I had done, and what I gotten away with; all of the crazy things that had gone on; the larger fears and the smaller triumphs; the joys and the disappointments. I was a little uneasy about returning home—alive and well, when so of many others, friends from basic training, AIT and from the First Infantry would not be going home at all.

When I stepped into the orderly room, Top and Captain Fairchild were chatting. I dropped my duffel bag, snapped to attention, and saluted, "Good morning, Captain; First Sergeant."

Top walked over to me, shook hands and handed me a cup of coffee. "I know this is a good brew because we stole some of your coffee," he said with a smile.

Until I headed for the plane, the three of us sat and talked like the old friends we had really become. I regretted not seeing Sergeant Mitchell again. He was staying for a second tour and was on a thirty-day leave home with his wife and daughter.

As the Boeing 707 lifted off the tarmac, I glanced at my watch. It was 10:05 a.m. In twelve to fifteen hours we would be landing at the Seattle-Tacoma International Airport. Looking around the plane, I didn't really expect to see anyone I knew. Most of the guys I'd come over with had gone back in September, but sitting just behind the bulkhead divider was my old friend BJ. The fellow in the aisle seat offered to trade places with me.

BJ and I chatted for a few minutes and I said, "Hey, you're the guy with a gorgeous wife back home. I don't understand why you extended."

"Well, it's very simple," he began. "Just like you, I get a six-months early out. My wife and I talked about it when I was on R&R. Prior to extending; I had just applied for college. I've been accepted at the University of Oklahoma starting winter quarter. All the paperwork is done, so the extension works out just fine. We'll have nearly two months to find an apartment near the campus and get settled. Then we can play house for awhile before I have to concentrate on my studies."

We continued talking for almost four hours. BJ wanted to be a schoolteacher. Seeing all those kids in the old temple had convinced him to choose that field. "History, I think," he said, "so that when the history books are written about the Vietnam War, I can tell the kids what is true and what is bullshit." Then with a somber look on his face he added, "Vic, I'm, I'm not very good at this, but I want you to know how sorry I am about you and Sam, and the two kids."

"Thanks, BJ. I appreciate that, " I said softly.

After awhile one of the stewardesses asked me to return to my own seat because we were preparing to land in the Philippines. BJ and I said our goodbyes. From the Philippines he was scheduled to take a connecting flight to Oakland, and I would fly on to Washington State.

In a short time I was airborne again, and the rest of the flight was uneventful. After visiting with two other guys, I slept the rest of the way to Seattle. Someone announced that it was 10:00 at night and we were getting ready to land at SeaTac. All those time zones can really be confusing. My watch was still set on Vietnam time.

As the plane touched down I could see it had been raining, and we taxied to a rather deserted part of the airport, where we waited for nearly half an hour. Finally one of the stewardesses opened the side door to let in a second lieutenant. He directed all personnel to gather their gear and proceed to the waiting buses. When it was my turn to step out the door, I was greeted by a refreshing light rain and clean-smelling air. We had gone from 100-plus degree temperatures and like humidity to a wet 45 degrees. I loved it. I was home.

It took us just thirty minutes to get from the plane to Fort Lewis. As we passed through the post gates, I could smell the smoke from the coal-fired furnaces. Now it was a welcome odor. When we stopped in front of a row of rather new, low-roofed buildings, I had to laugh to myself—this was a far cry from my first introduction to the Fort and to the Army. Well, at least they didn't lose us this time.

Picking up my bags, I stepped off the bus and followed the group into one of the buildings behind some barracks. Once inside, someone near the front hollered "Au-ten-hut." I looked toward the front. This group was enlisted men only. The officers had gone into another building. No one snapped to attention; we were too tired. Immediately, an officer gave the order, "Rest. Smoke if you have 'em," and introduced himself as Colonel-something.

This building had several little cubicles that went down a long hall. We were to strip to our shorts so that we could have another Army physical, including an X ray. I remember seeing several doctors standing in the corridor along with a dozen or so nurses.

As I walked down the hall, wondering which cubicle I was to use, I felt a warm hand on my bare arm and a soft voice that flashed me back to Nam. "Vic, is that you?"

Turning my head, I saw a face I almost recognized.

"Do I know you?" I asked.

With a smile that could melt Mount Rainier, the nurse pulled me out of line. "My name is Janie. I was one of the nurses assigned to the Long Binh post hospital."

"Yes, I do remembered you," I said, smiling. "Yeah, you always treated us with dignity. You made us feel like we were more than a medical chart or a body in a numbered bed." I had been in that hospital in Long Binh for food poisoning and dehydration. Janie was always friendly and considerate; she was the only one who would call my friend, the chaplain, for me. She was so gentle; she cared for each GI (at least this one) as though she were caring for a child. Oh yes, I remembered Janie.

"Your husband — is he still in Nam?" I asked.

"No, he's in the next building. He was on your plane," she answered.

I was glad he was okay. While we visited, she did her part of the examination, and I was back in the hall before I realized she had even begun.

"This is strictly against regulations," she said, and then she kissed me on the cheek and wished me well. Over the past nineteen months, I had found there were several things that were against regulations that I liked quite well; I believe I did my best to find them.

By 12:30 I had passed the physical and was climbing into a clean bunk with non-gritty sheets and two soft, woolen blankets. The room was kept at 75 degrees to help compensate for the temperature and weather changes we had experienced.

Morning found me still in the Army, but just barely. At 7:00 a.m. two sergeants came through the barracks to wake us—quite humanely, I might add. I showered, shaved, and dressed, and was eating breakfast by 8:00. Nineteen months earlier, all of this would have taken only fifteen minutes. In Nam, there were times we were quicker than that. But most of us were in the "I'm home now, and I really don't give a shit" mode.

Things were moving very quickly, and within a couple hours thirty of us were on an Army bus heading back to the airport. In my pocket were new orders to a nonexistent reserve group in Saint Louis, an airline ticket to San Francisco and two months' pay and bonuses, in cash and check. Before leaving Fort Lewis, I called family members to give them my arrival time in the Bay Area.

Seventy-five days before leaving Vietnam, I had ordered a new car through the PX: a '69 Chevy Corvair Corsa sports model. I had hoped to find it waiting for me in San Francisco, but because of everyone's favorite consumer watchdog, the Corvair line had been discontinued. I phoned the Seattle dealer, who told me the "good" news: the car had missed being built by just ten units. I still bought a Chevy— a used 1964 Impala hardtop.

I stayed with my sister and her family near Santa Cruz for a few days. She had arranged to have my son Michael there. Being reunited with him was truly a joy. I took Mike, my sister, and her two children to visit my mother in Palm Springs.

It was still warm by California standards, and I was slowly getting acclimated to the cooler weather. Being in California for a month or so was probably much better than starting off in Seattle's winter, which I learned was one of the worst on record. With a little swimming and the dry 85-degrees, I was able to hold onto my marvelous Southeast Asian tan a little longer too.

A few days after leaving Vietnam, my extra pounds quickly evaporated. I was reminded during my discharge physical that drinking less soda and more water would certainly help. This, coupled with some light running, took care of the weight problem. Not only did my old Levi's fit better, I was just feeling better. There's no substitute for a good night's sleep and regular food.

We all had a nice three-day visit, and then my sister and her family returned to Santa Cruz. After taking Mike back to his mother in Los Angeles I went to visit my older brother and his family nearby. He took me to a Rams game at the Los Angeles Coliseum. I don't believe I've ever had a better tasting hot dog. I stayed with them for a couple of days and then headed north to Santa Cruz for a Turkey Day celebration with other family members and my dad.

I had made a lunch date with a former girlfriend for couple of weeks after Thanksgiving. She worked in Palo Alto. Leaving my sister's home in Santa Cruz around 11:00 a.m., I arrived at my friend's office a little before noon. She suggested we walk to a nearby restaurant. As we crossed the street, I heard someone yelling on a bullhorn, and I saw a crowd of people gathering in a small park. I couldn't understand much of what was being said, but as we approached, it was clear this was an antiwar demonstration. My friend wanted to avoid the area, but other than what I had seen on TV news, I had never witnessed anything like this. Frankly, I was curious. In hindsight, I suppose I should have listened to my friend.

As we got closer, I saw placards with statements like: "How many babies have our GIs killed this month?" and "We murder young mothers and children." Several young men were burning their draft cards. As we tried to walk past, I shook my head in disgust. Two or three of the protesters approached me, asking, "Why is it so hard for you to believe the truth?"

I was quiet for a moment, then said, "I just returned from Nam. I was there nearly fifteen months, and I never saw infants or young children mistreated or killed by our soldiers. I'll tell you what I did see, though. I did see babies staked out and used as booby-traps by the Viet Cong. It killed the child and usually the GI's who tried to help. I also witnessed Vietnam's blood cleansing of Amer-Asian infants and the killing of their mothers by so-called religious leaders. That's the truth!"

Someone spat in my face, and as I turned around to identify the culprit, I saw three people holding an American flag and a fourth person pouring kerosene over it. Wiping my face, I heard someone in the group say something about burning the flag.

Seeing the flag in flames, I become so angry that I broke into a mad twenty-yard dash at the four people. My one intent was to rescue the colors. My heart ached for all those men still serving in Vietnam, all the wounded, and those who had been killed or were still missing in action. I kept remembering a statement that had been burned into a large plank that hung above the gate to a company compound. It read: "Though my country be right or wrong—My country—right or wrong!"

I tackled all four protesters: a young woman (the leader and flag burner), and three men. We all fell onto the flag, smothering the flames. The girl was only bruised, but two of the men were more seriously injured. The third man was unhurt but made a nearly fatal mistake. He kicked me in the ribs as I was trying to get up. As he made another attempt, I grabbed his foot and flipped him over. He broke his arm as he landed. I tried to help the others up, but two of them weren't able to stand.

Suddenly a large man grabbed me from behind and wrapped his forearm across my throat. I wasn't able to see him and I wasn't able to breathe. So, with my free right arm and fist, I struck him in the groin and brought my elbow up sharply into his solar plexus. He went down like a wet newspaper.

I was on one knee gasping for air, and as my breathing and my head cleared I heard someone holler, "Get the pig's gun. Kill the pig!"

Since I didn't have a gun, I knew they weren't talking about me. Turning toward my assailant, who was still lying on the ground gasping, I recognized the crumpled blue of a police uniform. "Oh shit, I've decked a cop," I said hoarsely.

A young man from the crowd reached for the officer's revolver. As he put his hand on the weapon I judo-punched the would-be gun thief twice in the back of the head and neck, knocking him out cold. Then I circled the downed policeman to keep any of the other demonstrators from trying to get to him or the gun. If only I had known it was a cop who grabbed me, all of this would have been avoided. Four police cars and five more officers came to our rescue. One officer had been across the street and had witnessed most of what happened, including my hitting his partner, but he had been too far away to hear anything but the yelling.

This was the second time I had ever worn handcuffs, and I still did not enjoy it at all. Even getting to ride in the squad car was no consolation. The police station was only a few blocks from the park. Once we were inside, the cops put me in a small office-like room, with a few chairs, a desk, and a telephone. They took off the cuffs, and after I sat there for nearly half an hour, two officers came in to get my side of the story.

"You do realize," the first one began, "that an assault on a police officer is a felony—and could mean some serious jail time."

I looked at both policemen and answered, "Yes, I understand that. He didn't announce he was a cop, and I thought one of the demonstrators had jumped me. Hell, I was simply defending myself."

The higher-ranking officer of the two told the other cop to take me down to booking, but just then a very well dressed, older man walked into the room. At first I thought he might be an attorney, but one of the others addressed him as Chief. He was the captain. He talked to the two officers for a few minutes in the hallway, then dismissed them and asked one of them to bring in two Cokes. He turned to me. "Are you a tough guy, son, or just stupid?" was his first question. "Neither, sir," I answered.

"You look military. Were you in Vietnam?"

"Yes, sir. I've just been back a few days. The people I tackled—are they seriously hurt?"

"Let's see." The chief looked down at the sheet of paper in his hand and read off, "One broken collarbone, a broken wrist, and a broken forearm. Nothing life- threatening."

"And the officer I hit? How's he, sir?"

"More embarrassed than hurt," he responded. "Tell me what happened at the park."

I explained the best I could and added, "I don't care what people say about the war—that's their right. But when someone tries to burn my flag, I'm going to make every effort I can to stop them."

There was a knock on the door, and the cop I had dropped walked in. "Hi, soldier, how ya doing?" he asked.

"I'm fine," I said. "Hey, I'm really sorry about all that out there, but I had no idea who you were."

The chief looked up at the young officer and asked, "Is that true? The witnesses and the other officers said that Mills' attack on you was unprovoked."

"No, Cap, that's not exactly how it was, but can I see you out in the hall for a moment?" Both men left the room just as our two Cokes arrived.

I could see my friend, the young lady, sitting down the hall, and we waved a couple of times as people came in and out of the small interrogation room. I had drunk most of my pop by the time the captain returned. The officer had explained to his superior that he had not identified himself. He said that while he had been lying on the ground he wasn't able to function, and that as soon as I had realized he was a cop, I had actually protected him by keeping the mob away from his weapon. He concluded, "Captain I believe Mills has acted as any person would have in a similar situation."

Verifying my first name, the captain asked, "Vic, what unit were you with in Nam?"

"I was with two MP companies, sir, the 552nd and the First Infantry."

The captain said, "Well, that explains how you were able to best one of my officers." Then he began telling about two very special nephews who were stationed in Vietnam. "One's with the Big Red One," he said in reference to my serving in that unit, "and the other is with the 9th Cav." Pausing and looking intently at me, he added quietly, "My two sisters, their mothers, are concerned because they haven't heard from them for awhile."

"Both good units, sir. You can tell your sisters that the First Infantry showed me how to survive and how to soldier, and the 9th is just as good. They couldn't be in better outfits."

The captain appeared relieved. He sat quietly for several seconds as if thinking about what I had just said. "How long will you be in the area?" he finally asked.

"Well, I was hoping to make one more trip to L.A. to visit my son, then head over to Palm Springs for a last visit with my mom and younger sister before I drive to Seattle."

He walked out into the hall again to talk things over with his men. The door was left open and I could hear most of what was being said. Apparently many of the officers had brothers, cousins, or close friends in Nam. When he came back into the room, several of the officers stood in the doorway.

"Look, son," he began, "I don't know where you are staying, and I don't want to know." Taking another sip of his drink, he continued, "But these clowns you put in the hospital are screaming for blood—your blood. I'm going to charge them with disorderly conduct and public endangerment with the flag burning, but that's all I can do." Walking over to the wire-mesh covered windows, he turned and said, "They want you for assaulting them. Hell, I wish I could have done what you did myself. But I can't—I'm a cop. Vic, my officers, these men here, are willing to lose all the paperwork about this incident, but you've got to help us too. You've got to get out of town fast, just in case this backfires."

He went on to say, "As far as my men and I are concerned, you were home on leave and have returned to duty in Vietnam."

I thought to myself, "If these guys, who don't know me from Adam, are willing to put themselves in jeopardy for me, I can at least do my part." I thanked the captain and the cop I had hit. Then shaking hands with each officer, I wished them all well.

Originally my plan had been to leave that weekend; however, my car was having some problems. The tranny had gone bad, and the dealer I had bought the car from told me he wouldn't be able to replace the transmission until the next day. I promised the captain and his men that as soon as my car was finished, I would head south. And that's what I did.

I picked up my car at 4:00 p.m. the next day and drove to my dad's place to meet everyone for a quick goodbye, then hit the road. While in L.A. and Palm Springs, I was able to have an early Christmas with my son, my mom, and my younger sister and her kids. Then it was time for me to move north.

About noon on December 23, I left Palm Springs and headed northwest through the San Bernardino Mountains and over to Highway 99. Reaching the turnoff, I pointed the hood ornament north and stepped on the gas.

Often in the past when I was on a road trip, I would join up with one or two other vehicles along the way. It was like a buddy system or caravan. This happened shortly after I turned north onto Highway 99. There was me in my Chevy, a young woman in a nearly new, sporty MGB, and a young man in an older Ford sedan. Late into the afternoon, just past Fresno, I stopped for gas and dinner. Traffic had been light all the way and it appeared that it was going to stay that way through the evening.

When I parked at the pumps, the attendant came over, and I said, "Fill 'er up with premium, please." As I got out of the car to stretch, I noticed the other two vehicles were also driving in. I smiled and waved. We had been playing follow-the-leader for the past one hundred miles. I asked the attendant to check the water and oil and to bring the bill to me in the restaurant. I exchanged greetings and joked with the other two travelers as they got out of their cars. The attendant said he would gas up their vehicles and bring their bills in to them when he brought mine in. (Where did that kind of service go?) Walking into the restaurant, I suggested the three of us share a table.

I had never visited with any highway buddies in the past, beyond saying "Hi" over the gas pumps. This was great! It was almost like traveling with friends. We introduced ourselves, and each of us shared a little of our back-grounds. The young man's name was Greg, and he too had recently returned from Vietnam.

The young woman was Jennifer, a second-year high school teacher in Salem, Oregon. She was teaching U.S. and World history, and seemed quite interested in hearing about some of our experiences in Vietnam.

The three of us talked for nearly an hour. A deputy sheriff came in for some coffee just as we were getting ready to leave, and I asked him if he had any road information for northern California.

Smiling, he said, "Wait a minute and I'll try to find out," and he walked over to the pay phone.

Greg decided not to wait any longer, and he paid his bill and headed for the highway.

After a few moments, the deputy came back to the counter and said, "The roads are clear all the way to Weed; there's some light snow past that point, but you shouldn't have any trouble."

"Do you think I could make Yreka tonight?" I asked.

"Yeah, probably," the deputy agreed. Taking a sip of his coffee, he added, "The roads are okay now, but that's normally a five-or six-hour run from here."

I assumed "normally" meant something close to the posted speed limit. Jennifer and I thanked the officer for his help and we headed for our cars.

Thinking out loud, I said, "Maybe I could cut a little time off of that."

"Do you have a place to stay in Yreka?" Jennifer asked.

"No, not by reservation, but I have stayed a few times at the Miners Inn Motel there," I replied. "I'm not anxious to try the pass at night, especially if it's been snowing."

"You know, I just may try to make it that far, myself," she said. "How fast are you planning to drive?"

Thinking for a moment, I said, "I hadn't thought about it, but I may try to keep it close to eighty-five or ninety."

She indicated that she could do that as well, so at least for the time being we could be company for each other on the road. We agreed that if one of us started to feel sleepy, that person would flash their lights and pull off at the first motel sign.

Back on the road, I gradually accelerated to eighty-five, keeping a wary eye in my rearview mirror for police. Jennifer's little car surprised me; I didn't think it could maintain that kind of a pace. About thirty minutes after leaving the gas and food stop, we saw Greg's car ahead of us. We slowly continued to gain on him. He was cruising at about seventy, and when we passed him, he increased his speed enough to join our convoy again. I don't know why, but it seemed reassuring to have that third car as part of the group.

For the next couple of hours, we saw just one car and a few semi-trucks. With all the coffee we had drunk at dinner, we were ready to pull off at the same gas station, at the same time, for the same reason.

We sped through Stockton, and just a few miles past Sacramento we picked up part of the new Interstate 5 that had been started three years earlier. It was a three-lane beauty, as smooth as silk. Eventually it would go straight through to the Canadian border. I was familiar with the part that ran through Seattle.

The new concrete made a pleasant contrast to the old asphalt of State Highway 99. It was much easier to see when driving at night. However, our exhilaration from racing along our own private speedway was rudely interrupted by unwanted company. A California Highway Patrol car appeared in our rear-view mirrors and was coming up fast with red lights flashing.

Jennifer had been in the lead, I was second, and Greg was third. We moved over into the right lane and slowed to seventy-five as the police cruiser continued to approach. The patrolman passed Greg, then me, and cut in behind the MG to pull Jen over onto the right shoulder. There was no indication from the officer that either Greg or I should stop. This made me a little curious, and apparently Greg as well. Since we all were speeding, why did the officer stop only her? We pulled over a few yards ahead.

The night was freezing cold, much colder than it had been in Fresno. Jennifer turned off her headlights, leaving only the parking lights on. As we walked toward her car, I glanced at her Oregon license plate. "Of course," I thought to myself. "She's an out-of-stater." I mentioned this to Greg and told him, "That must be the reason the officer singled her out."

It had probably been a slow night for the CHP, and the fact that this patrolman was going after just one of us, a female in an out-of-state car, looked to me to be a simple case of harassment.

As the patrolman advanced to Jen's car, he told us to get back in our cars and leave, adding, "This is none of your concern, boys."

For some reason his referring to us as "boys" rubbed us both the wrong way. The officer was about our age, but even if he had been older, he should not have used that term with us. Regardless of age, anyone who has served his country in the military is no "boy" (or girl) in my book.

Greg said, "She's a friend of ours and we're all traveling together."

I chimed in right behind, "Her name is Jennifer and we two *boys* will just wait for her."

He took her license and registration and told her, "You know, I had you clocked at over one hundred miles an hour back there."

She protested slightly, stating that her car couldn't reach that speed. It was true, and Greg and I interjected our two-cents worth in her support.

When the officer pulled out his ticket pad, Greg and I took our Army IDs and driver's licenses from our wallets and handed them to him. He gave us a hard look and asked, "Just what the hell do you guys think you're doing?" (At least we had gone up a notch from mere "boys" to "guys.")

I said, "If you write her a ticket, then you'll have to write one for me."

Greg held up his hand and added, "Me too."

"And," I added, "You'll have to be the one to explain to your watch commander and the court why it was that you stopped just one of us to issue a ticket. That means an early morning court session and all the paperwork to explain it!"

Still glaring at me, he asked, "Just who do you think you're talking to? I ought to run both your asses in, just on principle."

"Look, I'm an Army cop just back from Nam," I told him. "There could only be two reasons in the world why you stopped only Jennifer and not all three of us. One, she's a young woman alone, or two, she's driving an out-of-state car." I paused for a moment and added, "Actually, there is a third reason, but whichever one you pick, it's called *harassment* or maybe worse, depending on what's really on your mind!"

I saw his body tense up, and I added, "You can stop this now. Chew us out for speeding or give us three tickets. Or you can radio for your supervisor." Then I shut up.

Greg wondered out loud if a certain CHP lieutenant he knew might be on duty right then.

"That's my supervisor," the patrolman said a little startled.

"Good! He's my neighbor," smiled Greg.

The officer slowly returned Jennifer's papers to her, saying with a growl, "You guys slow it down some."

My guess was that like most of us cops, the patrolman hated paperwork. But I had to admit that the remark Greg made about his neighbor was a neat touch.

"Is that lieutenant really a neighbor?" I asked as we started back for our cars.

"Hell no. But before Nam, we *were* on a first name basis. Something about my driving."

I was still laughing as I climbed back into my car. I cranked the heat up and then accelerated to eighty. I had to leave the cop with a little dignity, so I maintained the slower speed for about ten miles. An hour later, Greg flashed his lights and exited the freeway for Red Bluff. Rolling down my window for a brief, cold moment, I waved and Jennifer blinked her fog lamps and tooted that cute little horn.

Jennifer and I continued up the freeway—our speed hovering around eighty-five. The night had cleared somewhat, and the moonlight on the surrounding countryside with its dotted snow-dusted ponderosa pines appeared like a fairyland. The scenery reminded me that Christmas was indeed in the air.

There was a light to medium dusting of snow along the outer roadway. The freeway had not yet been completed, and stopped abruptly as we entered the small town of Weed. Jennifer tooted her horn, pointed to a lighted motel sign, and waved goodbye as she turned into the driveway. I could certainly understand her desire to get some sleep. I was doing a lot of yawning myself, but Yreka was less than an hour away.

I picked up a cup of coffee at an all-night truck stop at the north end of Weed, and managed to clear a few of the cobwebs out of my head. The radio didn't help much, though. That late at night, and in such a remote locale, I couldn't find anything but static. To help myself stay awake, I sang every song I knew.

Although it was not snowing as I continued along the old highway, there was a good amount of powder on the ground. Fifty minutes later, I pulled into Yreka. Miners Inn Motel was only a couple of blocks from the highway exit. It was a good thing because I was exhausted and nearly out of gas — both me and the car. I was truly looking forward to a hot shower and a warm bed.

Walking into the lobby, I saw the same huge grandfather clock near the fireplace that I had admired on previous trips; it was exactly 11:45.

The man at the front desk greeted me, "Good evening sir. A room for one night?"

"Glad to see someone on duty so late," I responded, "Good evening to you too. Yes, just for tonight."

As I filled out the little card the man had given me, his wife came out and commented, "You look awfully familiar. Have you stayed here before?"

"Yes ma'am, several times," I told them. "I'm on my way home to Seattle from Vietnam."

Although my room should have cost me thirty dollars, they charged me only ten.

I thanked the couple for their kindness, then I added, "I'm not sure— perhaps I'm just tired—but there may be a young lady in a dark green MG looking for a room. Her name is Jennifer." I had no logical reason for mentioning anything about Jen, but from the time I left Weed, I had felt uneasy, continually looking into the rearview mirror for those familiar headlights. Picking up my bag and heading for my room, I noticed the vacancy sign now flashed "no vacancy." I was getting rummy. "Jen's fast asleep in her own motel room right now," I argued with myself as I carried my bag up the stairs.

Within a few minutes, the room was nice and warm. The hot shower felt good, and I snuggled down into a warm, soft bed. It didn't take long for the sleepies to catch up. As I drifted off, I sent a silent prayer to God for my friends, and for all our men and women back in Vietnam. Then I was out.

In my dream I seemed to hear a persistent knocking. I kept responding, "Come in," but the knocking continued. Finally I roused myself enough to realize that someone was actually knocking on my door. I turned on my lamp and glanced at my watch. It was nearly 1:30 a.m. Slipping on my jeans, I wobbled to the door and opened it. There stood Jennifer. She was a dreadful sight.

Half crying and visibly shaken, she said, "I got here just as you disappeared into your room."

"That was over an hour ago," I answered from deep within my foggy brain.

"I've been sitting in my car trying to figure out what I should do."

I picked up her small bag and took her by the arm to lead her inside, and I sat her down in the chair nearest to the heater.

When my head cleared a little, I asked, "What the hell happened in Weed? The last I saw of you, you were pulling into the driveway of a motel."

Shivering, she explained, "When I got to my room some boys jumped me and stole my purse. One of them was the motel owner's son. When I confronted the owner, he called me a liar. He sent me away and suggested I quit trying to cause trouble."

I could see that during the mugging she had managed to get a couple of good bruises on her face and arms.

"So did they get all your money?" I asked as I handed her a towel.

"All but three dollars and some change. Fortunately, my wallet with my gas cards and driver's license was locked in the car." Soaking up some warmth from the heater, she continued, "I was so scared, I just grabbed my stuff and drove away. I didn't know what to do. I remembered that you were going on to Yreka, to this motel, so I decided to come here." Starting to cry harder, she added, "Halfway here I realized that I didn't have any money—just oil cards." Looking up at me, she said, "I'm so tired, and I know this looks and sounds really dumb, especially since we're strangers, but I just can't go another mile. Could I please stay here? I don't know what else to do!"

"There are two beds here," I pointed out. "Yeah, you can stay. Why don't you get a hot shower? Things will look better in the morning."

As I headed into the bathroom to clear out some of my clothes, I saw her looking forlornly at the bed. "Oh, a real bed," she muttered. "It looks delicious."

She dropped her wallet, moved a few feet from her chair, and landed prone on the bed. In less time than it took me to turn off the lights, she was sound asleep. This was the last available room. I honestly wasn't sure what to do. I had no reason to disbelieve her—she really looked her story. I certainly couldn't throw her out, and this obviously was not a rendezvous of passion.

I pulled off Jennifer's boots, turned down the bed for her, rolled her into it, covering her up. Then I went back to my bed, whispering to myself over and over, "No, I'm not interested. I'm just too tired." I stripped back down to my briefs and T-shirt, something I wouldn't usually do in the company of a stranger, especially a young woman, and got back into my bed. All I was feeling at that moment was sympathy. I was fast asleep again in nothing flat.

I woke up slowly the next morning, and for a few moments my thoughts had me still in Nam. The smell of coffee permeated my brain, and I could hear the shower running. There on the nightstand, Jen had left me a steaming cup of coffee. I was definitely not in Vietnam.

After we loaded our things into the cars, I took Jennifer to the motel office to introduce her. I explained the situation to the same couple that had greeted me the night before. They wouldn't accept any additional money. Jen and I thanked them again.

I still had plenty of money, so I treated her to breakfast at the Denny's next door to the motel. We gassed up, and once more we were on our way. It was just past 8:00 a.m. and I wanted all the daylight possible for our drive through the Siskiyou Mountain pass. Some snow had fallen during the night, and we worried that we might run into more of it. I had never driven in snow before and was wishing I had bought a set of snow tires. The traffic was very light though, and we did just fine.

We crossed the pass into Oregon and gradually descended to a lower elevation. We were able to keep our speed up to seventy miles per hour in most places. But due to highway construction or small town speed zones, we occasionally had to slow to a snail's pace.

After another few hours, a light snow was falling again, and Jennifer was in the lead. I pulled off behind her at Salem to say goodbye, but she insisted on treating me to an early dinner. I agreed and followed her to her apartment a few minutes away. She was a great cook. I have a list of many things that I wish I had followed up on or done differently. Jennifer is definitely on that list.

Early evening found me driving through Portland, and as the lights of that city disappeared in my mirror, I crossed the Columbia River into Washington State. I had never traveled through this area before. When I helped my friend move up two years earlier, we had driven through Bend, Oregon, entering Washington near the Dalles, and driving up through Walla Walla.

Even though this route was new to me, a sense of belonging began to settle in my thoughts. It was winter and dark, a little past 6:00, so I couldn't see what the countryside looked like. In Portland the local radio station had forecast snow for most of the Pacific Northwest, promising a white Christmas, but there was hardly a flake for most of the distance from the Oregon border to Seattle.

It was the holiday season, and there should have been a lot of people trying to get somewhere else—but except for a few semi-trucks, the traffic was really light.

My mind hit recall as I sped past Fort Lewis where I had been just five weeks earlier, and where I had started out twenty months before that. It was now a little after 9:00 and I could smell the pungent odor of those same old coal furnaces that I had learned to stoke. It didn't seem as if it had been that long since I had learned what clinkers were and how to pull them out.

Before leaving Palm Springs I had phoned ahead for a motel reservation. As I turned off Aurora Avenue into the parking lot of the Marco Polo Motel in Seattle, the radio announced the time as 11:30. It had begun to snow as I entered the city, and now larger snowflakes were falling, slowly building up on the ground. My thoughts tumbled over and over like scenes from a favorite old movie. Sitting in the car with Christmas carols softly playing on the radio, I remembered Sam and all she had meant to me, and still did. I thought of all the kids at the orphanage; the narrow, winding, hot, dusty roads; and the many Vietnamese people whom I had grown to love. As I remembered, I could almost smell the country. I was overcome with a bittersweet nostalgia for the good memories I would always carry with me.

I thought too of the double standards that had been so prevalent in my unit. Here I was, back in Washington State, while half a million GIs were still slugging it out overseas. I thought about all that had happened during my tour of duty. Had I contributed anything of value during this unpopular war? Did my efforts make any difference in the big picture? I didn't know for sure. I didn't even know for sure if I had killed anyone. I hoped I hadn't, but I was glad to be alive and well. I was more fortunate than many who had gone through the worst horrors of the fighting; and I was grateful to have survived. There were lots of questions, but not too many answers—at least, not then. I had done my job as I had seen it. So had most of the other GIs, and many of them had paid a higher price: their lives. There were a few things I did know for sure. It was Christmas Eve, and the radio was softly playing "Silent Night." My strange odyssey was finally over. I was home!

Epilogue

Two months after my return to Seattle, I took up my job again with Seattle Transit. It was good to be a civilian again. The Vietnam War has long since been dubbed "the only war America has ever lost." Not in my book! In 1968 we convinced the North Vietnamese government to come to the treaty table. Finally, in 1973, they signed the peace accord with the joint Allied Forces in South Vietnam. The government of the North promised no further aggression against the government of South. Like so many of the communist governments of that day, the North reneged. They simply used the cease-fire order that had been in place for over two years as an opportunity to rebuild. The Viet Cong crossed into South Vietnam, enmasse, in 1975. In less than a month, they captured Saigon.

I was working the day the news broke about the collapse of South Vietnam. On a short layover at the end of the line at West Seattle's Alki Beach, I read the newspaper accounts with tears streaming down my face. Gripped by fear and concern for the orphanage we had established and for everyone there, I wondered what would become of all the children, their mothers, and the two women who had taken it over.

One of my regular passengers reached out in comfort. As it turned out, she was in upper management with the American Red Cross in Seattle. She asked me the specifics about the location of the orphanage, and she promised that she would do all she could to find out what had become of those families.

The following week, she asked me to meet her for coffee at a small fish-and-chips restaurant on Alki. "I have some information for you," she said when we had settled in. "Your kids, *your families*—everyone—got out and were flown to Thailand the night before the Viet Cong came through the area." Our tears of joy blended with our coffee.

God Bless!